AF480794

# BIG MAN

# Big Man

An Incredible Journey from Mississippi to Hollywood

Tim Shea and Willie Harris

Davenport

# CONTENTS

# Introduction

Willie Harris was many things: loyal, persistent, charismatic, sensitive, wise, confident, welcoming, proud, inspirational, determined, loving, and very, very tall.

The first time I heard him speak was in February 2016 while I was driving to work and listening to a segment of NPR's *StoryCorps*. I was struck by the sound and character of his voice as he talked about his time growing up in Mississippi under Jim Crow and his battles against racism with the Black Stuntmen's Association in Hollywood. I could hear the passion. He had seen a lot, and felt a lot, and he wanted you to know about it. All of that came clearly through my car radio and I knew that his life story needed to be told. I knew it was an improbable tale of struggle, sacrifice, and accomplishment. I immediately knew all of that, and the segment was only two and a half minutes long. That is how compelling Willie was.

When I called him at his home and told him I wanted to help him tell his story, he immediately and enthusiastically said he would be happy to partner with me on this project.

After I started talking to him a few times a week I learned so much more about his life in Mississippi, his year in Chicago, his service in the Air Force, and his time with the Black Stuntmen's Association, and it was all much richer and more fascinating than I could have fathomed.

Willie's height helped him navigate life in many ways. When you meet someone who is 6'8" you are not likely to forget him, especially someone who has something important to tell you, whether you like it or not. When he saw something that he thought was wrong, he would talk to anyone who he thought could help make it right, and he would talk to them again if he didn't succeed at first. His height got people to notice he was there, but once they started talking to him, they didn't want to stop because he was so engaging. His height also helped make him an exceptional basketball player, but it contributed to some intense physical challenges that he dealt with for most of his life.

This book tells the entirety of Willie's life story, and his personal journey is complemented by insights and scenes from the lives of those closest to him, as well as historical information that contextualizes all the events depicted here. The stories of Willie and his family and friends are presented as they were told to me. There is language that is difficult to read and incidents that are painful to think about, but they are all true.

Willie's story, and the millions like it, are stories we cannot turn away from. They are stories that define and illuminate the American character. The Black experience in America is at once the most heartbreaking and inspiring saga in our history, and we must embrace it.

I found all aspects of Willie's experience to be enthralling and educational, and I wrote this book as a tribute to his legacy, as well as for those in our country who have faced the same challenges. I hope you find it to be eye-opening, entertaining, energizing, and worthwhile.

Tim Shea
February 2024

The barrel of the gun was pointed at Willie's face.

"Nigger, are you callin' me a liar?" Bill Turner said as he took a pistol from under the counter of the country store, reversed the chamber, dropped in a bullet, and leveled it at Willie. It was two feet from his nose, and he could smell the metal.

"I'll blow your damn brains out," Turner said, his teeth clenched and rage etched in the lines of his forehead.

"No, Mr. Turner, I'm not callin' you a liar, but I didn't steal your cigarettes," Willie said.  At 15 years old and 6 feet, 2 inches tall, Willie was big, and strong, and often defiant. But now he was terrified. As a Black teenager in Mississippi in 1956, he had gotten used to being treated a certain way by whites in the tiny sharecropping community of Howard, but this was different. No one had ever put a loaded gun in his face before.

# 1

## A WORLD NOT OF THEIR OWN MAKING

Willie Darnell Harris came screaming into this world in a sharecropper's cabin on the eighth day of the eighth month in the year America entered World War II. The four-room shack where he was pulled from his mother's womb was the only home he would know for the first 19 years of his life. He was delivered by Laura Rimpson, a midwife who presided over the births of all the little Black boys and girls in their part of rural Mississippi in the 1930s and 1940s, as the nearest hospital was 12 miles away. A year earlier, she delivered Willie's older brother Robert, and over time, she did the same for up to a dozen of his cousins who lived on a neighboring plantation.

The cabin was located on Clifton, a 1,000-acre plantation in the small community of Howard, which rests in Holmes County. It is due west of Lexington, the county seat, and the 10-mile trip to Lexington on Howard Road winds through thick forests and fields pregnant with cotton and corn in late summer. The county is lush, green, and sparsely populated, and an hour's drive west of Howard brings you to the east bank of the Mississippi. On your way to the big river, your ride can take you by the birthplaces of Delta Blues pioneers B.B. King, John Lee Hooker, and Mississippi John Hurt, all of them born into sharecropping families.

The Harris cabin—as well as the other 15 on the plantation—had no electricity or indoor plumbing in 1941, and they were all set up pretty much the same way: two bedrooms, one for the parents and one for the kids; a kitchen with a wood-burning stove; a room with a table for eating, and maybe a couch and chairs, if you were lucky. Kerosene lamps provided light, and there was a well and outhouse in the yard.

Willie and Robert were raised by their parents Evie and Oscar Harris. Evie was born in 1900 in neighboring Carroll County, and her family moved to the Howard area when she was a young woman. By the time Willie was born she had spent most of her more than 40 years picking cotton, never having learned to read or write. Oscar was there, but he wasn't. He was known to take up with women in the area and he would disappear for days at a time, often taking some of the family's paltry wages or food with him to share with his girlfriends. When he was home, bad things often happened. He would hit Evie, and when Willie got to be 6 or 7 years old, Oscar would smack him around, too, when he got sassy. Oscar was 6 feet tall and 200 pounds, a strong dude, and when Willie talked back, Oscar would whack him upside the head with a left jab. Robert was calmer than Willie and could usually avoid Oscar's wrath by doing what he was told to do, but Willie was harder to handle. There was a fire burning inside him that was tough to contain, and it certainly could not be extinguished.

So Evie, Robert, and Willie clung together in their little shack and tried to survive each day as best they could. By the mid-1940s Evie was an illiterate, middle-aged Black woman with no marketable skills—other than being an extremely hard worker in the fields—who was stuck in an unhappy marriage with an abusive husband, eking out a hand-to-mouth existence on a plantation in the heart of the Jim Crow segregated South. Whatever dreams that made her heart leap as a young girl had long since floated away on a Mississippi breeze, but now she had a new mission to sustain her: do anything she could to help her boys get away from the dead-end existence of sharecropping and make something out of their lives.

Before the boys could make something out of their lives, they had to make it through childhood. Evie taught them everything, from working with the animals in the pen, to cultivating the peas, okra, sweet potatoes, collard greens, snap beans and more in their vegetable garden, to picking cotton. If the family was going to have chicken for dinner, she would send Willie out to the chicken coop to grab one of the birds and get it ready. He would hold the chicken under his arm and spin its head round and round with his other hand until he snapped its neck. Then he would yank the head off and drop the decapitated chicken in a pot of boiling water on the wood-burning stove to get the feathers off. Now they were ready to slice it open, pull out the intestines and other internal organs, and drain the blood before frying and eating it with biscuits and gravy. They kept the bones to make chicken soup the next day, but unlike some of their neighbors, they didn't eat the chicken's feet or head. They were happy with the rest of the bird.

Hogs provided much more bounty than chickens, and they also required much more work. It started in the spring when Willie and Robert would go out to the forest that surrounded the plantation fields and cut down a hickory tree, saw it into smaller pieces, pile it on the back of a mule they had borrowed from the plantation owner, and haul it back to the cabin where they would cut it, split it, and stack it, so it could become seasoned throughout the summer and fall. The family usually had a half dozen hogs, and they would slaughter them in November or December so they would have enough food to get them through the cold winter months. When they killed a hog, they would cut up and eventually eat all the meat: the ham, ribs, bacon, hock, neck, and butt, as well as the feet, ears, snout, cheek, and tongue. Almost no part of the hog went to waste, and about the only parts they wouldn't eat were the teeth and eyeballs. Many families would eat the hog's small intestines, known as chitlins—boil them up and season them with greens. Willie didn't like that; the ham was his favorite. After cutting up the hog they would use the chopped hickory sticks to start a slow-burning, smoldering fire in the smoke-house, which was a small wooden structure in the backyard near the outhouse.  They would hang the meat in the smokehouse for a few days to preserve it and then would take a little here and there to make meals over the next several months. The hog fat was very important because Evie would render it in boiling water in a pot on the stove to create lard, which was used to fry chicken. Buying soap from the store would have been a luxury, so Evie made their soap for body washing and doing laundry from a mixture of lard and lye.

In addition to smoking meat from the hogs to get through the winter, the family would preserve potatoes by digging a hole in the ground, dropping them in, and covering them with straw. Evie was also a master at canning peaches, pears, and apples in mason jars. With lessons handed down over many generations, she knew exactly how long to cook the fruit, how much sugar to put in, and how to can them so they didn't spoil. Willie made himself many a meal from canned peaches and biscuits.

It was a subsistence living, to be sure. The vast majority of what they ate they had raised or grew. On most days, everything they consumed was a product of their labor, except the sugar and salt they would buy at the Howard Store at the bottom of the hill. Share-cropping was designed so the sharecroppers would always have just enough money or food to get through the day or week, and they need-ed to keep working incessantly to sustain their meager way of life. It is a system in which landowners provide housing and a plot of farmable land to families in exchange for their work raising and harvesting the crops. Sharecropping became widespread in the South during and after Reconstruction (1865-1877) following the Civil War. Plantation owners had plenty of land to raise crops, but no longer owned slaves who worked the land. Most free Blacks had no land and very little or no money, but they could work to earn their keep. In most cases, the landowner provided each family with a ramshackle cabin, tools for farming, and a small plot of land behind their cabin for raising a few animals and growing their own vegetables, known as the truck patch. At the end of the year, about a week before Thanksgiving, each family would settle up with the owner and receive their share—or more accurately, the amount the plantation owner said was their share—of what the crop, usually cotton, brought at market, hence the term "sharecropping." The sharecroppers were supposed to be paid one-third to one-half the value of the crops they brought in during the harvest, the idea being that the landowner would keep one-half to two-thirds, since he provided the land and housing. However, like just about every economic, political, legal, educational, or social system devised by whites who held power in the South in the century following the Civil War, its ultimate goal was to maintain the power and economic security of whites and to keep Blacks mired in hopeless poverty, undereducated—or utterly uneducated in terms of an academic education—and under the thumb of the ruling class.

The amount each family received from the owner depended in large part on how much or how little the owner chose to give them. Many sharecroppers were illiterate, and even those who could read and were skilled in arithmetic had no recourse if they knew they were getting cheated. The owner controlled everything: he owned the land and the tools needed for farming; he provided housing, such as it was; he created, maintained, and interpreted the plantation's financial records; and he ran the plantation store where the sharecroppers would buy the sundry items needed to supplement what they were able to grow and raise on their own. On top of all of that, he was white, and if a Black man questioned the actions of a white man in the South in the mid-twentieth century, he was likely to get a gun pointed at his head, or much worse.

The system was designed to keep sharecroppers perpetually dependent on, and often indebted to, the plantation owner. The year started in late winter with the owner providing each sharecropping family with a monthly loan to help them survive until the crop came in.

"Starting in about March of every year if you had four in the family, he would give you about $30 for March, April, May, June, July, and August; you start picking cotton in August. So those months, he would give you something to start, about $30 a month, but at the end of the year he would take that back," Willie said.

Robert recalls how hard his family worked and worked, only to end each year with nothing to show for it, and the system continued to work as it was designed, keeping families like the Harrises dependent upon their plantation owner.

"They would work all year long and come to the end of the year, they didn't get anything. The man told him that they owed money instead of getting money. The way it supposed to be, once he sold his crop off, we were supposed to get some money back, but we never did. And we just kept workin' and workin'. You'd scrape every little bit you could. There was nothing you could do about it. It was what it were. Like I say, we raised our own gardens, we raised our own hogs, and we had our own cattle, one or two cows, and that kept us goin'."

There were peach and pecan trees on Clifton Plantation, as well as peanut and alfalfa fields. But like most plantations in Mississippi, the dominant crop was cotton. The calendar and daily life of everyone on the plantation revolved around the cultivation and harvesting of cotton. It started in March or April when the seeds were planted on the owner's fields, as well as all the plots assigned to each sharecropping family. These were anywhere from 3 to 10 acres, depending on the size of the family. The bigger the family, the more cotton they could pick, the larger the plot. A few weeks after the planting, the choppin' would start. Choppin' cotton was the most physically demanding and exhausting part of the process. Once the cotton plant has grown to be about 6 inches tall, the grass that grows around it needs to be cleared away, so it doesn't smother the burgeoning stalk. Clearing the grass away with a hoe is called choppin' cotton. It might take two weeks for a family to chop cotton in their field, and then they would have to go back and do it all over again until the plant was strong enough to survive on its own. The workday was from "can to can't," which means you start working at sunrise, when you can see, and you stop at sunset, when you can't see.

Willie and all the other little boys and girls would start working the fields when they were old enough to handle a hoe, about seven or eight years old. Before that, some would be given the job of bringing water to those toiling in the cotton rows. Choppin' and picking cotton was brutal work, and Willie hated it. "You get up in the mornin' and go out in the cotton field and it's wet from the night's dew and all of that stuff, and that cotton is over your head, and it would be cold, too, but you had to do it." He would end the day wiped out, often hungry, with his sweaty clothes stuck to him. Washing clothes was a laborious process, and with so many other things to do, it only happened once every couple of weeks. Willie would have to wear the same clothes for a few days in a row, and the cabin would smell pretty rank at times.

The cotton plants would grow to maturity during June and July, and during that time the sharecroppers would work on the crops in their truck patches, bale hay, and do other work for the plantation owner. On a hot summer day Willie would be standing in the field, sweating while he walked behind the hay baler, and watch the white boys playing Cowboys and Indians, and ask his mom why.

"Mom, why do we have to work so much? I want to play like the white kids."

"Well, son. That's just the way it is. There ain't nuthin' we can do about it, so you just have to deal with it," Evie would say.

It was the late 1940s, almost a decade before the civil rights movement gained any momentum. Life was just as hard for Blacks in Mississippi in 1948 as it was when Evie was a girl in 1908, so she had no reason to believe it would ever change. The Southern Way of Life, with its well-known written and unwritten rules, had been ensconced since the late nineteenth century, when it had been altered slightly to accommodate for the abolition of slavery. The social and economic caste system was clearly defined: white plantation owners and professionals at the top, and Blacks, sharecroppers in particular, at the bottom. Evie taught Willie and Robert everything they needed to know to survive: "Whenever you speak to a white man you address him as sir, or mister. Whenever you are in town, if you see white people walking toward you on the sidewalk, you step off to let them pass. Whenever you are standing in line in a store and a white person gets in line, you step off to the side to let them go ahead of you. When a white person tells you to do something, you do it, and you don't sass them. And perhaps most important of all, whenever you see a white woman or girl, do not look her in the eye and do not speak to her."

Willie, Robert, Evie, and millions of other sharecroppers were living in a world not of their own making. They did not choose any of this. They were born into it and boxed in. The concept of the American Dream holds that if you work hard and play by the rules you can build a better life for yourself than your parents had. For these people, in their situation, that notion was a pathetic farce.

Willie felt the shackles of segregation from a young age. He hated the fact that he had to work so hard and couldn't have any of the things the white kids had. While others put their head down and plowed ahead because that is just the way it was, Willie asked himself, Why? Why do I have to deal with this crap? Why do I have to be careful about everything I say, work almost all the time, and never have anything? And nothing crystallized this growing anger more than cotton picking season. When August rolled around and the white kids were getting ready for the start of school, the Black kids from the sharecropping families were getting ready for two to three months of hard labor.

A cotton field in full bloom is a beautiful sight: a sea of brilliant white speckled with green stretching to the horizon, shimmering in the September sun against the backdrop of a gorgeous blue sky. It is a beautiful sight, that is, unless you are one of the people who has to pick all that cotton. In that case, it can practically be hell on earth. Mechanical cotton harvesting machines were not widespread in Willie's area of Mississippi until about 1960, so throughout his entire childhood all the cotton on Clifton Plantation was picked by hand by the 15 sharecropping families. He and Robert would get up in the morning in late summer and early fall and head out to the fields. When they were eight or nine years old, they were given a small sack that Evie had stitched together, and it would hold about 10 pounds of cotton. As they got bigger, they got bigger sacks, until eventually they were lugging sacks that held 100 pounds of cotton on their backs. They would quickly, yet carefully, pluck the fluffy cotton fiber from the boll with two fingers and a thumb, then stuff it in the sack. Again, and again, and again. It made your fingers ache, and your hunched back sore, and it was so monotonous and mind-numbingly boring.

After many a long day of working in the cotton rows, Willie would finally be free to rest. When the lamp was extinguished, there was nothing left to do but lie there in bed—often damp, and cold, and hungry—and count the stars through the holes in the roof. In the still of the Mississippi night he would listen to the crickets and cicadas sing, hoping that someday, some way, he might hear a rare and different tune.

There were bright spots in Willie's childhood; they didn't have to work all the time, and they did have some fun with the other kids on the plantation, as kids will do. The family had two pet dogs, including Ted, a mutt who survived on Harris table scraps. Willie and Robert and the other kids would bring him along to help hunt rabbits and squirrels. Back in the day, they shared many a tasty meal with squirrel as the main course. Lope was a registered collie, but he was no Lassie. Robert named him Lope because he meandered along at a casual pace and liked to lay around in the shade, just chillin'. Like any kid, Willie was happy when he was with his friends. His infectious smile, outgoing personality, and impressive height made him a natural leader among his peers. Many of his friends didn't know he was angry inside; they just knew him as Willie D. When they didn't have to work, the boys often played baseball and the game that would become Willie's lifelong obsession, a blessing, and in some ways, a curse: basketball.

When Willie was growing up, there were four or five other working cotton plantations adjoining Clifton or within walking distance—Brock, Beall and Ellison, and Powell among them. This area, known as Howard Bottom, is very flat and consists mainly of acre upon acre of cotton fields bounded by forest. Every now and then you would see a dwelling, a red wooden barn, or a silver grain silo. The nearest town is Tchula, four miles away, and it had only 900 residents back then. This was true country living. Dirt roads, lots of dust, and people who were self-sufficient, because they didn't have any other choice. The nexus for the community was Howard Store, where household necessities were sold, and right next to that was the cotton gin, where everyone would bring their cotton to have it weighed and processed. To get to Clifton, you went up a steep gravel road that began next to the gin.

Once you ascended the hill, the land flattened out again and the plantation spread out before you. Jones Road ran straight down the middle of the plantation, with cotton fields stretching symmetrically for an eighth of a mile on each side, and behind them, the sharecropping cabins, about one every 100 yards. Willie's next-door neighbors were the Johnsons on one side and his friends Curtiss and Winford Ross on the other. Pinky Patterson, whose little sister would become

Willie's high school sweetheart, lived next to the Rosses, and the other families included the Hendersons, Nelsons, Simmons, Fords, and Jergens.  A half mile down at the end of the road, past all the cabins, was the focal point of Clifton Plantation, The Big House.

Constructed in the late 1840s by slaves, its formal name is Clifton Plantation House, but all the sharecroppers who ever worked there knew it simply as The Big House. Built in the Greek Revival architectural style, it is roughly a 50- by 50-foot square, with tall sash windows, white clapboard siding, and topped by a pyramidal, grey shingled roof, with dormers on all four sides. Supporting the roof across the front of the house are eight elegant white pillars that sit on a generous U-shaped covered porch which wraps around the left and right sides. Inside, the impressive main entry hall is flanked by a parlor and library, and behind them are an expansive dining room, the kitchen, and two bedrooms. The truncated second floor also houses several more bedrooms. The front porch is a comfortable place where the owner and his family could sit and sip on a glass of lemonade, watch the swaying boughs of the majestic magnolia trees in the front yard, thumb through a book, and watch the slaves and their descendants, the sharecroppers, hard at work in the sweltering tropical heat. It is a great source of pride to the family who owned The Big House from the 1870s to the 1980s that it is widely considered to be the architectural model for Beauvoir, the post-Civil War home of Jefferson Davis, President of the Confederate States of America. Beauvoir was constructed in Biloxi down on the Gulf Coast just a few years after The Big House, and the homes are so similar that without looking closely it is difficult to tell them apart.

The Big House was entered into the National Register of Historic Places in 1985 and its application stated that its significance includes its representation of "an agriculturally-oriented lifestyle that is a rare survivor of the Civil War, Reconstruction, and the modern age."

*Former Ross family cabin, Clifton Plantation, 2017*

*The Big House, Clifton Plantation, 2017*

The contrast between The Big House and the sharecroppers' cabins was as dramatic as that between a sunlit mountaintop and a murky ditch. The Big House exuded elegance, refinement, and attention to detail, while the cabins provided the bare minimum of a roof, four walls, and a floor.  In the 1940s all of Clifton Plantation was commanded by Mr. Peyton Abbott Jones. In rural Mississippi, the plantation owner's decrees were akin to the law. Peyton Abbott Jones ruled Clifton like a king, and The Big House was his Buckingham Palace. Born in 1894, the plantation had been in Peyton's family since shortly after the Civil War. His grandfather, who had the improbable name of Major Liberty Constantine Abbott, and his grandmother Maria were the first in his family to run the plantation and reside in The Big House. Major Abbott was from a small town south of Buffalo near Lake Erie. He had volunteered to fight for the Union in New York's Fifth Cavalry and had come to Mississippi as a carpetbagger in the late 1860s to work on behalf of the federal government. He never left.

Peyton Abbott Jones started running the plantation in 1930, and he was feared and loathed by the sharecropping families who lived on Clifton. Willie tried to stay as far away from him as he could, since he was, in Willie's words, a complete jackass. When Willie or anyone had to talk to him, they needed to remove their hat, bow their head, and meekly ask "'Scuze me, Mr. Jones, may I please ask you something?" If you didn't treat him with the proper deference, you were likely to get slapped in the head or kicked in the ass. It didn't matter that he wasn't a big man, you had damn well better not hit him back if he struck you. He controlled everything and everyone on the plantation. If you did something he didn't like, he just had to say the word and your family was gone, with no place to go.

He often told the sharecroppers that "Niggers don't need no damn education." When he saw 8-, 10-, or 12-year-old kids going to school when there was work to be done in the fields, he would tell them and their families: "We need this boy working in the fields, not goin' to school."

How did this happen? How is that 80 years after the end of the Civil War Willie found himself growing up in a system that felt like a watered-down version of slavery, minus the whips and iron shackles? To understand interactions between whites and Blacks in Mississippi in the 1940s, we must consider what came before. What historical events, economic and social systems, and traditions and beliefs helped shape the environment Willie was born into in 1941? It all began with the settling of the South by whites in the 18th and early 19th centuries, and the growth of its agricultural economy. In W. J. Cash's classic 1941 delineation of the history, temperament, and social order of the American South, aptly titled *The Mind of the South*, he explains that the white Southerners' resistance to external authority has its roots in the pioneer spirit of the men who settled the deep Southern states. They had access to generous tracts of inexpensive, fertile farmland, and in order to succeed, they had to rely primarily on themselves to make the most of it. While most Americans grow up and make their way in a community, relying on others, and usually being bound by the rules of their community, this was foreign to the men who settled the South as farmers, many of whom eventually became plantation owners when the cotton boom occurred at the turn of the 19th century. Cash explains that the dominant trait of the white Southerner was individualism. This mindset was fostered by the conditions present throughout cotton country: the need to work the land effectively to survive, and the isolation inherent in living up to a mile or more from your nearest neighbor. This individualism in turn bred a chip-on-shoulder swagger in all classes of white Southerners—be they wealthy plantation owner, common farmer, or the poor white who drank his moonshine and played his fiddle—and the swagger was usually accompanied by an ever-present threat to "knock hell out of whoever dared to cross him."

The demand for cotton—and the ability to produce it more rapidly—exploded in the first few decades of the 19th century. King Cotton was a juggernaut, with the Southern states producing the majority of the world's supply, and no state producing more than Mississippi. During the decade prior to the Civil War, there were actually more slaves than white people in Mississippi. Economically, slave labor became a necessity to ensure the profitable production of cotton—or so it was thought—and consequently, the concept of slavery as an acceptable, normal, and just practice became a foundational component of the worldview of most white Southerners. People have the ability to justify almost anything, especially when money is at stake. Slavery as an institution needed to be protected from any external interference, especially from any do-gooder Northerners—the infamous outside agitators—trying to meddle in the South's business.

Of course, it would be unfair and wholly inaccurate to suggest that an entire population of millions of people spread out over thousands of square miles—the white South—thought and acted in lockstep by supporting slavery, with every man and woman also fueled by the same fierce resistance to authority and an ironclad determination to choose their own path. Perhaps surprisingly, the vast majority of abolition societies formed in the first half of the 19th century were founded in the South. But the pro-slavery forces, led by plantation owners, many of whom became state legislators and U.S. congressmen and senators, dominated Southern society and politics in the mid-19th century, and it was their determination to maintain the status quo that sent them flying headlong and with fury into the disaster that was the Civil War.

Following the war and collapse of Reconstruction around 1890, Southern state legislators and governors enacted discriminatory laws that prohibited almost any public or private mingling of Blacks and whites, and the legal segregation of public and private spaces became the norm. That strict separation between the races was just as clearly defined and impermeable in 1940 as it had been in 1890. In one respect, Peyton Abbott Jones wasn't too far removed from the Civil War and slavery—really just one generation. While his grandfather on his mother's side was a Yankee carpetbagger, his father,

Peyton Tabb Jones, was born in Virginia in 1854 and lived in Mississippi most of his life. He would have been very familiar with slavery, the Civil War, and their aftermath, having lived through all of them. Beliefs and values are handed down from generation to generation—however misguided or malignant they may be.

In 1908 the United Daughters of the Confederacy erected a 25-foot-tall granite monument in honor of the Holmes County soldiers who fought in the Civil War to recognize their "patriotism and their heroism, and to commend their example to future generations." This same organization erected a monument to the Ku Klux Klan in North Carolina in 1926. The Holmes County monument stands today in Lexington on the courthouse grounds at the epicenter of the county's political, social, and commercial life. It is topped with the likeness of a noble-looking Confederate soldier who calmly holds the barrel of his rifle. For more than a century he has stood next to the American flag—though the rebel soldier is conspicuously higher than the stars and stripes—and he gazes out on the bustling town square at a hardware store and insurance agency. The following is carved into the base:

> *The men were right who wore the gray, and right can never die.*

The fields of Holmes are filled with memories. Ancient footprints are everywhere.

**2**

— · —

# SEPARATE AND UNEQUAL

Willie had just turned six years old in the fall of 1947 and he was a little nervous. He was going to go to school for the first time, just like his brother Robert and all the other older kids on the plantation. He was nervous because he would be going to school with kids from all the other nearby plantations. He would be going with kids who were six to sixteen years old, and he hadn't met any of the kids who weren't from Clifton Plantation. The plantation was like a self-contained universe, and young children like Willie rarely had the chance to venture off it. All this uncertainty worried him. Would they be mean to him? Tease him? Beat him up? He didn't know. Then there were the academics to think about. Would they teach him to read and write? His mom couldn't read and write. How could he do something that his mom couldn't do?

Mt. Zion School served the plantation children from first through eighth grades. It was a modest one-story building nestled amongst the plantations and was a two-mile walk from their cabin. Its exterior was plank wood covered in redwood stain, the window and door trim were painted white, and it was capped by a galvanized tin roof. There was no insulation in the building and the floors, walls, and ceiling were all made of tongue and groove lumber.

Evie bought Willie a new button-down cotton shirt and crisp khaki pants before his first day of school.

"Willie, when you walk through the door after school you take off that shirt and those pants and you hang them up. You have to wear them to school every day," Evie said.

"Yes, mama."

"If you don't, you gonna get a whoopin'," she said.

"Yes, mama."

Evie talked tough, but inside she was glowing with pride that her boys were going to school and might someday have a chance to get out of this nowhere land.

Mt. Zion School was built in 1926 to serve the Black children who lived on the plantations and farms east of the town of Tchula in the rural community of Howard. The construction cost was $2,500, with half being raised by the local Black families, and about one-third was provided by the Rosenwald Fund. Julius Rosenwald was from Illinois and was the President and CEO of Sears, Roebuck and Company in the early decades of the twentieth century. As a Jew, he understood the persecution his people had endured for centuries, and he was determined to use his vast wealth to help others who were suffering. He established the fund "for the well-being of mankind" in 1917. He gave to many causes, but he became particularly interested in improving the difficult state of African American education and donated funds for the construction of more than 5,000 schools for Black children, most of them in the South, with more than 600 of them in Mississippi. Mt. Zion School had five rooms for the eight grades, so most rooms housed two classes. It was heated by a wood stove in each of the classrooms and lit by coal oil lamps. It was in use until 1961 and it never had a science lab, or cafeteria, or even indoor plumbing. Its grounds didn't have a baseball field or basketball court, and only in later years was a playground erected. But the parents who sent their children there were proud of it, and they did what they could to support it. While many of them had never been to school for more than a few years themselves, this was their community school, and it was a symbol of hope.

While Willie was anxious and excited about going to school for the first time, he would have to wait two months longer than the white kids in the area. Every morning from mid-August through mid-October he would be sweating in the cotton fields, hunched over with his fingers aching from the monotonous picking, and he would look up to see the sun shimmering on a school bus as it rumbled down the road that cut through the middle of the fields, puttin' a ton of dust in the air. It would stop at The Big House and pick up Frank Abbott Jones, Peyton's son, and bring him to the white school in Tchula four miles away. The white schools were beautiful brick buildings located in the towns and cities, not on the edge of plantations. They had electricity, cafeterias, baseball fields and tennis courts. School segregation was perfectly legal in the United States until the 1954 Brown vs. Board of Education Supreme Court decision ordered states to desegregate public schools. Despite the ruling, many schools in Mississippi, particularly in rural areas and small towns, have never truly integrated. The white folks have found ways to avoid it.

Willie resented the disparity between the quality of the white schools vs. the Black schools.

"It's just like you go into a nice restaurant, or you go into what you call a hash house, you know, it's filthy, dirty, and all of that. And it was cold, we had wooden heaters, and half of the time they didn't have enough wood to keep the classrooms warm. You sit in class all day, if you had a coat to wear, you keep the coat on so you could stay warm."

The white children went to school on a traditional schedule, their academic year beginning in mid-August and ending in early June. The school year for Black children ran from mid-October through mid-May. There were two reasons for the school year being truncated for Blacks: cotton picking took until at least mid-October to complete, and the sharecroppers started choppin' cotton in mid-May. The academic calendar was secondary to the need for child labor—Black child labor. If you lived on a plantation and you were

Black, you had to work in the fields, it didn't matter if you were six or sixty years old. Perhaps the only reason the whites who controlled the school system even reluctantly allowed Blacks in rural areas to attend school at all is because there wasn't much to do in the fields from November through April.

According to the Southern Way of Life, with one of its main pillars being the presumption and preservation of white supremacy, an education for Black children was not supposed to be part of the equation, at least as far as the white plantation owners were concerned. The reasons are simple. A) If Black children are in school, then they can't be working in the fields, and B) if Black children get an education, they are likely to leave the plantation altogether, and then the system would start to crumble. Before mechanical cultivating and harvesting machines were commonplace in the late 1950s, Black labor was essential for the plantations to function, just as it had been for the century prior to The Civil War when slave labor was the bedrock of the South's economy.

No one was more staunchly opposed to Blacks receiving an education than Peyton Abbott Jones. As soon as Robert and Willie started going to school, he confronted Evie about it in the fields.

"I hear your boys are goin' to school," Jones said.

"Yes, that's true, Mr. Jones," Evie said.

"Haven't I done told you that niggers don't need no damn education? They need to be out here workin', not goin' to school."

Evie stuck her hoe in the ground and glared at him.

"My boys work in the fields before school, and they come back to work in the fields when they get home from school. They're doin' what they need to do. I see your boy goin' to school, so my boys are goin' to school, too, Mr. Jones," she retorted.

Jones just looked at her and shook his head.

"Goddamn niggers," he said as he walked away.

Robert marveled at his mom's determination and courage in standing up for them.

"Anyone that bothered the two of us, my brother and myself, my mom would kill a brick over us. We used to have a sayin' down there: 'There's only two free people back there on the plantation, that was a Black woman and a white man.' 'Cause most of the time they didn't deal with a Black woman. They would have a conversation with her, but they wouldn't push her around," Robert said.

Though school opened for Blacks in mid-October, that didn't mean all the kids would be able to go right away. A particularly robust cotton crop or a rainy fall often meant it would take till early or mid-November to finish the cotton picking. Joseph Smothers grew up on nearby Beall Plantation, and he met and became friends with Willie at Mt. Zion. Like many parents, his mother found a way to allow him to finish getting the crop in and get an education.

"Oh no, they didn't want you to get no education. See now, when you gatherin' the cotton crop in, I didn't go to school till November. 'Cause I had to gather that crop in. What my mother would do, she would send one of us to school when school started, one day, to get all the lessons and everything that we could study at home. Whenever we went back to school the teachers would give us a test on it, and that would catch us up with the other students. The schoolteachers knew what situation we was in so they worked with us. They know you couldn't come to school until you got that crop in so they'd make it where you could still learn. We had some caring teachers. If not, we'd have been still down there not even knowing how to read, but I thank God that we had those kinds of teachers," Smothers said.

So a nervously excited Willie headed off to Mt. Zion School in a pack with Robert and his plantation friends Samuel and Henry Mitchell, and Charlie Bell and Willie Andrews.

"You be a good boy, and don't get in any trouble, because I will hear about it," his mom told him on the first day of school.

As they walked down the dusty dirt road, the bus carrying the white schoolchildren would go by, its occupants yelling at them out the windows, calling them names, and trying to scrape the backs of their necks with wire coat hangers. Terrorizing Blacks was part of the way of life, and they were getting an early start.

"If it was raining, the bus driver would deliberately run in water to slice water on you or run you off the road. That was plain miserable," Willie said.

Evie would send Willie with a chicken or baloney sandwich and he quickly learned that he would have to run over the hill at lunchtime with the other young boys to avoid having their lunch confiscated by the older bullies. Sometimes he didn't make it, and he went hungry that day. Devotions were held every day at noon, and the children would sing hymns and pray to the Lord, thanking him for all their blessings. The highlight of the day was definitely recess when the kids could run around, play ball, or throw rocks in the Fannegusha Creek that wound by the school. Before heading back into the building they would all run to the pump at the back of the school to get a bellyful of water that tasted like iron. When it was cold the older boys would be sent out in the afternoon to forage for firewood to heat the school the following day.

Teaching in Mt. Zion School was certainly challenging. The space was cramped, there were very few resources, and the students had many barriers to their success, such as a lack of electricity in some of their homes and the need to be working the fields during planting and harvesting time. And teaching in those schools certainly did not pay well. At the start of the school year in October some of the women who taught at Mt. Zion would end their days by joining their students' families picking cotton in the fields so they could make a few extra dollars.

Willie's first and second grade teacher was Mrs. Bertha Coleman. She was short, plump, and stern. She lived in Lexington, but during the school year she stayed in a room she rented across the street from Mt. Zion School, as there was no way for her to travel the 10 miles each way between her home and the school. Bertha didn't smile much, and she wasn't someone you could reason with. She was right, and if you didn't agree with her, you were wrong.

"You had better learn something in Mrs. Coleman's class, because back then they would whoop your ass in school. There was a vine that used to grow right behind the school called rattan. They would go cut one of those and whoop you with it," Willie said.

Though his mom had told him to be a good boy, and Willie always wanted to please his mom, he couldn't help being a rascal. That was who he was. Corporal punishment would be meted out for not doing your schoolwork or for misbehaving. When Willie was punished, it was usually for the latter. He would disrupt the class, get in a fight at recess, or just generally act like his rambunctious self. Bertha would tell Willie to come to the front of the class, bend over, and she would whoop his ass with the vine. This happened to Willie two or three times—every month. Robert was much more studious and calmer than Willie, and he was almost never disciplined. He would just watch Willie's antics and shake his head.

"I was the bad boy," Willie said.

Things got better for Willie in third and fourth grade when Miss Loretha Land was his teacher. Miss Land was tall, light-complected, and sweet. She was someone Willie could talk to, and she was kind to the children. In other words, she was soft. When Willie would misbehave, she would call him up to the front of the class.

"Willie, I don't know why you do the things you do," she said.

"I'm sorry, ma'am," Willie said, gazing up at her with a sad and repentant face.

"You know I have to punish you, Willie."

"Yes, ma'am."

Miss Land looked at Willie for a long moment.

"Well, Willie, I think you can be better. I know you can be better. Will you promise me that you will be a good boy and I won't have to call you up here again?"

"Yes, ma'am, I promise."

"Okay, Willie, then I am going to let you go this time, but you need to be better," Miss Land said.

"Yes, ma'am, thank you," Willie said, and he turned around and went back to his seat, a big grin on his face.

Receiving an education is considered the right of every American. It is the first step for people who wish to achieve the American Dream of having a better quality of life than their parents, especially when those parents endured great hardship. This was especially true for sharecroppers living on plantations in rural Mississippi in the 1940s. Their knowledge of the world was very limited. Evie and many others couldn't read or write, so their days were spent working and surviving on the plantation, with occasional trips into town. There were no televisions or even electricity in their homes, so other than word of mouth, the only source of information that reached them was through the radio, if they had a friend or family member who was fortunate enough to have one. In this context, acquiring an education has the potential to be liberating from the sharecroppers' point of view, and dangerous from the plantation owner's point of view. The teachers knew this, so they had to walk a tightrope. It was their mission to educate the children to give them a chance at a better life, but they could not explicitly say: "You need to get an education so you can get a job that is more fulfilling and lucrative than picking cotton, a job that likely will take you far from here." They could not say anything that would anger Mr. Charlie, slang for a white man who oppresses Blacks.

"They wouldn't talk about how you get off the plantation, because they didn't want that to get back to Mr. Charlie. They would talk about getting an education, and learning. That is what they talked about. They would talk about how you must learn here to achieve to go higher. But they didn't talk about how to get off the plantation, because they knew that somebody would talk and it would get back to Mr. Charlie, and their job was gone," Willie said.

Willie was not the best student in the class. In fact, he wasn't a proficient reader until the fourth or fifth grade, and he clearly was not the most well-behaved child. However, when the teachers talked about the importance of getting an education, and how they knew some people who had left the plantation, and where they had gone, he listened carefully. He was energetic and free-spirited and charming—on the outside, but inside he was angry and bitter. He hated picking cotton. He hated being told what to do by any and every white person he met. He started thinking about getting off the plantation at a young age. Nationally famous role models for Blacks in the middle of the twentieth century were not plentiful. A young Black boy like Willie in 1950 could look up to the incredible athletic achievements of Jesse Owens, Joe Louis, and Jackie Robinson. As he progressed through elementary school, musicians such as Louis Armstrong, John Lee Hooker, and B.B. King achieved nationwide fame and stardom. But there were very few well-known Black political or business leaders at the time. It appeared to Willie and those around him that sports and music were the two most likely paths to freedom from the plantation.

"The only two ways to get you out of there: being a musician, or playing sports, was the two easiest ways to get out. The education was the third way to get out," Willie said.

The textbooks used in Black schools at the time were hand-me-downs from the white schools. By the time Willie and his classmates got their hands on them, half the covers were torn, and they were badly beaten up. The texts were written by white men and intended for use by white children. One thing Willie noticed is that there were little to no references to Black people in them.

"In grammar school I never seen anything in a book about a Black person. We didn't have those books," Willie said, and it is likely that those books didn't exist.

One of the American History textbooks that was in use in American public schools at the time was *The New World and its Growth*, by J. G.

Meyer and O. Stuart Hamer, published in 1948. Though the text is 441 pages long, the brief sections on slavery and cotton are the only references to Black people. The text refers to "Southerners" and "Negroes" and it is clear that Southerners is used to describe white people only. The discussion of slavery is centered on how important slaves were to the production of cotton in the first half of the nineteenth century. There is no mention of whipping, rape, torture, tearing families apart, or the use of dogs to hunt down runaway slaves.

The book seeks to inform America's impressionable young minds about what happened to slaves after they were freed in 1865:

> At first the Negroes had a hard time getting used to freedom. Some thought that since they were free they did not have to work. It was difficult for them to realize that they had been given freedom—not from work, but to work for themselves.

The authors' intent is clear: to inculcate in the minds of white children the notion that Blacks are lazy, the same people who had worked harder than anyone else in America since their involuntary arrival in 1619.

The description of how cotton is produced in 1940s America delineates the sharecropping system and it includes a photo of a long line of mule-drawn wagons stuffed with cotton, waiting for their turn to have their cotton weighed at the gin. All the wagon drivers are Black, and in the foreground are two young men, sitting casually on their wagon, smiling as if they did not have a care in the world. Life looks grand. The caption reads:

> Cotton picking is almost over. Cash will soon be jingling in the croppers' pockets—cash to pay last year's grocery

bills, cash to buy some new clothes, cash for stick candy
for the children.

The textbook does not mention the many harsh realities of life for Blacks in the first half of the twentieth century: segregationist laws, lack of educational and economic opportunity, voter disenfranchisement, or the terror wrought by the Ku Klux Klan.

A report by the Equal Justice Initiative in 2015 finds that about 4,000 Blacks were lynched in Southern states from 1870 to 1950. "Lynchings were violent and public acts of torture that traumatized Black people throughout the country and were largely tolerated by state and federal officials," the report said. The number of lynchings identified in the report only accounts for known lynchings, and there are likely many others that occurred but were not chronicled. Importantly, the threat of lynching was omnipresent and often psychologically omnipotent, and it was an integral feature of the Southern Way of Life. Meyer and Hamer's *American History* textbook makes no mention of lynching. It does, however, include a section praising the achievements of General Robert E. Lee, the man who led an army in revolt against the United States government.

In terms of Black leaders and historical figures, there is no mention of Frederick Douglass, Harriet Tubman, or W.E.B. Du Bois. The only Black leader whose accomplishments are described is Booker T. Washington. This is perhaps not surprising, since though Washington has been praised by historians for doing many things to improve the lives of Blacks in America, he has also been criticized for accommodating white segregationists and not demanding true equality for Blacks. He was a pragmatist, and while he worked to improve the economic situation for Blacks at the Tuskegee Institute by educating them in trades and farming, the notion of true equality was a battle he did not think he could win, so he didn't push it.

Washington was the only Black leader who Willie ever read about in his grammar school textbooks, and the only other Black person he ever learned about in school was the famous scientist George Washington Carver, who preached the virtue of farmers planting crops other than cotton to prevent soil depletion, and to improve their ability to be self-sufficient. So the only two Black people Willie ever heard about in grammar school were helping Blacks become better farmers. Well, Willie hated farming, and he knew his future would be different.

# 3

## ONCE IN A WHILE YOU GET SHOWN THE LIGHT

Even as a young boy, people were drawn to Willie due to his outgoing personality, ready smile, and infectious laugh. His friends found him fun to be around, but behind that persona he was battling some demons. He hated working in the cotton fields and being told what to do by Peyton Abbott Jones, his son Frank, or any other white man who he met. He had some fun at school, but he struggled academically, and being such a rascal, it seemed he was always getting in a fix. A piece of him enjoyed the notoriety of being known as the bad boy, but it wasn't always as glamorous as it seemed, especially when he was getting a whoopin'. He loved his mom, but his dad, well, he was just plain nasty. He smacked Willie in the head every time he got sassy—and even when he didn't—but worse than that, he treated his mom horribly, hitting her and bossing her around. It made him furious, but there wasn't anything he could do about it.

When he was about seven years old something strange started to happen. A few Saturdays a month his mom would tell him that Mr. Davenport was coming to pick up Willie and Robert and they were going to spend the day with him. Now Mr. Davenport was a different story altogether. He was almost six and a half feet tall and Willie thought he looked like a giant. He owned his own car, which was incredible because only three or four Black families in the area owned a car. What was even more amazing was that he had a big house with three bedrooms and acres of land that he also owned. He was a farmer who had several dozen head of cattle and he raised cotton, corn, and soybeans. Mr. Davenport wanted them to feel at home and he told the boys to call him Andrew.

Willie never did anything fun with his dad, but when they were with Andrew, it seemed like all they did was have fun.

When Andrew would pull up next to the fields in his 1948 Chevy to pick up Willie and Robert, his mom Evie would look up and a big smile would come across her face, but Oscar Harris would just scowl. The boys would be bursting with joy. They had waited for this all week. They would hop in the back seat and drive off the plantation, smiling at their friends who were playing games or working in the fields. Andrew would take them to a little burger joint in Tchula that was run by a Chinese family, where cheeseburgers were 10 cents. Then it was over to the Frosty Freeze for a chocolate milkshake that cost 25 cents. All the restaurants had two windows with signs above them, one that said, "Whites Only," and the other that said "Colored." The same signs hung over the water fountains, and Andrew always told Willie don't ever mess around and go where it said Whites Only. But oh that milkshake tasted so good on a hot summer day. His dad had never bought him a milkshake. Not once.

The highlight of the day was when Andrew would take them to the movie theater, where admission was 15 cents. There was a sign with an arrow that pointed up to the top floor that read "Colored." They would hike up the stairs and sit on the wooden benches of the second floor that looked down over the white section on the first floor with its plush velvet seats and carpeted floor. Willie didn't care about that too much in those moments. He was just happy to see the pictures roll with stars on horseback like Rex Allen, Lash LaRue, Johnny Mack Brown, Roy Rogers, Gene Autry, Whip Wilson, and of course, John Wayne. Almost all the popular movies were westerns back then, and Willie marveled at the open spaces, the mountains, and all the excitement of the Wild West. He watched them herding cattle and fighting Indians. It sure looked like it was a lot more fun than picking cotton.

The boys would also enjoy playing with the kids who lived near Andrew's house.

"He had a cousin lived right across the road from him and his cousin had kids me and my brother's age. So we would love to go down there 'cause we would play with his cousin's kids. Then we had a good meal and we didn't worry about what are we gonna eat," Willie said.

The boys would often spend the night at Andrew's and the Davenports didn't have any children, so it was just the four of them in the house—Willie, Robert, Andrew, and his wife Ruby. The bedroom had two comfortable beds in it and pajamas for them to wear. Pajamas! They never had any pajamas at home—they just slept in their underwear.

The boys would lie awake in bed and try to figure out why they were there.

"Robert," Willie asked, "what are we doing here?"

"We are sleeping in a nice comfy bed, that's what we're doing."

"No, I mean, who is Andrew, and why is he so nice to us? I mean, he ain't mom's brother," Willie said.

"No, he ain't."

"I don't think he is related to mom at all," Willie said.

"No, I reckon he ain't."

"Then what are we doing here?"

"I don't know, Willie, and I really don't care. I'm not complaining or saying nothing 'cause this is the sweet life. The one thing I ask is that you don't blow it for us, you little shit," Robert said, smacking Willie's arm.

"I won't," Willie smiled, and he went to sleep.

Andrew would also take the boys to Lexington a couple of times a month. It was twice as far from the plantation as Tchula and while it only had 3,000 residents, it was the closest thing to a big city that

Willie would see in his childhood. Willie loved these rides because Andrew would tell them about the Negro league stars and his own baseball playing days. In the 1940s and early 1950s, baseball was the number one sport in America, as football and basketball had not yet ascended in popularity. On those magic carpet rides Willie would hear Brooklyn Dodgers baseball games on the radio—Jackie Robinson was playing, and practically every Black man, woman, and child in the South immediately became a Dodgers fan. Robinson was a god to Willie. He had made it to the big time, and it helped Willie to dream that it was possible for him to make it someday. They also talked about Otis "Big Smokey" Smothers, a man who grew up on a nearby plantation and became a famous musician in the Chicago jazz scene in the late 1940s and early 1950s. Just like they said in school: the two surest ways to make it off the plantation were sports and music.

On Saturdays the businesses around Courthouse Square in Lexington were bustling with shoppers, both white and Black. For a rural county, it was their version of Times Square. It was the place everyone from many miles around went to do their business on Saturday. All the restaurants around the square were for whites only, and Willie knew not to even think about going in them. Running south off the square was Yazoo Street and it was filled restaurants for Blacks and juke joints that were packed on Friday and Saturday nights. They called it Beale Street in honor of the entertainment district in Memphis. The big department and clothing stores around the square were run by Jewish merchants, including Cohen's department store and N. Shure's clothing store, and Andrew would take the boys there to buy their school clothes and shoes. Since there were not enough stores to service both Blacks and whites, the Blacks were allowed to shop in the same stores as whites, but they always had one Black employee who took care of all the Black customers.

Lexington also had a cattle auction on weekends where Willie would go with Andrew so he could sell his cattle. Willie watched how Andrew interacted with the white men. He always showed them respect and tipped his hat when he said hello. Willie noticed that the white men called him Mr. Davenport when they said hello, and not "Boy." Willie could sense that it was because he owned land and cattle, and he was seen as more prominent than Black men who were sharecroppers. He also noticed that Andrew was always very calm and polite around white men. No matter what he saw or what he knew that was wrong, he always said "Yes, sir" and "No, sir," and went about his business. Years later, Willie realized that this approach helped him maintain his standing in the community and decreased the chances he would be terrorized or attacked.

"As long as they would tell you to mind your own business, and long as you didn't get involved with what they was doing, and speak out or nothin', you was alright. 'Cause most of the Blacks that owned their own land, they didn't say anything, even though the white people got paid more for cotton then they did, but they kept their mouths closed."

As long as successful Blacks like Andrew didn't speak out against the omnipresent economic, social, political, and educational racial injustice that defined life in Mississippi, the whites would let them work their land and not bother them. There were not enough of them to be a threat to the whites anyway. While there were hundreds of Black families in the area around Howard in the 1940s, only three owned land: Andrew Davenport, Cornelius Richardson, and Alan Lewis. The rest were sharecroppers, with a few tenant farmers sprinkled in.

Half a dozen Black men worked on Andrew's farm, and if you were a laborer on a farm in Mississippi in 1950, working for another Black man was a sought-after job.

"Working for another Black was better work, 'cause you didn't worry about nobody cussin' you out, trying to slap you upside the head, or kick you, or whatsoever," Willie said.

The circus came to Lexington every year and Andrew would take the boys. Whites sat on one side of the tent and Blacks on the other. Willie loved seeing the elephants and tigers and other exotic animals, but the performance also included a minstrel show, with white performers putting on blackface and portraying Blacks as stupid, lazy, superstitious, happy-go-lucky buffoons. Minstrel shows had been touring the United States since the 1830s and it was considered the most popular form of public entertainment in America in the nineteenth century. The openly racist themes of the minstrel show were in line with the attitudes of the majority of Americans during the genre's heyday. Frederick Douglass pointedly denounced white performers who put on blackface as "the filthy scum of white society, who have stolen from us a complexion denied them by nature, in which to make money, and pander to the corrupt taste of their white fellow citizens." Willie would watch the white half of the audience laughing uproariously during the minstrel show, and he would just sit there, uncomprehending.

There was also a meat freezer in Lexington where Andrew would store meat after his cattle had been butchered. Willie would ride up there with him and he would take out some meat a few times a month, take it home, and cook it up. This was so much different than what they had back on the plantation, where on the first of the month Evie would get her $30 loan from Mr. Jones and the boys would go with her to the Piggly Wiggly market in Tchula to buy groceries. If they were lucky, they could buy meat that would last for the first couple of days, and then they would spend the rest of the month surviving on what they grew and raised or caught. Willie, Robert, and Evie would go down the road to Black Creek where they would fish for catfish, smallmouth bass, or mudcat. And then there were the squirrels that the boys would hunt for in the forest next to the plantation.

Willie didn't know why, but every once in a while Andrew would give his mom a few steaks and she would serve them along with some homemade peach cobbler, but those scrumptious meals were rare.

It was a hand-to-mouth existence and there were plenty of days when Willie was hungry and there was no food in the house. What little money they had, his dad would blow it doing some foolish thing. Evie said he had "outside girls." The Davenport farm was about a half-hour walk from the plantation, and one day when he was really hungry, Willie walked over there by himself with the hope of getting something to eat. He headed down the hill, past Howard Store, down dusty Blissdale Road and over the bridge that spanned Black Creek to the Davenport farm. Andrew wasn't home, but he walked to the screen door to speak to his wife Ruby.

Ruby stared at him blankly through the door.

"Boy, what do you want?"

"Excuse me, Miss Ruby, I'm sorry to bother you, but I'm real hungry. Can I please have something to eat?" Willie asked.

"Don't be comin' around here begging for food. Go back to your shack on the plantation and let your mama take care of you. I ain't your mama," Ruby said.

"But we ain't got nothin' to eat, that's why I came here. Please?"

"I ain't got nothin' for you. Now get on along," Ruby said as she shut the door.

Willie walked across the street and stood under a sugar magnolia tree and waited. About an hour later he saw Andrew's car coming slowly down the road, the gravel crackling under its tires. Andrew got out of the car and saw Willie standing under the tree.

"Hey, Willie! What are you doing here?"

"Andrew, I'm sorry, we don't have no food in our house, and I'm real hungry, and I came over to see if I could get something to eat, but Miss Ruby said she don't have nothing for me," Willie said.

"You walked all the way over here?"

"Yes," Willie said.

"You hold on a minute. I'll be right back."

Andrew walked toward the kitchen door, staring at Ruby who had been watching his conversation with Willie through the screen.

"Ruby! What are you thinking, turning Willie away? If that boy ever comes here again, ever, you give him what he asks for. All he wants is a goddam sandwich, for chrissake."

A few minutes later, Andrew walked out of the house with two sandwiches and a glass of milk for Willie, and they ate lunch together.

When Willie was 11 years old, he started hearing things that confused him. He would be walking in Tchula with his dad and someone from another plantation would walk by, smile at Willie, and say "Hey, Davenport, how you doin', little man?" Willie didn't know what to say, but whenever it happened, his dad would whack him hard in the back of the head. This went on for a couple of years, rumors reaching his ears and older kids teasing him, saying "Who's your daddy?"

Finally, when he was 14, he asked Evie about it.

"Mom, you know I've been hearing rumors."

"What kind of rumors, son?" Evie asked.

"Rumors about Andrew Davenport, and you, and me and Robert."

"Oh, son, I wouldn't listen to those fool rumors if I was you. Ain't never done nobody no good," Evie said, and turned away.

Willie started to get angry.

"C'mon, Mom! I'm old enough. I deserve to know. People are saying that Andrew is my father! Well, is he?"

Evie whirled around, hurt. She looked at Willie and she could see the pain in his eyes. She sat down at the kitchen table and put her head in her hands.

"The truth is, yes. Andrew is your father," Evie said, holding back tears.

"And Robert's, too?"

"Yes," Evie said, "and Robert's too."

"Well, your dad—I mean Oscar—I don't have to tell you how awful he is, he has outside girlfriends and such, and we haven't gotten along since I don't know when. And you know that your grandmother lives down Blissdale Road near the Davenport farm. I would go visiting and see Andrew Davenport, and he was so tall and handsome, and his first wife had just died. And I would talk to him over the fence, and actually I knew him many years ago, when I was in my 20s. But anyway, we would talk and laugh and well, you know, one thing, and then another, and then along came Robert, and then you came, and you boys made me so happy. I knew I would have to tell you someday. I just didn't know how," Evie said.

Willie sat there thinking about what to say next, and Evie continued.

"I just wanted somebody to make me feel good. Somebody to make me feel like they cared. Everybody deserves that at least once in a while."

"Let me ask you something, Mom. If you knew Andrew back when you were young, why didn't you get together with him back in the day?" Willie said.

"I would have loved to, son. That was my dream. But Andrew is educated, and he owns that beautiful farm. Look at me. I was just a girl from the plantation, cleaning and cooking for the white folk, can't even read or write. I just didn't fit in with him and his friends."

"Well at least now I know why that man never cared for me," Willie said.

"Now you know, and I'm sorry."

The knowledge of his true bloodline gave Willie some peace. He no longer felt guilty that he had such a poisonous relationship with Oscar Harris and for not respecting the man. However, knowing that his father lived nearby on a big farm that he owned made it all the more difficult to get through the days and nights on Clifton Plantation. Every time he had to work in the fields, every time he had to make a meal out of peaches and biscuits, and every time he went to bed in their darkened cabin, he would think why—why can't we be living on Andrew's farm all the time, not worrying about our next meal, and living with a dad who actually loves us?

Willie always looked up to Andrew, but now he listened more intently to his advice, which wasn't given very often. The message from Andrew about how to behave was similar to what his Mom had told him: don't do anything to incite any whites and get away from any situation that could escalate into violence as quickly as possible.

"It was very seldom, he always told me, don't be a fool. Do not act the fool in front of them. Whatever they said, if I didn't want to deal with it, if I see 'em coming. Get out the way. Just leave, and if they would say something to you and cuss you out, then go ahead and get on out the way," Willie said.

The message was basically that we can't win in any confrontation with a white person, and if you say something or do something that they don't like, it can get real ugly, real fast. So the smart thing to do is avoid any confrontation, because we can't win. That's the system. It doesn't matter if you are right or if you didn't even do anything; the only thing that will matter in the end is how the whites perceive what you did, and how they react to it. We can't win. That's the system.

As Willie continued to get taller his fear of Oscar Harris slowly subsided. Oscar was a strong man, but Willie was looking forward to the day when he would no longer have to take his physical abuse.

When Willie was 15 Oscar ordered him to come outside the cabin to help fix the fence surrounding the pig pen, which had come undone and was blowing in the wind. Willie came out to help, but Oscar was impatient.

"Get your ass over there and hold the fence before I whoop your ass," Oscar barked at him, as he struggled to nail the rusty wire to the fencepost.

Willie, now almost 6‘ 4“ and half a head taller than Oscar, said "those days are over."

This is a pivotal moment for Oscar. If he allows the boy to talk back, his dominance over him is finished. Needing to do something to try to hold onto his power over Willie, he flings the hammer at his head. As it hurtles toward him, Willie hears it whistlin' in the wind. He ducks, and it just misses his head. A lifetime of fire and fury swells in Willie's breast and he pounces on Oscar. As he is about to beat the hell out of him, he says "This is for my mom, too!" Evie, who had been watching this unfold from the back door, rushed out and pulled Willie off Oscar.

From that day on, Oscar never mistreated Willie again. They just avoided each other.

# 4

## BOILING WITH RAGE

Living in a segregated community meant that you were required to act a certain way if you were Black. You couldn't go into restaurants reserved for white customers, or use water fountains or bathrooms that were clearly marked Whites Only, or use the same libraries. These weren't just customs, they were laws. But it was more than that. Young Blacks were also taught how to act around whites, how to speak around whites, and how to avoid getting into trouble with whites.

Willie was an extremely spirited child, and his mom Evie took great care in explaining to him how he needed to behave. Evie was 40 years old when Willie was born, and she had cooked for white people when she was a younger woman. She had seen a lot.

"My mom, when she was in her early age, her 20s or 30s, somewhere along there, she used to cook for white people and she would tell me how to act, and what to do if they would say something to you. Don't be, what they'd call it then, don't be sassy, 'cause you would pay a price for that, and she didn't want her son to be beat up and there was nothin' she could do about it. And if it happened, they would probably have to kill her, because she would step in. I learned most everything how to behave, 'specially when it came to white people, from my mother. I guess my mother had seen, and been around stuff that I was never privileged to see. 'Cause she would tell me about when she was a youngster growin' up how white people would beat you, and she'd seen a lot of it. I didn't, but I'd heard about it. So she's the one taught me how to behave," Willie said.

What Willie's mom taught him, and what the other moms and dads in the community taught their kids, was to be submissive. Even though it cut against every notion they had of dignity and self-respect, they taught them this simply for the sake of self-preservation. This submission included routine activities such as stepping off the sidewalk when whites approached to give them a clear path; keeping your head down when speaking to a white person, and never contradicting what they said; and never striking a white person, even if they struck you.

Evie needed to spend more time with Willie than she did with Robert, teaching him what he should and shouldn't do.

"My brother didn't speak out. My mom was afraid for me that I was the one that would speak out and say things. And she thought that if I didn't get out of there, I might wind up being killed or hurt or something," Willie said.

One of the things Black males had to endure was how they were addressed by whites. Peyton Abbott Jones had a son named Frank, and when Frank, and all other white males turned 14 years old, Blacks had to start calling him Mr., so Frank became Mr. Jones. But for Black males, that transition never happened. The whites called a Black male "Boy" when he was a boy, when he was an adolescent, and when he was a man. Then maybe when he was 50 years old, they would start calling him "Uncle," skipping right over the terms "Mr.," or "Sir." Those terms of respect were almost never applied to Black males, and it was intentional, letting them know their position in the Southern hierarchy.

When Willie became a teenager, living in this stifling environment really started to bother him.

*Robert Harris and Willie Harris, circa 1955*

"Day in and day out, livin' in a segregated community. You'd be walking down the road and the white people would come along in their cars and they'd run you off the road. If it rained they'd make sure they had a water puddle to wet you up. They'd call you names. That's why I was angry. You couldn't fight back," Willie said.

Willie got bigger and bigger, his outgoing nature made him very popular, and the girls started to notice him. That was all good, but inside his heart and mind, a furor was brewing.

"It was because of my size, because most of the white men in the area where I grew up was real short, and they would say 'Come here, nigger. Fetch me this or fetch me that.' And you know, you may be sittin' there talkin' to somebody and they would say 'Hey, nigger boy, come over here,' and it was just plain humiliation. And you better not say anything, you better just smile and say 'Yes, sir, mister.' And you was just completely handicapped. And I was just boiling with rage that one of these days I'm gonna get my opportunity, and whoop one of these white dudes' ass. When you have somebody abuse you, and keep abusing you, and you can't do nothin' about it, frustration sets in. Anger sets in. Hatred sets in. And that was me," Willie said.

Willie couldn't talk much to Robert about how angry he was, as Robert was much calmer and didn't have the same overt fire. Robert was certainly unhappy about how Blacks were treated, but he was the introvert in the family. He kept his head down and plowed ahead. Willie was able to vent his frustration to his good friend Henry Mitchell who lived just a couple of cabins away on Clifton Plantation. Willie and Henry played basketball together, hung out all the time, and were like-minded. They would frequently make plans to get back at the white guys who had abused them and do it so they wouldn't get caught.  Nothing ever came of it, but it felt good just to talk about it.

When Willie was seven years old in 1949, he woke up in the middle of a hot summer night to the sound of a pack of bloodhounds barking and howling.

"Ma, what's that?" he asked Evie.

"The boss man from the next plantation got a posse and they are chasin' Will," Evie said.

Willie pulled his bed covers tighter around him. He knew what Will was like, and this didn't sound good.

Will's full name was Willie Lee Wilkes. He was a sharecropper who lived on Ellison and Beall, a plantation that bordered Clifton. He was in his mid-twenties and had served in the United States Army during World War II. Even before he went into the Army, Will was known as the kind of guy who stood up for himself. He wasn't the submissive type, and his boldness—which in a white man would have been viewed as admirable—was an uncommon and dangerous trait for a Black man of his time, especially in rural Mississippi.

Everyone in the community knew what had happened the day before Willie was awoken by the scream of the bloodhounds. Will had been at Howard Store, as the male sharecroppers would hang out on Saturday behind the store and shoot craps, drink beer, and tell stories. On this Saturday Will went into the store and bought a bag of loose tobacco. All the sharecroppers bought loose tobacco back then and rolled their own cigarettes, since they could not afford pre-rolled. The man behind the counter threw Will's change down on the counter and some of it rolled onto the floor at Will's feet.

"Pick it up," Will said to him.

"What did you say, nigger?" the clerk asked.

"I said pick it up," Will said.

The clerk came out from behind the counter and started to push Will out of the store.

"Get the fuck out of here, boy!" he screamed.

Will went outside and got a pistol and fired a shot in the air, and then he took off. The clerk and the store manager got a posse together, which included the local sheriff, and they started hunting for Will.

Dennis Smothers is Will's younger half-brother. He was only six years old at the time, but he remembers being terrified.

"They made some telephone calls to gather the posse and they were hunting him down. They were going to kill him," Smothers said.

Late that night the posse caught up to Will. He was hiding in some bushes at the top of a hill. He put his hands up and was about to surrender, but then he thought better of it, knowing that they would probably kill him. He used his military training and did a duck and roll down the hill, and he took off, the men in the posse shooting at him, and missing. He made his way to town and hopped a freight train to Yazoo City, which was 30 miles away.

The next morning Will's mom went to talk to the plantation owner and pleaded for her son's life. Please don't kill my boy when you find him, she said. The owner said they wouldn't kill him, but he wasn't welcome on the plantation anymore and he had better not come around again. Will stayed away for a full year, and at the end of the next summer he came back and was helping his family pick cotton when the plantation owner spotted him. He called the sheriff and they grabbed Will and brought him into town. Will's mom again went and pleaded for her son's life. She was told they would let him go if he never came around again. She agreed to move the family off the plantation right away. They moved to another plantation in a different community where no one knew Will. His mom said she couldn't stay in a place where her children were not welcome.

An entire family with a half dozen kids moved their home because a Black man talked back to a white man. It wasn't that what Will had done was so terrible. It was the idea that if we let him get away with it, what else will he think he can do? And then what else will other Blacks think they can do? Before you know it, they will think they can vote and talk to white women. No, it must be stopped before there is any crack in the system of white supremacy. Dennis Smothers knew that his brother had done something that was forbidden for Blacks in the South.

"They weren't going to let him get away with that. You didn't talk back to white people at the time, and you don't sass white people.

Whatever they say, it don't have to be the law, it was the law. It was well known all over the community that Will had violated the code, the white code. You know, you don't do nothing like that," Smothers said.

As Willie grew, so did his interest in sports, particularly basketball. But while the NBA wouldn't have any Black players on the court until 1950, other sports had integrated earlier. Joe Louis, himself born into a sharecropping family in Alabama, became the heavyweight boxing champion in 1937 and reigned for a dozen years. Jackie Robinson was born into a sharecropping family in Georgia and broke the color barrier in Major League Baseball when he started playing second base for the Brooklyn Dodgers in 1947, earning Rookie of the Year honors that year, and the league's MVP award two years later. It was a huge deal for Blacks to be able to follow the exploits of these two pioneering heroes. Hearing about all their success was a tremendous source of pride for Blacks in America, and it helped kids like Willie believe that they, too, could do something special. It was like Willie's teachers had told him: the best way to get off the plantation and be successful is by being really good at sports or music. Essentially, do something that will entertain white people.

"The biggest thing then was Joe Louis and Jackie Robinson. The fights would come on on Friday night, brought to you by Gillette razors. And Black people, as I can remember, back when I was six, seven, eight years old, didn't have a TV. It was a radio. And everybody would go to one house and cheer for Joe Louis. And also Jackie Robinson, because my dad was a great baseball fan, and when we would go places with him, he would have the baseball game on the radio. Most of the Black people didn't listen to nobody but the Dodgers, because the Dodgers was the only one that had a Black," Willie said.

Willie distinctly remembers hearing Red Barber, himself a Mississippi native who had a folksy style, calling the Dodger games on the radio. When Barber first learned that Robinson would be coming to play for the Dodgers, he said he was going to quit because, having been raised in the South, he didn't think he could call a game with a Black player on the field. However, he changed his mind about quitting, and soon after seeing Robinson play, and seeing what kind of man he was, he became a big supporter of him and the other Black players that followed.

Shortly after Robert turned 18 years old in 1958, he took a walk to downtown Lexington on the first Tuesday in November. He was headed to the courthouse to vote.

When he walked into the courthouse he saw a middle-aged white guy sitting at the table in front of the voting booths. Robert had never seen him before.

"What you come here for, boy?" the man asked.

"I came here to vote, sir," Robert said.

"Oh, you don't need to vote, boy. I'll vote for you," the man said.

"You can't vote for me. I have to vote for myself, sir."

"Oh, I don't think so, boy," the man said, and then he picked up a double-barreled shotgun and casually pointed it at Robert.

"I guess you're gonna vote for me then," Robert said, and he turned around and walked out of the courthouse.

Blacks had been prevented from exercising their right to vote in Southern states in the century since the Civil War, usually through poll taxes, literacy tests or intimidation. Robert knew he probably wouldn't be able to vote, but he had to try.

"I figured that being at that age, and you're supposed to vote, and I wasn't totally illiterate, I figured I'd try it. I figured he wasn't going to let me do it, but I figured I'd try it, otherwise, it would have been on me by not going. Because a lot of people didn't ever test the system." When Robert did finally get the chance to vote, he relished it, and never took it for granted.

"That is why today, anytime there is an election, if it's for dog-catcher, I'm going to vote." When he was twenty years old in 1960, Robert got a job at the local Ford dealership, cleaning and preparing cars before they were sold. At that time, Blacks weren't allowed to sell cars, and were kept in the background. After he was there a few weeks, the owner brought in a young white guy and told Robert to train him to prepare the cars. When they got their next paycheck, the new guy showed Robert his check, and it was almost twice as much as Robert's. He went to see the owner.

"How can he be getting' twice as much as I am, and I'm training him?" Robert asked.

"Well, you know, he's white," the owner said, "you can't get paid as much as he does."

Robert quit the job that day and was hired at Tidwell's service station in town. One of his duties at the station was to go to the house of one of the station's employees, a white woman, and cut her grass every Thursday. It was understood by everyone at that time that Blacks did not go to the front door of a white person's house. If they wished to speak to them, they had to go to the back.

Robert would work at the white woman's house with another guy from the station, a poor white guy. One afternoon they were working in her yard when the white guy started talking shit to Robert.

"I'm better than you, nigger," the white guy said.

Robert seethed inside, but kept his cool. They were doing the same job, and Robert was doing a better job at it, so who is this guy to say he is better than me? Robert knew it wasn't the safest thing to confront or contradict a white man in a small town in Mississippi in 1961, but he couldn't keep his mouth shut.

"You ain't better than me," Robert said.

"Yes I am, nigger," he said.

"Okay, if you better than me, then go up and knock on that lady's front door," Robert said.

Silence.

"You can't," Robert said, "'Cause you ain't nothin' but poor white trash."

"Fuck you, boy," he said," and started to walk around the house toward the front door. Robert followed him, trailing by about 30 feet, waiting to see what would happen.

"He went up there and knocked on that lady's front door, and she come out there and cursed him out, callin' him everything 'cept a child of God," Robert said, "and after that, the guy sat on the corner and drank wine every day. Never did go back to work. He just couldn't understand: he was white, and he couldn't go to that white lady's door. He had to go to the back, same as I did. Poor white people had the same problem I had."

After the white guy stopped working, Robert would go up to the woman's house by himself every Thursday. Gradually, she started asking him to come do some work for him in her house. She was pretending that her sink was clogged and said she needed Robert to get down under the sink and fix it. She really just wanted to get him inside the house. Oldest trick in the book. My pipe is clogged. Robert knew it was risky, knew he shouldn't be in there, but he didn't want to say no, so he did it. As soon as Mr. Tidwell down at the station started to hear about Robert doing work in the woman's house, Robert had to quit.

"That lady almost got me killed. I'm not supposed to be in there. You have to be careful because you can get killed quick and it's not your fault," Robert said.

Robert and Willie and all their friends knew the rules, and if this wasn't Rule Number One, then it was at least near the top: Don't mess with white women, don't talk to white women unless spoken to, and just stay away from them altogether.

"Sometimes, you couldn't even look at one. If you did, you better glance at a quick pace and move on."

Yale sociology professor Elijah Anderson has written in the twenty-first century about the difficulty American Blacks have faced navigating "white space" since the end of the civil rights movement. White spaces, such as white neighborhoods, restaurants, schools, universities, workplaces, etc., are spaces that are populated almost entirely by whites, and where Blacks are typically absent, not expected, or marginalized when present, according to Anderson. Even more than 50 years after the murder of Martin Luther King, Jr., Blacks still must approach these spaces with care. And yet there was Robert, a twenty-year-old Black man doing his best to navigate the white space in a small town in Mississippi in the early 1960s.

Howard Store sat at the bottom of a hill, just a few hundred yards from Clifton Plantation. A small, square building with a hot metal roof, it was nestled in the nexus of Jones Road and Howard Road, on the same dusty patch of land as the cotton gin. With the closest town being five miles away, the store and cotton gin provided vital resources to the people of Clifton and the neighboring plantations. The gin was where they would bring the fruit of their labor, and the store is where everyone would go to buy the items they couldn't raise or grow themselves, such as sugar, salt, and flour.

One painfully hot summer afternoon when Willie was fifteen, he was in the store with Henry Mitchell. They were just killin' time, and Willie noticed there was a little white boy in the store, and he was maybe five or six years old. And there was no one else there except the proprietor, a surly middle-aged white guy named Bill Turner. Willie and Henry went home, and a couple of hours later, Henry showed up at the door of Willie's cabin.

"What's up, Henry?" Willie asked.

"Willie, Bill Turner wants you to come down to the store."

"Why?" Willie asked.

"He said you stole his cigarettes," Henry said.

"What? Why would he say that?"

"I don't know," Henry said, "I guess maybe that little white kid told him you did it."

"That's bullshit," Willie said. He hadn't stolen any cigarettes, but he knew he had better go down there. He walked down the hill to the store and went in. Bill Turner was standing behind the counter.

"Mr. Turner, I was told that you wanted to talk to me," Willie said.

"Slim," Turner said, "you stole my cigarettes."

"No, Mr. Turner, I didn't steal any cigarettes," Willie said.

"Nigger, are you callin' me a liar?" Bill Turner said as he took a pistol from under the counter of the country store, reversed the chamber, dropped in a bullet, and leveled it at Willie. It was two feet from his nose, and he could smell the metal.

"No, Mr. Turner, I'm not callin' you a liar, but I didn't steal nuthin'," Willie said.

Turner raised the pistol some more. It was now at Willie's eye level.

"I'll blow your damn brains out," Turner said, his teeth clenched and rage etched in the lines of his forehead.

At 15 years old and on the threshold of manhood, Willie was 6 feet, 2 inches tall, big, strong, and often defiant. But now he was scared. More than scared. As a Black teenager in Mississippi in 1956, he had gotten used to being treated a certain way by whites, but this was different. No one had ever put a loaded gun in his face before.

He was momentarily paralyzed by terror, but then he had one thought: get out. He turned and ran as fast as he could, up the hill and back to his cabin, his breathing as heavy as an Olympic sprinter.

"That was the closest I came to, maybe if I stayed there he woulda shot me, I don't know. I still don't know today why he didn't pull the trigger. It ain't no good feeling having a loaded gun stuck in your face.

But I never forgot," Willie said, and he never went back to the store again as long as Bill Turner was there.

Before the civil rights movement gained momentum in the late 1950s, some white preachers and congregations used flimsy religious arguments to defend segregation, citing biblical verses that they claimed proved God intended different races be kept separate. In doing so, they ignored dozens of other verses in the old and new testaments which instructed people to love everyone equally and be good to everyone. At the same time, millions of Blacks took solace and emotional refuge in their Christian faith. Spending Sunday at church was, for many, the highlight of their week. In the church they could find peace, deliverance, and salvation.

Most of the whites in and around their area attended First Baptist Church of Lexington, located just one block north of Courthouse Square. A large brick building with heavy oak doors, it boasted a massive organ to the right of the altar, narrow floor-to-ceiling stained glass windows, and seating for a few hundred of the faithful. The Blacks who lived on Clifton and the nearby plantations attended Mt. Zion Church, a smallish, white wood structure just down the dirt road from the cotton gin and Howard Store. While Mt. Zion lacked the impressive physical stature of First Baptist Church, it was no less beloved by its parishioners.

Willie's family attended church occasionally, but not on a regular basis like so many of their neighbors. Willie and Robert would often go with their dad when they stayed with him on the weekends, and Evie would go with her friends to a church that was closer to where she grew up in Carroll County. Evie didn't attend mass as regularly as many other Black women in the area, and she told Willie it was because she had a hard time with the hypocrisy of some people who acted one way all week and then presented themselves as pious and spiritual on Sunday. Willie inherited his mom's keen eye for hypocrisy, and he also struggled with the notion that faith in the Lord would help him escape his horrible circumstances, something that others in his situation believed.

When he was 15 years old he asked his mom about something that had been bothering him.

"Ma, how is it that if you go to church, you're a Baptist, whether you Black or white, you pray to the same God, but this God tell you if you white you better than us?"

"What do you mean, son?" Evie said.

"What did we do for God to hate us so bad?" Willie asked.

"Oh, my child, it ain't God. God don't hate you. God loves you. It's the people," she said.

"Them white people go to church, 'cause I see them going to church, who are they prayin' to? It got to be the same God, it ain't no two different gods. God can't be tellin' them one thing and tellin' us another," Willie said.

All the thoughts and pain and confusion that had been churning in Willie's mind came spilling out.

"I hear the old people talking about how great God is and how he saves us. If God is so great, then why does he let the Black people suffer so much? The Blacks live in a shack and go hungry, and never have anything to wear. That makes me think there is no way that a Black person could die and go to hell, because we already living in hell. Why should any human live in hell in the so-called U.S.A.? Why did God make it that way?"

Evie just gazed at Willie and a sadness overtook her face. He had seen too much, thought too much, felt too much, and suffered too much for someone so young.

"Ma?" Willie asked.

"Yes, Willie."

"Do you even think there is a God?"

"Well," Evie said, "I know there is a fountain that was not made by the hands of any man."

"Well, God or no God, he doesn't seem to be helping me at all," Willie said.

"Well, that's how it is, and son, you've got to prepare for it, and live with it," Evie said, "or you've got to prepare to get out of here."

"Well, Ma, I will not survive stayin' here. I've got to get out of here. I don't know when, or how, but I've got to go.'"

A few years before the start of The Civil War, a prominent American made a clear public statement about his beliefs regarding race, particularly what he believed to be the difference between whites and Blacks, and how they should co-exist in this republic. It was very important to this speaker that his words were clearly understood, so much so that before he began, he asked the crowd to observe a profound silence so that they could hear everything he was about to say:

> I will say then, that I am not, nor ever have been, in favor of bringing about in any way the social and political equality of the white and black races; that I am not, nor ever have been, in favor of making voters or jurors of negroes, nor of qualifying them to hold office, nor to intermarry with white people; and I will say, in addition to this, that there is a physical difference between the white and black races which I believe will forever forbid the two races living together on terms of social and political equality. And inasmuch as they cannot so live, while they do remain together there must be the position of superior and inferior, and I as much as any

other man am in favor of having the superior position assigned to the white race.

Those words were not spoken by a future Ku Klux Klan leader, nor by a Southern plantation owner, nor by a young man who several years later would take up arms against Northern aggression in the name of Dixie and fight to defend her honor and beloved Southern Way of Life. They were not even spoken by a Southerner. Those words were uttered by then 49-year-old U.S. Senate candidate Abraham Lincoln in a debate with Stephen Douglas on September 18, 1858.

## 5

—·—

# YOU GOT TWO GOOD EYES BUT STILL DON'T SEE

For a young Black man in Holmes County during the 1950s, there was perhaps no greater symbol of white oppression, injustice, and corruption than the sheriff.

His name was Dick Byrd. Richard F. Byrd. The Notorious RFB. He enforced—and often fabricated—county and state laws, and his most frequent targets were the Black citizens. He pretty much did whatever he wanted, and if he felt like it, he might come round and bust you for smilin' on a cloudy day. To make things worse, he was physically imposing. Six foot two and stocky, he was as tough as dried out beef jerky.

Byrd was a Chevrolet salesman when the all-white voters of Holmes County elected him sheriff in 1952. He ran on an anti-corruption campaign, promising to shut down bootleggers, cattle rustling and gambling. He did shut them down, but then allowed the bootleggers to revive their businesses as long as they bought their supplies from his good friend, and of course, paid the sheriff his weekly allowance, like a mafia don demanding "protection" money from all the neighborhood businesses.

"We didn't live that far outside of Lexington, and where we lived, there were three juke houses that sold whiskey. And he would make his rounds and collect money from letting Black people sell whiskey. I would see Dick Byrd, probably every Monday morning making his rounds, he would come out in the country collecting his money from lettin' people sell whiskey," Willie said.

Abusing Blacks was a sport for him, and while Willie and everyone he knew tried to stay as far away from him as they could, numerous contemporary accounts indicate that Byrd would roam the dirt roads of the county and always find plenty of people to terrorize.

"He would pull you over and say Nigger, roll down the window. He'd say stick your head out. Then say roll the window back up on your head. Then he'd start beating you with his nightstick," Willie said.

If Willie was ever inclined to sass someone or take a chance that might violate the code of conduct, it wasn't when Dick Byrd was around.

"At that time, whatever a cop said, you better do what he said, especially that man," Willie said.

One night Willie's friend Clarence was with another Black teenager when a fight broke out between a white guy and a Black guy. The sheriff showed up and asked Clarence and his friend if they had seen the Black guy hit the white guy. When they said they hadn't seen anything, Byrd jailed them for "unseen conduct," a charge that didn't exist. He let the white guy go home, and that night he asked the three young men in the jail cell if they wanted baloney or chicken for dinner. Two of them said baloney, but Clarence made the mistake of asking for chicken. Byrd whacked Clarence in the head with his nightstick and said "Well, goddammit, here's a drumstick."

"He wasn't goin' to give you no chicken," Willie said, "baloney was real cheap."

In a vast and remote rural county that spanned almost 800 square miles, there really was not any person or other authority to tell Byrd what he could or could not do. He worked with a staff of just two deputies, but by extension, because the laws and culture of Mississippi were based on the maintenance of white supremacy, the white residents often acted as surrogate deputies themselves. They were free to treat the Blacks as they wished and to accuse them of whatever crimes they wished, and Byrd would be happy to charge them.

"They didn't have to call the sheriff. They called the sheriff or the police or something after they got you and said come get this dude, I caught him stealing my chickens, or sellin' whiskey, or you name it. It really wasn't about the police in a lot of cases, because the white people was the police," Willie said.

One example of how the system worked involved a nineteen-year-old Black man named Curtis Freeman. In late September 1955 he was riding in the back of a pickup truck early one morning in Tchula when it passed a school bus stop and he called out "Hey, Sugar, you look good to me." When later questioned by Sheriff Byrd, Freeman said he was speaking to a friend of his, a Black girl at the bus stop whose nickname was Sugar. However, Mary Ellen Henderson, a ten-year-old white girl at the bus stop, believed that Freeman was speaking to her, and became greatly upset. She told the bus driver what happened, he told the Tchula elementary school principal, and the principal immediately called the sheriff. Dick Byrd leapt into action, rounding up Freeman and the other young Black men who were in the back of the pickup and questioning them for hours. The sheriff told Freeman it didn't matter who he was speaking to because what he said had been heard by a white girl, and so he charged him with "unlawful use of vulgar and obscene language." A county court sentenced Curtis to six months hard labor on the county farm.

There was one person in Holmes County who had both the courage and position in society that allowed her to stand up to Sheriff Byrd and expose his horrific treatment of the citizens he was elected to protect. Hazel Brannon Smith was a white woman who grew up in Alabama in the 1920s and graduated from the University of Alabama in 1935 with a degree in journalism. She moved to Mississippi and over the next decade she bought and revitalized the weekly newspaper in nearby Durant, a small town in eastern Holmes County, as well as the major newspaper in the county, *The Lexington Advertiser.* Her office and printing press were on Yazoo Street, due south of Courthouse Square.

Smith wrote a column on the front page of her 8-page newspaper called "Through Hazel's Eyes," and it was there that she opined about the social and political situation in Holmes County. She became known as a friend to the Blacks in the county because she wrote about fairness and justice for all people. Willie and his friends knew she was different.

"Hazel Brannon Smith always treated Blacks respectful. She was one of the few white ladies you would see on the street, and you didn't have to get out of her way, she would speak and stuff, and talk to you. But the rest of them wouldn't," Willie said.

Smith became known as someone who annoyed the white establishment with her pen, reporting on political corruption and social injustice, but she didn't start to become a public enemy to the majority of whites in Holmes County until the summer of 1954. It was the July 4th weekend and around twilight a group of Blacks were congregated on a street in Tchula. Dick Byrd drove by with his deputies and then got out of his car to disperse the crowd. He whacked a few young men with his flashlight and nightstick and told them to "Get goin'." Several of them turned and ran, including 27-year-old Henry Randle, a local resident who had come into town to buy food. As they ran, Byrd pulled out his pistol and fired several shots at their backs, with one striking Randle in the back of the thigh, dropping him to the ground. Byrd got into his car and drove off.

Hazel heard about the shooting the next day and went to Tchula to talk to witnesses. When she was confident that she had her facts straight, she printed a blistering editorial on the front page of the next edition that included the following:

> The laws in America are for everyone—rich and poor,
> strong and weak, white and Black and all the other races

that dwell in our land ... Laws were made to protect the weak from the strong. This man was shot in the back. He was running only because he had been told to "get going" by the sheriff. He had not violated any law... He just made the one mistake of being around when the sheriff drove up.

That column started a world of trouble for Smith, but she never backed down. Byrd sued her for libel and was awarded $10,000, but the judgment was overturned by an appeals court. As the civil rights movement gained momentum over the next decade, she frequently wrote in support of the cause of equal treatment of all people, and her enemies, particularly the White Citizens Council, hit her back. Hard. The council orchestrated the firing of her husband, a county hospital administrator. They organized an economic boycott of her newspapers and started a rival newspaper in Lexington to try to put her out of business. She fired back by comparing them to Hitler's Gestapo. Two of her newspaper offices were bombed, including the one just off Courthouse Square. A cross was burned in her front yard.

In 1964 Smith was awarded the Pulitzer Prize for editorial writing, the first woman to receive such an honor. She was lauded by other journalistic bodies for her determination to report the truth, despite the intense harassment and obstacles placed in her way. But the economic boycott and her status as an enemy of the white establishment did not end. She had to borrow heavily to keep her newspapers afloat and she eventually filed for bankruptcy, left the state to live with family, and died penniless. The Holmes County white establishment had won, at least economically.

On August 31, 1955 two boys were fishing in the Tallahatchie River, about an hour north of Clifton Plantation, when the bloated, disfigured, lifeless body of a 14-year-old Black boy floated toward them. It was the corpse of Emmett Till. A Chicago native, young Emmett had been visiting relatives in northern Mississippi when he was abducted, tortured, shot in the head, and tossed in the river by two white men who accused him of flirting with one of their wives. The ensuing investigation, murder trial, and acquittal of the murderers received intense national news coverage. For the first time, the ugliness of segregation was crystallized in a horrific crime that shocked all of America. The events metaphorically put the entire state of Mississippi, and segregation itself, on trial as well. Three months later in Montgomery, Alabama, city bus driver James Blake ordered Rosa Parks to move to the back of his bus. When she refused, she was thinking about Emmett Till's murder, and it made her so angry that she stayed in her seat. Thus, Till's murder and his killers' acquittal is considered the true spark of the American Civil Rights Movement.

Willie and everyone around him paid close attention to the Till news coverage and trial. They, too, were horrified, and scared.

"I remember that very well. How they brutalized him, and all of that. See, that was the thing then with Black people. You couldn't say hardly anything," Willie said.

Emmett and Willie had a lot in common: Emmett was born exactly two weeks before Willie; both had infectious smiles and magnetic personalities; both had strong mothers who endured life with abusive husbands; and both of their mothers had instructed them that they needed to be submissive around white people. But they had one major difference, and this proved to be fatal for Emmett: Willie was raised in Mississippi, and Emmett was raised in Chicago. Since he was a toddler, Evie had taught Willie to keep his head down and say "Yes, Mister," and "No, Mister," whenever he was addressing white men. Before Emmett left Chicago to visit his cousins in Money, Mississippi, his mother Mamie told him that if he ever angered a white person in Mississippi he needed to get down on his knees and beg for forgiveness. Having grown up in the less restrictive North, Emmett was not inclined to do what his mother told him, and it likely cost him his life. As feisty as Willie could be at times, he had been brought up to understand how he needed to act, simply for self-preservation. He swallowed his pride, no matter how bitter it tasted going down.

Emmett was excited to go to Mississippi in the summer of 1955, having heard about the Delta region from his great uncle Mose Wright when he had visited Till's family in Chicago.

On the evening of Wednesday, August 24, Emmett and a group of his cousins and their friends drove to Money, Mississippi, having just dropped Wright and Emmett's great aunt off at church services, where Wright was preaching. The group went to Bryant Grocery and Meat Market to buy candy at about 7:30 pm, as it was the only store open in town that late in the day. The store was owned by a young white married couple, 24-year-old Roy Bryant and 21-year-old Carolyn Bryant. Roy was out of town and Carolyn was working the store alone that night. Exactly what happened in the store will likely never be known. It appears that Emmett was in the store alone with Carolyn, though it may have only been for a very short time, Carolyn testified that Emmett said things to her in the store that made her feel uncomfortable, and it was said that he whistled when he left the store, theoretically at Carolyn. Whatever happened in the store, the perception was that Emmett had broken one of the ultimate taboos of the South—a Black male interacting with a white woman in a sexually suggestive way. Regardless of what 14-year-old Emmett may or may not have said or did, it really makes no difference—nothing he said or did could have justified what followed.

When Roy Bryant returned home three days later on August 27, his wife told him of her encounter with Emmett. Outraged, Roy asked around town and learned that Emmett was staying at Mose Wright's house. He and his half-brother J.W. Milam drove to Wright's house between 2:00 and 3:30 am the next morning. Armed with a pistol and determined to take Emmett, the two men barged into Wright's tiny home and Milam asked for "the nigger who did the talking." They abducted Emmett, tied him up and threw him into the back of their pickup truck. They drove to the next town over and beat Emmett in a barn, his cries being heard by terrified Black neighbors. After beating and torturing him, they drove to a nearby cotton gin, took a 70-pound steel fan, wrapped barbed wire around Emmett's neck and attached the fan to him to weigh him down. They shot him in the head above the ear and tossed his body off the Black Bayou Bridge in Glendora, Mississippi. Three days later, his swollen and mutilated body was found by the two boys who were fishing.

This was the vigilante justice inflicted upon "the nigger who did the talking," a 14-year-old child.

And there was Willie, another 14-year-old child, bound to his plantation not all that far from where Emmett was murdered, knowing that one misstep that broke the unwritten laws of the South could visit the same fate upon him or any of his friends. The difference between Willie and Emmett was that Willie had seen the system play out his whole life. He knew how restricted he was, and that was the source of the anger that was building inside him. His mother had instructed him practically since birth about how he needed to act around whites. He listened to her and obeyed, but it was far from easy.

Emmett's murder may not have become such an important and powerful moment in American civil rights history, were it not for the courage and determination of his mother. Mamie acted quickly upon his death to ensure that his body was sent back to Chicago, preventing a rapid burial in Mississippi. And most significantly, she demanded an open casket at his funeral, so the world could see what they had done to her child. Thousands of mourners filed past the casket at the A.A. Rayner and Sons Funeral Home on the southside of Chicago. A grotesque photo of her son's bloated and disfigured corpse lying in his casket was printed in Black newspapers and magazines, and generated outrage from coast to coast. As with so many other atrocities—the Holocaust, parts of the Vietnam War, 9/11—it was the unfathomable and sickening image that most fully represented the anger, disgust, inhumanity, and despair. Just hearing about something heinous and revolting is often not enough to move people. They need to see it with their eyes.

The trial? While it was closely watched and received immense national media attention, it went pretty much the way everyone expected it would. Less than a month after the kidnapping, torture, and murder, Roy Bryant and Milam were tried in the Tallahatchie County Courthouse in Sumner. On September 19 the all-white, all-male jury was sat—there could be no other kind, as Blacks and women were forbidden from serving on juries in Mississippi at the time.

Sheriff Henry Clarence Strider and an expert medical witness testified falsely that the body fished out of the river could not have been Emmett's. During the trial, Strider also locked up two young Black men who were prepared to testify for the prosecution. Should anyone wonder why Blacks felt so much despair regarding their chances to make it in the Deep South when someone who is sworn to uphold the laws of the state of Mississippi is actively engaged in thwarting the prosecution of two murderers?

Bryant and Milam were found not guilty after 4 days of testimony that was followed by 67 minutes of jury deliberation. One unforgettable moment was Mose Wright standing and pointing at Milam, identifying him as one of the men who kidnapped Emmett from his home. It sounds like such a rudimentary part of the American justice system: a witness confirming on the stand that someone accused of a crime had committed the crime. But in that time and place, with its history and hierarchy suffocating just about every action Blacks were "allowed" to take, a Black man calling out a white man was seen as unprecedented and heroic—and it was both.

Following the trial, Bryant and Milam were free to admit that they had tortured and murdered the 14-year-old child because they had been acquitted of the crime in court and could not be tried again for murder. Milam provided the following rationale for why they murdered Till in an interview with *Look* magazine in 1956. Milam's explanation certainly does not reflect the attitude of all whites in the South in the 1950s, but his views were typical of many of his brethren and are embedded with so many themes reflecting the mind of the South: the entitlement, the two-tiered society, frustration with "outside agitators," and the perceived necessity of using vigilante justice to enforce unwritten laws devised by the ruling class.

> Well, what else could we do? He was hopeless. I'm no bully; I never hurt a nigger in my life. I like niggers—in their place—I know how to work 'em. But I just decided it was time a few people got put on notice. As long as I live and can do anything about it, niggers are gonna stay in their place. Niggers ain't gonna vote where I live. If they did, they'd control the government. They ain't gonna go to school with my kids. And when a nigger gets close to mentioning sex with a white woman, he's tired o' livin'. I'm likely to kill him. Me and my folks fought for this country, and we got some rights. I stood there in that shed and listened to that nigger throw that poison at me, and I just made up my mind. 'Chicago boy,' I said, 'I'm tired of 'em sending your kind down here to stir up trouble. Goddam you, I'm going to make an example of you—just so everybody can know how me and my folks stand.

To Milam's way of thinking, Till has crossed an uncrossable line: a Black cannot be allowed to act in any way that would indicate anything approaching equality with whites. That's how it had always been, and that's how it would always be, if there was anything Milam could do about it.

One woman who was able to see the racial divide from the perspective of both whites and Blacks was Betty Bobo Pearson. Betty was born in 1922 into a well-established white, plantation-owning family in the Mississippi Delta. Her family history in North America dates back to before the Revolutionary War, when her ancestors came to the colonies from England after fleeing religious persecution in France in the middle of the 18th century. Her great, great, great grandfather was a soldier in the Revolutionary War, fighting on the American side, and her great grandfather was a cavalryman in the Civil War, fighting on the Confederate side.

She grew up with Blacks as her servants, caretakers, and playmates. A college graduate who served in the Marine Corps during World War II, she and her husband Bill stood out in their community because they believed Blacks and whites should be treated equally and they were against segregation.

Having grown up in the Delta in the 1930s, Pearson explains the mindset of the vast majority of whites who embraced segregation as just the way things were, particularly because conforming to the status quo is the easiest path.

"For many people it's just easier, or maybe they just don't think through it enough, for whatever reason, it's just easier for them to just go along with whatever that flow is. You know, whatever the preacher says, and whatever my parents say, and whatever this society says, just go with that flow as if you were in a current or stream, don't fight it."

Pearson's father was raised by a Black mammy named Alou. She bathed him, put him to bed every night, and took care of him. Her father couldn't remember his own mother taking care of him the way Alou did, but her father firmly believed Blacks were an inferior race and whites needed to take care of them. While her father would never dream of physically harming a Black person and took good care of those who worked for him, he believed whites and Blacks were separate and unequal. This baffled Pearson.

"I still can't, almost 96 years old, I don't understand why I thought that they were people just like me, which they are, of course, and my father who had been raised by this woman and who loved her, thought they were inferior. I couldn't understand that," Pearson said.

Betty doesn't know exactly when or how her notions of human equality developed. Growing up on a cotton plantation and then in the town of Clarksdale, she was immersed in a culture that understood white supremacy as ostensibly a fact of life. She certainly did not have any role models—either in the community or in her home—who taught her that all people should be treated equally.

"By the time I left for college I was absolutely sure that human beings were human beings and that this racial superiority thing just was not true. And where that came from, or exactly why, too many people have asked me: why, if my brother and I were raised in the same household, did we end up with such different ideas? I can't answer that, I don't know why. But I do know that by the time I got to college I was sure where I was as far as the Black-white question was concerned, and I realized that I did not agree with either of my parents," Pearson said.

The notion of white superiority, particularly Southern white superiority—because many white Southerners hated Northerners as much or more than Blacks—was reinforced and practically etched in stone by the blows suffered by the South: losing the Civil War, punitive measures enacted by the federal government during Reconstruction, and the fall of the price of cotton in the late 19th century, which crippled the Southern economy. These forces led to white Southerners forming an ideological ring around themselves, and heaven help the fool who was brave enough, or stupid enough, to voice a different opinion. W.J. Cash wrote in 1940: "Tolerance, in sum, was pretty well extinguished all along the line, and conformity made a nearly universal law. Criticism, analysis, detachment, all those activities and attitudes so necessary to the healthy development of any civilization, every one of them took on the aspect of high and aggravated treason."

Pearson agrees that the aftermath of the Civil War contributed to the hardening of the mind of the South.

"The South is the only part of the country that has experienced losing a war, and I do think they have a chip on their shoulder in that sense. I don't think people in the North really realize how bad Reconstruction was and why there was such a backlash against it for the white people in the South. I think that it just crystallized a lot of those prejudices that they already had, and made it worse, and put the chip on the shoulder. You know, 'We've been picked on by those damn Yankees,'" Pearson said.

To understand just how unusual it was for Betty to defy her family and friends with her views about racial equality, we need to remember just what the majority of white Southerners in the mid-20th century thought about Blacks, which mostly ranged from hatred to a paternalistic belief that it was the white person's duty as a Christian to care for Blacks because they were inferior and needed help.

Betty's father, for example, adhered to the doctrine of *noblesse oblige* (nobility requires), a rationale employed by moderate whites which held that Blacks were an inferior race, and it was their duty to take care of them.

"My father was extremely kind to Black people. His generation, he was born in 1902, I think. His generation had been raised by people who had gone through Reconstruction, and I guess some of them had lived through the last part of slavery as well, and they were absolutely convinced that Black people had been made by God to be inferior to white people. And my father was always extremely good to the

Black people that worked for him. They all adored him, even until he died. He thought it was his duty, as a Christian man, to take care of them in the same way that he took care of my brother and me. And of course that was very dehumanizing for grown people, but he just didn't understand that, but he was a kind person," Pearson said.

Regardless of where their prejudices fell on this spectrum, the bedrock was the idea that Blacks were by nature inferior and segregation was necessary, and in the minds of many, ordained by God. So whether the intent was malevolent or seemingly beneficent, the end result was the same: Blacks would continue to be segregated educationally, economically, legally, and socially, and of course, that means having less access to quality education, less access to good jobs, and fewer legal protections.

Betty and Bill's radical—by white Southern standards at the time—views on racial equality did damage their relationships with many of their family and friends, but they needed to do what they knew was right.

"There was definitely a price we paid socially, and I think that for a lot of people that was more price than they wanted to pay, and so it's easier just to go along with whatever the climate and attitude is, and say oh, well, someday it will get better," Pearson said.

That price also included being ostracized, even decades after her liberal views became known in the community.

"One of the sad things that happened to me maybe 15 years later: I had an itinerant white carpenter who did some work for me, and he did a good job, and I really liked him a lot, and I called him and I said 'I have a little job I want you to do for me,' and he said, there was a pause, and he said 'Well, I don't think I can do it.' And I said, 'Well, I'm not in any big hurry, we don't have to do it right now, just let me know when you could do it.' And he said 'Well, Mrs. Pearson, I'll tell you the truth,' he said, 'my wife told me she'd leave me if I worked for them nigger-lovers again, and I love my wife and I need her, and I don't want her to leave me, and so I just can't work for you anymore'.

And I said 'Well, Mr. Coleman, I'm very sorry, but I understand, and thank you.'"

Pearson's home county is Tallahatchie, the site of the Emmett Till murder trial. Even though the torture and murder of Till occurred in two neighboring counties, the trial was held in Sumner, the seat of Tallahatchie County, because his corpse was found in the county. Pearson knew everyone of social and political importance in Tallahatchie County at the time. Her uncle Bill was editor of the local newspaper and he obtained two press passes for Pearson and her dear friend Florence "Flossie" Mars. Both were in their early 30s in the summer of 1955 and Flossie, like Betty, had grown up in a well-established family in Mississippi, and also like Betty, she had defied her family and friends with her liberal, progressive thinking and concern for the plight of Blacks in their segregated state.

Pearson was motivated to attend the trial after seeing the white reaction to the murder in her county. She perceived a difference of opinion amongst whites regarding the case, at least initially.

"There had been a change in sentiment. When Emmett Till's body was first found, all the people that I knew in Sumner, and Webb, and Clarksdale and all those places were horrified, they thought it was a terrible thing to have happened, and they wanted whoever did it caught and convicted immediately, and that sort of thing. But once the national and international press got hold of it, they became very defensive, because they felt that Sumner, for example, was being blamed for something that they had had nothing to do with, and agreed it was a terrible crime, but it was as if Mississippi was really the criminal and not those two men. And, of course, in a way, the whole culture of segregation was sort of being put on public trial. But they became very, very defensive. So that the sort of feeling you got went from 'this is terrible, we need to find out who this is and lock 'em up,' to 'everybody's pickin' on us, and we didn't have anything to do with it.'"

Though many in the community were horrified by the crime, there was also a lot of support for the defendants. Sumner residents rallied to raise funds for their legal defense, and the lawyers in town, none of whom wanted to be singled out for representing people accused of such a crime, banded together to represent the defendants together.

"There was in every grocery store and drug store, almost every one, there was a gallon jug thing with a big top on it, asking for contributions for the defense of Bryant and Milam, and they were almost always full of quarters and dimes, and some dollar bills stuck down in there. I think that the class of people that they came from, that ended up being defensive of them, they came to the trial, they were all for 'em. They were glad they were exonerated. I mean, even if they had killed them, that class of person would have thought 'Well, it's okay, if an n-word boy insulted her or tried to hold her hand, or whatever, then he deserved to be killed.'"

Though it was late September when it started, the temperature flirted with 100 degrees throughout most of the 5-day trial, and it certainly felt much hotter than that, with 280 people packed into the courtroom and the anger and hatred boiling inside many of them, mostly toward the victim, but also toward the press and the Northerners who had shaped this murder as an indictment on Mississippi as a whole, and Tallahatchie County in particular.

"When the jury walked in, just seeing the expressions on their faces, and I knew a few of 'em, I didn't know all of 'em by any means, but I knew two or three that lived in Webb, I said 'Flossie, they'll never convict.' Even before the trial started," Pearson said.

Betty and Flossie sat at a table for white reporters, and they had a good view of the jury, defendants and scores of Bryant and Milam's supporters who packed the courtroom. The Black spectators who attended were allowed to sit behind the whites in the last few rows, and they also crowded into the standing area. She also had a clear view of Mose Wright when he stood up and pointed at Milam, identifying him as the man who came to his home and kidnapped Till.

"He was a short man. I don't think he was any taller than I am. To me, it was just shivering because it was very difficult for a Black man to stand up and point his finger at a white man and accuse him of something because that's just the way it was between Blacks and whites in Mississippi in that day. So it was very brave of him."

Within days after testifying, Wright had to be relocated to Chicago for his safety, abruptly leaving Mississippi after having lived there all of his 64 years.

What Betty and Flossie saw during the trial helped spur them to lives devoted to civil rights activism, and Betty was instrumental in the establishment of the Emmett Till Interpretive Center more than 50 years later.

This is the world that Willie, his family, friends, and all other Blacks in rural Mississippi grew up in during the 1940s and 1950s. Segregated, denied opportunities, unable to vote, seemingly destined to a life of hand-to-mouth poverty unless they fled the South, and perhaps most perniciously, deemed to be intrinsically inferior by the whites who controlled all the levers of power in Southern society.

# 6

## Hoop Dreams

Baseball was America's favorite game in the 1940s and 1950s. It was the sport Americans played, watched, and talked about more than any other. Football and basketball would ascend decades later, but in the middle of the twentieth century baseball was the game. Willie knew a lot about baseball. Andrew Davenport played when he was younger and loved to tell him about it, and he would hear the old men talking about the Negro League players when he would go down to Howard Store on the weekends. Many people in Willie's community—both Black and white—also enjoyed going to watch a game between local Black teams on Sunday afternoon after church. And, of course, Willie and all Blacks, young and old, followed the pioneering exploits of Jackie Robinson, Larry Doby, Roy Campanella, Satchel Paige, and others when they were finally allowed to play in Major League Baseball beginning in 1947.

Playing baseball, though, that was a different story for kids like Willie. The nearest baseball field was in Tchula, four miles from Clifton Plantation. After leaving Mt. Zion elementary school Willie attended Mileston High School. It was a 10-mile bus ride to Mileston, and he went there with all the other Black teenagers within a wide swath of western Holmes County. Mileston didn't have a baseball field or a baseball team, and Willie never had a chance to play baseball in any organized league when he was growing up.

Mt. Zion did have two basketball hoops and a dirt court. They would mark out lines in the dirt and Willie would play with kids from all the neighboring plantations during recess. Back on Clifton, he would play with his friends Henry and Samuel Mitchell.

"There was a pasture that was between my house and their house, and they had a basketball thing they had put up there in the pasture, so we would go down the hill in the pasture and play," Willie said.

The boys crafted their first hoop with the rim of a bicycle tire that they nailed to a backboard made of wood and tin. Willie started playing consistently when he was 10 or 11 years old and he knew right away that he liked this game. It was one of the few times he had fun on the plantation. When he was working in the fields, he would constantly ask himself "Why? Why am I here having to do this? Am I going to be here doing this forever like my Mom? What can I do to get out of here someday?" He would also think about the abuse he and his mom took from Oscar Harris and how badly he wanted to make that stop, but felt powerless to do so. Playing basketball with his friends took his mind off all his troubles. It was his therapy.

Mileston High School was set out in the country, nestled amongst several plantations. Though its students came from a large rural area of Holmes County, they numbered only about 250 young men and women in the four grades combined. Willie entered Mileston High School in 1956, two years after the U.S. Supreme Court's historic decision in Brown vs. Board of Education in which the court unanimously determined that "separate educational facilities are inherently unequal" and in 1955 the court ordered all segregated school districts to desegregate "with all deliberate speed." The only thing deliberate about the reaction of school boards in rural Mississippi was that they were definitely not going to desegregate. School boards and local governments were all controlled by whites due to the disenfranchisement of Black voters, and they would be damned if they were going to let outside agitators tell them what to do, again. The white response to the court order to desegregate was to generally ignore it for the first decade, and then when the civil rights movement received federal support with the passage of the Civil Rights Act and Voting Rights Act in the mid-1960s, whites began pulling their children out of public schools, setting up private Christian academies with the financial support of the White Citizens Council. This practice continues well into the 21st century.

If Blacks had been allowed to vote in Mississippi in the 1950s, things likely would have been different, as there were about twice as many Blacks as whites in Holmes County. However, since they could not vote, they could not control the fact that the educational resources provided to them were significantly less than what was provided to white schools. Mileston High did have a basketball court and a football field, but other sports like baseball and tennis were not part of the extracurricular offerings. Willie's high school basketball teammate Stanford Murry remembers when he started to realize how unequal things were.

"Well see, the thing of it is, that's all we knew. That's how we had grown up and that's all I knew. Of course there was no television, there was very little radio, and we didn't know any better. Especially early, and then when I realized, probably late in high school, ready to graduate and stuff, and you start to see a little bit differently. Sometimes you're passing and you see the white schools playin' football, and you see the equipment that they use. They had the finest, and our equipment was cast over from theirs, they would give us what was left over from theirs. And the Black schools never got new football equipment, you know. Now we could get new basketball equipment because it was not as expensive, you know. You can get uniforms. Our gymnasium was about 20 feet shorter and about 5, 10 feet narrower than an average gymnasium. I remember when we went to Greenwood to play in a tournament and we walked in their gymnasium and it looked like a mile long. Our chemistry lab had nothing in it. Nothing. It was just a classroom. So when I started to look around and see, it is frustrating, and it does make you mad," Murry said.

Willie's anger sprang from many sources. Having subpar educational and athletic opportunities bothered him, but it was just another brick on the load. What made him seethe most intensely was the system of segregation and white supremacy—the knowledge that those who control your society consider you less than the whites, and that manifested itself on a daily basis. While many of his friends adopted the attitude that they didn't like the system and they didn't accept the system, they tried to "make the best of it" because no one believed it would ever change and they felt powerless to help make it change.

"A lot of my anger was the treatment. You could be walkin' at night, or even during the day, and some of them young white boys would come through in their cars and they would try to run you over. There wasn't nothing you could do about it. And they would call you all kinds of names. You know, all kinds of stuff. That is the part that I really hated. 'Cause I couldn't speak out, and I couldn't fight back, knowin' that you could whoop a lot of these guys' asses. But you couldn't do anything. That's stressful. Real stressful. That you got to let some jackass call you a name, and tell you 'Get out the way, nigger!' or 'Pick that up over there for me,' or 'Go in there and get me a soda.' Stuff like that," Willie said.

As Willie gets bigger, he gets more defiant, even if that defiance must by necessity be internalized. He dreamt of hurting white men who had mistreated him. He couldn't talk to his brother Robert about it, as that wasn't Robert's style. Robert took after Andrew Davenport and had a measured approach to everything. Willie, on the other hand, had inherited his mama's fire.

"His ideas were a little different from mine. He was, I wouldn't say he was a radical, but compared to me he was a radical. I was on the calmer side," Robert said.

Willie could talk to his good friend Henry Mitchell about it. They would often plot how they could get back at somebody who had abused them, but the most important part of the scheme was how could they pull it off so that no one knew they did it. They never quenched their thirst for vengeance, but it was cathartic to talk about it. Thinking in detail about how you could hurt someone is not healthy for a 15-year-old kid, but the environment he was living in often guided Willie's thoughts to very dark places.

His mom Evie saw Willie getting more and more frustrated as he got bigger, and that started to scare her. She worked relentlessly to try to keep Willie under control so he wouldn't get hurt. When Willie was a teenager, it appeared to him that virtually all white people were racist because they kept the system of white supremacy in place. It was only when he got much older that he understood it wasn't that simple. There were good white people, but he just couldn't see that when he was a teenager. His world literally looked black and white.

"A lot of white people back in that day wasn't as bad; some of them went along with it because of what the other white people was doing, and they didn't want to buck them. So they went along with some of the stuff. They didn't like it, but they had to go along with what the neighborhood was doing. All white people that lived in the South at the time wasn't racist," Willie said.

Surviving high school was Willie's immediate concern, but he was also at the age when people start thinking about their future. What will I be when I grow up? He watched his mom work endlessly and never end up with a dollar to her name. He would have loved to go live with his dad Andrew Davenport and help run the farm, but Andrew's wife Ruby didn't like Willie, so that wasn't going to happen. If he stayed in his community, the best prospect awaiting a young Black man was to get a job driving a tractor. Working in the fields paid $2.50 a day. Driving a tractor paid $3.00 a day. That held no appeal for Willie and was sure to lead to a life of continuing to live hand to mouth. He saw some of the older teenagers either quitting high school or moving to Chicago or Detroit to work right after they graduated from high school. They were part of the Great Migration, the movement of more than 6 million Blacks from 1916 to 1970 from

Southern states to cities like Chicago, Detroit, St. Louis, and New York. Most would have family already living in the big cities of the Midwest and Northeast who would provide the newcomers with a place to live until they established themselves. In Willie's part of Mississippi, this movement was often a risky proposition. The plantation owners exerted economic control over their sharecroppers lives under the system that kept many of them perpetually indebted. Blacks who were planning to move didn't tell anyone about it, especially the plantation owner. One day they would just be gone. In Willie's case, leaving the plantation would be especially difficult because he came from such a small family. Taking away any healthy body that worked in the field could jeopardize the family's ability to get all their work done.

"A lot of the Black people that worked on the farm had relatives that left Mississippi, and a lot of them had relatives in Chicago. Then, you wouldn't tell the plantation owner you was leavin', you just take off , 'cause you tell him you was leavin' you'd be in trouble," Willie said.

So Willie stewed about it when he was picking cotton or baling hay. He could eventually go north and live in a big city, but he wanted to do something special. He had been told his whole life he wasn't worth a damn, whether that was by Oscar Harris or the society at large, but he knew better.

"Why me? How in the hell did I wind up here? How can I get out of this? What's the prospect of a Black kid ever gettin' out of here? And the two things that mostly that was got you out of there were sports, and every once in a while, music. Otherwise, you were pretty well stuck," Willie said.

Everyone in Willie's community looked up to the Mississippi musicians who had become famous playing the blues: Muddy Waters, Howlin' Wolf, Mississippi John Hurt, John Lee Hooker, B.B. King, and so many more. Willie's friend Joe Smothers had two older brothers, Otis "Big Smokey" Smothers and Abe "Little Smokey" Smothers, who had left the plantation in high school and went to Chicago where they became successful musicians. They taught themselves how to play guitar when they were kids after their aunt made them a guitar by crafting it from a wire broom. Willie's good friend Lee "Shot" Williams also left the plantation in high school, moved to Detroit, and started a 50-year career as a professional rhythm and blues singer. His mama gave him the nickname Shot when he was young because he loved to dress up like a big shot. Much of his songwriting explored a man's quest for female companionship, including the hits "The First Rule of Cheating," "I'm a Nibble Man," "Drop Your Laundry Baby," and "Wrong Bed."

These musical success stories were a source of pride and gave hope to Black folks in Mississippi, but Willie wasn't musical, and he didn't like to dance. But when he entered high school Willie's family got their first television and his world started to open up. His mom told Willie and Robert that they needed to watch the evening news every night so they would know what was going on in the world. Having a TV meant Willie could also watch NBA basketball games. The NBA integrated in 1950, but for most of the next decade, the impact of Black players was modest. Only a handful of Blacks were allowed to play, as the league didn't want to upset their fan base which wanted to see big, tall white guys succeed. The Black players were told not to score, just pass the ball and rebound. They were scattered throughout the league, like flies in buttermilk. But Willie saw them. He saw people who looked like him, many of whom came from the South. He saw them playing the game he loved on television in front of thousands of fans. White fans. He was a freshman in high school, and he was tall and still growing. And he could play. He could do this. He could be a professional basketball player. He knew he could. It was his ticket out.

"I think we got TV, I think in '55, and I started watching professional basketball. I remember watching the Boston Celtics, the Fort Wayne Pistons, and Knicks and all of that. And watching these few

Black guys that was playing basketball. And at that time in '55 I think I was about 6' 2", somewhere along there. And I was playing basketball, and I figured it out for myself, this is my meal ticket. That's when I really started to focus my time, every spare time I had I was playing basketball. That's how I figured out how to get out of there. No one figured it out for me, I figured this out for myself. I couldn't sing or dance, or nothin', but I could play ball," Willie said.

During Willie's junior year Wilt Chamberlain entered the NBA as a member of the Philadelphia Warriors. He averaged 38 points and 27 rebounds in his rookie year. This is someone Willie could look up to: a Black guy dominating a league that was overwhelmingly white at the time. He looked like a man playing amongst boys.

As much as he wanted to stay focused on basketball, Willie was a young man and other enticements pulled him in different directions. He started dating Emma Patterson his freshman year in high school. She was a sweet girl who lived on Clifton Plantation and had five brothers who Willie was friends with, including her older brother Pinky. Her parents were strict so she would sneak out to see Willie and they would try to avoid being seen at the juke joints together, because then people would talk, and it would get back to her parents. Their romance lasted less than a year when Emma found another boy who could offer her more than what Willie had.

"There was another guy who dropped out of school and he drove a tractor and he bought a car, and I didn't have a car," Willie said.

As soon as they became teenagers, Willie and his friends would look forward to heading into Tchula on weekends in a pack. The town of 2,000 residents felt like a big city to them, and they would get there any way they could. Very few people had a car back then, but Jimmy Bailey did, and he ran a little taxi service. If you gave him a quarter, he would give you a ride to town. Louis Quinn was a bus driver who had a flatbed truck and the kids would pile onto the back to get to Tchula. When there were no rides available, they just walked the four miles each way. Sometimes it would be so dark you couldn't see your hand in front of your face, and so quiet that the only sound was the rocks crunching under their feet.

The restaurants and bars in town were segregated. Willie and his friends would head to one little street that had four or five cafés that sold beer, soda, and hamburgers. They steered clear of the cafés where the white folks congregated.

"We wouldn't go close to them because the younger white guys, teenage white guys would be out there, and, you know, you would definitely be in for trouble if they see you walkin' by, so we mostly avoided those places, didn't go close to them, 'cause they'd be out there drinking beer and acting the fool, then if they hit you and you tried to hit back, you knew that Dick Byrd and them was gonna beat your head in so you tried to avoid that," Willie said.

The Blacks were allowed to get together at their places in downtown Tchula until 10:00 pm on Friday and Saturday nights. At that time, the one police officer in town would go out into the street and blow a whistle as loud as he could, and that meant only one thing: all Blacks had better leave the downtown area immediately. You had your fun, now go on and get out of here. People started running around in all directions so that you would have thought there was a dragon with matches loose on the town. If they didn't leave, they either got thrown in jail or hit in the head with a nightstick and told to get lost. Some would go home, but most would head to the juke joints that were lined up on the road leading out of town.

Juke joints were institutions created, perpetuated, and celebrated by Blacks in the South following their emancipation from slavery. They were part unlicensed bar, part gambling hall, part dance hall, part music venue, but they were all fun. The idea was that you worked all week and then went there on Saturday night and tried to commit as many sins as you could before you got up to go to Church on Sunday morning. There was a gambling room in the back where you could roll dice or play poker, music would be provided by a juke box or someone playing a guitar or harmonica, and the drinks for sale would be beer or locally crafted moonshine whiskey. In Willie's community most juke joints were set up on the outskirts of Tchula, but there were also a few within a half mile of the plantation. Most were set up in private homes, and many of them were owned and run by women.

"You work all week and make two-fifty a day and the tractor drivers made three dollars a day. But on weekends they have to have somewhere to go let their hair down, get drunk, and there were juke joints where they would go. We couldn't go, you know, to the nicer white folks' café and their places, so the Blacks had what they called juke joints, and that's where they went to spend their money. And not only that, most of the people that ran juke joints were in with Dick Byrd. He let you sell whiskey for a price."

Teenagers were welcome in the juke joints because as long as they had money and were tall enough to put it on the bar, they would sell you a drink. Willie especially never had any trouble getting served because his height always made him look older than he was.

Willie loved going to Tchula with his friends on Saturday night to have some fun, gamble, and try to hook up with girls. When he didn't have to work in his family's field, he would either bale hay for Peyton Abbot Jones or do day work on other plantations, earning $15 for the week, five of which he would give to his mom, leaving him with $10 to blow that weekend. When they couldn't go all the way into town, they often played dice behind the cotton gin next to the Howard Store. On nights like this they would pool their money together and buy a gallon of moonshine for two dollars. If they didn't have even that much money, they would spend 15 cents on a bottle of Dr. Tichenor's Antiseptic, pour it into a bottle of Coca-Cola, shake it up, and suck it down. They didn't know why, but it made them as high as a Georgia pear because Dr. Tichenor's formula was 70% pure alcohol. The label said it was to be used for "cuts, bruises, sprains, superficial burns, sunburn, and mouthwash—Keep out of reach of children." They also didn't know that Dr. Tichenor was a Confederate Army surgeon from Kentucky who concocted his antiseptic formula during the Civil War to save his own leg which was badly injured and scheduled to be amputated. His formula quickly became widely used to treat injured Confederate soldiers, but he refused to allow it to be used on Union prisoners of war.

Willie loved to shoot dice. He loved the thrill of it, the chance that he could win some money and go have a big night on the town, buying drinks for the ladies and his friends. If he lost, it didn't bother him. If he won, he was ecstatic. One night he was rolling dice with his friends behind the cotton gin near the Howard Store.

"Slim, it's your shot," Willie's friend Mitch said to him.

"Okay," Willie said, "Four," as he called one of the most difficult numbers to roll.

He was getting himself pumped up by shaking the dice in his hand and cussin', shaking the dice in his hand and cussin', and he was squatting down with his back to the road.

"Slim, I think you'd better look over your shoulder," Mitch said.

"What the hell for?" Willie asked, and then he turned around and saw Andrew Davenport towering and glowering over him, not saying a word.

"Oh, shit," Willie said, and then Andrew poked him in the ass with his foot and knocked him onto the dice game. Andrew still didn't say anything, so Willie scooped up his money and ran away as fast as he could.

Andrew never mentioned the incident to Wille, but if Willie asked him for money he would say dryly "Are you going to gamble?"

As Willie was transitioning from being a boy to a young man in high school his life was focused on three Gs (and none of them were God): Girls, Gambling, and Getting the hell out of Mississippi. It was a lot to handle, but he managed it well. Willie did work hard to get better at basketball and it helped him become a four-year starter on the Mileston High team. They didn't have a JV or freshman team, and while Willie played forward as a freshman, by his sophomore year he was 6'5" and was installed at center. He was a ferocious defender in the paint and Naylond Hayes, the team's point guard, remembers what a strong offensive game he had.

"Willie D., he was the man, especially on defense. He had a nice little power move around the bucket. Nice little turnaround jumper going away from the bucket falling back. Then going to the middle, too. Then turn to his left and shoot a little jump shot. He was a real good ballplayer," Hayes said.

Willie loved playing basketball because it was the one thing he could do where he was special, he was dominant, and people looked up to him. When you grow up in a society where you are always told you aren't worthy of respect or equal treatment, it felt really good to be great at something. He would have loved to share the game with his dad, but Andrew Davenport didn't like basketball and Willie never saw him at his games until one night when one of his teammates said to Willie during warmups "Willie, Mr. Andrew is here." Willie scanned the bleachers and spotted his father sitting alone. When he saw Willie, he nodded and gave him a little smile. Willie played with a special fire that night.

Eli Grayson was the Mileston basketball coach during Willie's freshman year. Friendly and easygoing, Grayson had played basketball at Jackson State University, an historically Black college that was named Jackson College for Negro Teachers when he attended. For Willie's final three years in high school his coach was Willie Thompson, who had played basketball at Alcorn State University, another historically Black college which at the time was named Alcorn Agricultural and Mechanical College, reflecting its role as more of a vocational school than a traditional college or university. Thompson was more of a hardass than Grayson, and he pushed Willie to get better.

"If you screwed up in the ballgame Willie Thompson would make you run a couple of miles the next day around the football field," Willie said.

*Mileston High School basketball team, circa 1959. Willie Harris is holding the basketball in the middle.*

Thompson also told Willie that if he stayed focused on basketball he might be able to earn a scholarship to play in college, which is exactly the motivation he needed to keep working to get better.

Willie's lifestyle did not go unnoticed by Coach Thompson. Coach saw the great raw potential in Willie, but he knew he was a rascal. One day he talked to him after practice, Willie sitting on the bleachers and Coach pacing in front of him.

"Harris, you been working hard on your game?"

"Yes, Coach," Willie said.

"You been working on the stuff I showed you with your inside moves?"

"Yes, Coach," Willie said.

"You sure?"

"Yes, Coach," Willie said.

"Really? Then why did I hear you were at the juke joint Saturday night, shootin' dice and actin' the fool?"

Willie looked up at Coach and said nothing.

"Were you at a juke joint Saturday night?"

"Maybe, Coach," Willie said.

"Don't sass me, Harris."

"I'm sorry, Coach," Willie said.

"Oh, I bet you think you're something special, don't you, going out gambling, drinking, romancing the ladies. I bet you think you're a really big man."

"Well, the boys do call me Big Man, Coach," Willie said, looking down.

"Don't sass me, boy!"

Coach slammed the ball that he was holding into the court and then caught it, squeezing it tight.

"Harris, you like picking cotton?"

"No, Coach," Willie said, starting to get angry.

"You like doing whatever the man in the big house tells you that you need to do?"

"No, Coach," Willie said.

"Listen, Harris, this is not the way for you to go. You've got a lot of God-given talent, maybe more than you deserve, but it's there, so you can't waste it. You need to focus on chasing the basketball, not chasing girls. If you spend every weekend in juke joints surrounded by hustlers and hoochie mamas, I can guarantee you that something bad is going to happen.  If you want to get out of here and do something special you need to work on your game, not on getting your noodle wet."

"Thanks, Coach," Willie said.

Though by the latter part of his high school career Willie had very little interaction with Oscar Harris, his hatred of his stepfather did not subside. He could not let go of the anger he felt toward him for the way he treated the family, especially his mom.

"I knew well that the man my mom was married to, that he knew all the time that he wasn't me and Robert's dad. I think that's why, see my brother was quiet and all of that, you know, he never would hardly say anything. But it wasn't me. You couldn't push me around the way that he would take things, I wouldn't. And I used to lay in bed at night, thinkin' about what I'm gonna do to this man when I get big enough? How can I get rid of him, or really do something drastic to him without somebody knowin'? That's how much I disliked the man," Willie said.

Then during Willie's junior year he learned that Oscar Harris was having problems with his prostate. One day Peyton Abbot Jones came to take Oscar to see a doctor in Lexington, and the doctor sent him to a hospital in the state capitol of Jackson, an hour south of the plantation. It was just two days later when Mr. Jones came by the house and told the family he had died. They never learned how he died, and Evie speculated that they might have just put him out of his misery.

The pain Willie felt from 18 years of living with a stepfather who mistreated him and having his real dad living so close by, all that pain would not go away, even after Oscar Harris died.

"And all of this stuff had built up in me. And I wonder today if that man hadn't have died, what would I have done to him. And it's bad to hate, 'cause hate poisons your whole insides. I would go to bed and get up thinkin' about wringin' his neck," Willie said.

On a practical level, Oscar Harris' death meant that the family was losing one-fourth of its workforce, and Willie, Robert, and Evie would have to do more.

Coach Thompson helped Willie improve by connecting him with Cleveland Buckner, who at the time was playing basketball on the

Jackson College for Negro Teachers team. Buckner was three years older than Willie and would go on to play in the NBA for the New York Knicks, including one memorable night in 1962 when he was given the impossible task of trying to guard Wilt Chamberlain during the historic game when Wilt the Stilt scored 100 points. Buckner, who was also 6'8", worked out with Willie and showed him how to play against a big man. Make him uncomfortable and don't let him do the things he wants to do around the basket. If he is right-handed, overplay his right side and make him go left, giving you a much better chance to block his shot.

While Willie was good enough to play basketball in college, there were only a handful of schools where he could actually get recruited, and these were limited to the Black colleges in Mississippi. Black athletes were generally not allowed to play on teams in Southern colleges and universities attended by whites until the late 1960s. The first Black athlete in any sport to play at the University of Mississippi was basketball player Coolidge Ball in 1972. Since someone like Willie couldn't play at a big school in the South, he could dream about playing at a school like Michigan State or Notre Dame or somewhere back east or in the Midwest, but the reality was that major college programs were not sending scouts to look at ballplayers in rural Mississippi. It wasn't just that colleges and universities in the South had white-only and Black-only teams, collegiate basketball teams across the country were very much segregated before the 1960s. In 1948 Clarence Walker became the first Black player in any college post-season basketball tournament, playing at what is now called Indiana State University. In order for him to play, the National Association of Intercollegiate Basketball had to reverse its policy of banning Black players from playing in its tournament, and it only happened because Walker was supported by the NAACP and his coach, the legendary John Wooden. Blacks were sprinkled in small numbers in major basketball programs across the country, usually no more than one or two on a team, so the schools wouldn't upset their rabid fan bases, which generally preferred white players. Having a small number of Black players on the team wasn't tokenism—that concept didn't exist in the segregated America of the mid-twentieth century. It was just the opposite; the Black players had to be some of the best in the country to be allowed to play. The first college team to win a national championship with a majority of Black starting players was the 1955 University of San Francisco team which featured Bill Russell and K.C. Jones, both of whom are now Hall of Famers for both their college and professional careers. As in other areas of their lives, these Black ballplayers had to work at least twice as hard and be twice as good as whites in order to be given a chance, or even be considered as an option. They were the same barriers that have been erected in the path of Blacks in America since they were dragged to its shores centuries ago. So to put it mildly, if Willie wanted to make it as a basketball player, he had a tough road ahead, but he was a fighter.

Before Willie could concern himself with playing basketball in college and beyond, he was focused on his high school team. Willie and all his teammates had one goal that none of them would ever be able to achieve: to play basketball against white high school players. Due to segregation, Black high schools were only allowed to play other Black high schools.

"They had put us down for so long, and we wanted to show them what we could do on the basketball court," Willie said.

There was not a basketball state championship for the Black schools, and the most they could achieve was to win the Delta Conference Tournament, and that was their goal.

Willie and his senior class teammates had stuck it out in Mississippi while many of their classmates had migrated north after their sophomore or junior years. His senior class had only 56 graduating students, but in their freshman year it had 80. The thirty percent who dropped out did not do so because they wanted to work full-time in Mississippi. There weren't any good jobs for Blacks in Mississippi, and if they left school, it was most likely to move to Chicago or Detroit or St. Louis where many had family and could find work that paid a decent wage, or at least it was decent compared to $2.50 a day.

Willie's teammate Stanford Murry recalls his mindset as a teenager in Mississippi in the late 1950s.

"My thought was to get out of there, 'cause I figured there was no hope of change. Blacks couldn't vote. Blacks held no political office. Blacks had no way of bettering themselves, except to leave Mississippi. I graduated May 19, something like that, and left within about 5 or 10 days," Murry said.

As the Delta Conference Tournament approached in February 1960, Willie did not yet have any college coaches who were recruiting him. A few days before the tournament Coach Thompson pulled him aside.

"Are you ready for the tournament, Harris?" Coach asked.

"Yes, Coach," Willie said.

"Well, you had better bring your A game, Harris."

"I always do, Coach," Willie said.

"But especially bring it on Friday, because E.E. Simmons is coming to the game."

"The coach at Alcorn?" Willie asked.

"Yes, sir, he is coming to see the center on Leland High School, a guy named McNeal. He is 6'8" like you, but he's got about twenty pounds on you. Simmons is real high on McNeal, but don't let him outdo you, Harris. You can change Simmons' mind," Coach said.

That night when Willie went to bed and looked up at the stars through the hole in the cabin's roof, he wasn't thinking about getting up to work in the fields. He was flipping a basketball up in the air and thinking about the tournament, and smiling.

On Friday morning the team boarded the school bus for the half-hour ride to the tournament, which was being held in Belzoni, nicknamed "The Heart of the Delta." It is another small country town surrounded by endless acres of cotton, soybean, and corn fields. Normally boisterous, Willie sat quietly and looked out the window and watched the fields roll by. They were just rows of soil in February, waiting to be planted and for the start of that endless cycle to begin again. Maybe he wouldn't have to do that again, ever. If he could play great and take care of McNeal, maybe he wouldn't be hunched over in the field in October, picking cotton. What a delicious thought.

The Delta Conference Tournament was an all-day affair. It started at 9 am and wasn't finished until 11 o'clock that night. If you made it to the championship game it was your fourth game that day. Mileston was a longshot to win the tournament. The smallest school in the conference with only a few hundred students, it was certainly the underdog, but Willie felt that any team he was on had a chance. They grinded out a few wins that morning and afternoon and later that night, in what may have been the biggest stroke of luck in Willie's life to that point, they found themselves in the championship game facing Leland High School and their big talented center McNeal. Willie was so keyed up before the game he thought he might explode.

"Harris, go do your thing," Coach said in the pre-game huddle.

When the game started and Willie posted up against McNeal for the first time he could tell it would be tough to move this guy off his spot, but he remembered what Cleveland Buckner had taught him and he kept battling. Willie loved to talk trash to his opponents, but McNeal was quieter. The only thing he said to Willie at the start of the game was "Don't bring that shit in here or I'll make you eat it."

"Okay, we'll see," Willie smiled.

The game was tied at halftime, but in the second half Willie took over, blocking McNeal's shots, fighting harder for rebounds, nimbly shooting over him, and outhustling him. Mileston won by 10 points and the underdogs were the tournament champions.

The following Monday after practice Coach Thompson called Willie over.

"Harris, I got something to tell you."

"What's that, Coach?" Willie asked.

"You played real good in the tournament."

"Thanks, Coach," Willie said.

"Coach Simmons thought so, too. He liked what he saw. He thought you whooped McNeal. He wants you to come play for him at Alcorn. He is giving you a scholarship."

Willie was shocked. He stood there with the biggest smile of his life on his face and thought about how his hard work had finally paid off.

He raced home and excitedly told his mom. Evie was stunned and so proud of her boy, hugging and squeezing him like she never had before, the tears rolling down her cheeks. Her pride and joy quickly morphed into concern about how Peyton Abbot Jones would react. With Oscar Harris gone and now Willie, how could she and Robert keep up with the fields? Evie, however, always put her sons' welfare ahead of hers, and she talked to Mr. Jones about it the next time she saw him.

"Mr. Jones, you know my son here, don't ya, Willie?"

"Yes."

"You see how tall he is?"

"Yes."

"Well, he has gotten a scholarship to go to Alcorn to play basketball."

Jones goes berserk.

"Hell, no! Niggers don't need no damn education! You can't live on my plantation and have this boy go to school!"

Evie straightens her back and speaks carefully.

"Mr. Jones, I can't read and write. I want my son to get an education so he can get a good job. What can I do so he can go to school?" Evie asked.

"Well. goddammit, if he's going to go to school, you've got to get someone to take his place in the field, pickin' and all of that."

Evie tells Willie to go get his father Andrew. Whenever Evie needed something, she would turn to Andrew, and he found someone to replace Willie in the field so he could go to school.

Willie would never pick another boll of cotton for the rest of his life.

**7**

**GET OUT**

The rest of Willie's senior year was a breeze, and all he could think about was getting to Alcorn. Working in the fields felt like part of his past, so he asked his mom if he could go to Chicago to work for the summer, and Evie set Willie up with his cousin Annie, so he had a place to live.

In late May one of Andrew Davenport's workers drove Willie to the train station for the long ride to Chicago, as Andrew could no longer drive, having had a brain tumor removed a few months earlier. Willie boarded the train late in the afternoon with his one little suitcase and sat in the "Colored" section. It was the first time in his life he was leaving the state of Mississippi. He marveled when the train approached Memphis. He had never seen anything like it.

"Especially coming in at night and seeing all of the lights and everything. You thought you had died and went to heaven if you grew up on a plantation."

The train continued through Kentucky and then crossed the Ohio River into Illinois.

"When you leave Mississippi, they had cars for what they called 'Colored,' and when you cross the Ohio River, what they say, now you crossin' the Mason-Dixon Line, you could sit anywhere you wanted to sit. At that time I was young, and I didn't know all the rules or regulations, so I just stayed in my seat."

Willie moved in with his cousin Annie in her apartment in the Woodlawn section of the South Side of Chicago. He had a friend from home named Charlie April who had moved to Chicago with his family. Willie and Charlie decided to take a walk downtown and go job hunting together. Willie landed a job bussing tables at O'Connor's Restaurant downtown and he was doing such a good job that after a few weeks they made him the cashier. He was making more money than he had ever made in his life, and he was able to eat as much as he wanted.

The South Side was more integrated in the late 1950s than it would ever be again. While the neighborhood he lived in was primarily Black, there were a significant number of whites living and working there as well. Compared to the strict segregation of Mississippi, life in Chicago felt much freer. He would go into a bar and there would be a white guy sitting at the barstool next to him. That would never have happened in Mississippi.

"You could go into restaurants and stuff like that and you didn't have a colored section and a white section. If you rode the bus you could sit anywhere you wanted to sit and all of that, you didn't have to go through that."

While it was freer in some respects, Willie understood there were limits. It was made clear to Blacks that it was acceptable for them to go to some areas of the city and its suburbs, but not to others. In general, the vast majority of Blacks in Chicago lived south of downtown, and the vast majority of whites lived north and west of downtown. That has changed very little since the 1960s, other than the fact that a cluster of Chicago's northwest suburbs now have a majority of residents who are Black.

"Yes, there was racism in Chicago, like Cicero, Illinois, which is right outside of Chicago, Franklin Park, and all of that. You didn't let the sun set on you in those little towns if you were a Black during those times. And certain parts of Chicago, like out where Wrigley Field is and stuff, where the Cubs baseball park is at, Blacks didn't go out there neither unless they worked out there. But it still wasn't as bad as Mississippi. If there was a bar in the neighborhood, well, you know, white people lived in the neighborhood where my nephew lived, and all of that. You could go in there and you didn't have any problems," Willie said.

Towns like Cicero had earned the nickname "Sundown Towns" due to their policy of not allowing Blacks to live in town or even be present in town at night or on the weekends. In the 1950s there were more than 10,000 Blacks working in factories in Cicero, but none living there. Sundown Towns were not unique to the Chicago area, to Illinois, or to the Midwest. They were all over the country—thousands of them. They enforced their racist policies through uniform housing discrimination, local ordinances, intimidation, and when all those failed, terrorism. In early June of 1951 the owner of an apartment building in Cicero rented a unit to Black Chicago city bus driver Harvey E. Clark Jr., his wife Johnetta, and their two children. Clark served his country in the U.S. Army during World War II and was a graduate of Fisk University, where he had met his wife when they were both studying there. The young family was living in a cramped tenement in the South Side and wanted a larger, more comfortable home. This is how the American Dream is supposed to work: you serve your country, get a college education, work hard, abide by the law, and improve your living conditions. However, when the Clark family tried to move into their apartment in Cicero they were barred by the police, who had been tipped off by a municipal official that a Black family was planning to move into town. The sheriff told them to "get out of here fast." Clark was from Mississippi, so he was intimately aware of the scourge of racism that infected America, but he was still baffled.

"We were denied admission to the building by the police themselves. I was a newcomer to Chicago, and being a Southerner, I thought I was in a free state, Abraham Lincoln's state," Clark said.

The NAACP filed suit on behalf of the courageous Clarks, and with the help of a court order they moved into the apartment in late June. Word spread throughout Cicero that a Black family had moved in and on the night of July 11 an angry mob assembled outside the apartment building. Women hurled stones through the windows of the Clark family's apartment. The mob grew to 4,000 people and many of them invaded the building, destroying much of the interior and setting small fires. The Clarks and all the other building residents fled in terror. The Cicero police were there, but they did little to stop the rioters, so Illinois Governor Adlai Stevenson called in the state's National Guard troops to finally quell the violence. All this happened because a World War II veteran and his young family had moved into an apartment.

The attack on the Clark family occurred several years before the civil rights movement in America was widespread and gaining traction. However, even 15 years later, after the Civil Rights Act of 1964 and the Voting Rights Act of 1965 had become the law of the land, the virulent racism of many whites in Chicago was as strong as ever. On August 5, 1966, Martin Luther King Jr. was leading a march to a realtor's office in Chicago so he could demand fair housing policies be followed, regardless of a tenant's race. A mob of 700 white people swarmed the march, hurling bottles, rocks, and bricks. One of the rocks hit King in the head, sending him down to his knees momentarily. He told reporters later that day: "I've been in many demonstrations all across the South, but I can say that I have never seen, even in Mississippi and Alabama, mobs as hostile and as hate-filled as I'm seeing in Chicago."

Fortunately for Willie, his Chicago summer of 1960 was uneventful. He was an eighteen-year-old kid and he didn't put himself in any situations where he was likely to have problems. He was only there a few months, he worked hard in the restaurant, and spent most of his time off in his cousin Annie's apartment. In August he packed up his suitcase and headed back to Clifton Plantation to get ready to go to college.

His stay on the plantation was brief, but he had one problem: he didn't have the clothes he needed to go to college. Having grown up on a plantation, he had never needed—and could never afford—a closet full of clothes so he could look presentable on a daily basis. Once again, his dad came to his rescue.

"I didn't have clothes to go to school and all of that stuff. So he told me to go and see Mr. Shure who had the clothing store and get four or five pair of pants and shirts, and all of that, and then go over to Mr. Williams shoe store and get me two pair of shoes. The hardest thing for me to find was shoes. 'Cause I was wearing a size 15 that time, and the most you could find was a 13. But Mr. Williams used to order them for my dad. That's how I got 'em. I never forgot that. So that was my clothes to go to Alcorn," Willie said.

When late August came and it was time to go to Alcorn, Andrew Davenport came to the plantation with a driver to pick Willie up for the two-hour ride to his new home.

Evie looked up at Willie with a mixture of pride and sadness. She hugged his torso.

"You make sure you pay attention in class," she said.

"I will, Mama."

"And don't be acting the fool and get yourself in any trouble," she said.

"I won't, Mama."

"Most importantly, make sure you write me," she said.

"I will, Mama."

"I love you, Willie," she said.

"I love you, too, Mama."

"Now I think you better go," she said, "'cuz if I stare too long I'll probably break down and cry. Oh, oh, oh, oh sweet child o' mine."

Willie and his dad drove through a thick forest to reach the campus. When Willie had told people he was going to Alcorn to play basketball, some had said "Why you goin' there? It's in the sticks!" They were right. Alcorn State University was founded in 1871 in southwestern Mississippi, five miles east of the big river and 50 miles south of the Delta's rich farmland. It was founded with the intent of training recently freed male slaves to learn a trade or the science of farming, and the school began admitting Black women in 1895. The campus is not adjacent to any town or city and is surrounded by miles of forest in all directions. Perhaps it was placed there so whites wouldn't have to see it and have any visual proof that negroes were beginning to get educated. Even 150 years after its founding, little has changed, and it still sits like an island in the wilderness. The school's most famous alumnus is civil rights icon and martyr Medgar Evers, who graduated in 1952. Prior to attending Alcorn Evers had served in the U.S. Army during World War II, and he was a decorated combat veteran. Upon returning home to Mississippi after the war, he found he was still unable to vote, just like so many other Blacks who had served their country. This discrimination energized him, and he became the NAACP's first field secretary for Mississippi in 1954. His activism and investigations of racially-motived crimes made him a target of White supremacists, and he was assassinated in his driveway in Jackson the early morning of June 12, 1963 by Ku Klux Klan member Byron De La Beckwith. Evers was returning home after meeting with NAACP lawyers, and his wife Myrlie and his three small children Darrell, James, and Reena were waiting inside the house for him. The killer was also waiting for him and he fired one bullet from a shotgun into Evers' back. It went through his heart and he was dead within an hour. He had been carrying t-shirts that read "Jim Crow Must Go." Much of the nation mourned his loss, but Martin Luther King Jr. and other civil rights activists were able to prevent any anger over his murder from devolving into violence.

Willie moved into the dormitory, a two-story building that resembled a military barracks, with his roommate Wade Murry. Wade was Willie's friend from Mileston High School and was the brother of

Stanford Murry, Willie's high school basketball teammate. The Murrys were sharecroppers on the nearby Nixon Plantation, and Wade was the youngest of their 10 children. When Wade graduated from high school his parents became some of the half a million Blacks over the past 40 years who had left farms in the South and moved to Chicago during the Great Migration, but they asked Wade to go to college because it would mean a lot to them if one of their children graduated from college.

"We were farmers, sharecroppers, and so my mom and dad didn't have any money and I didn't have any money, so I went with probably the money that I made in Chicago one year, you know, and my brother gave me some money, and my sister gave me some money, and that was it. I guess we both went to school with one suitcase. I just went 'cause I was the baby, and nobody in my family of 10 kids had ever gone to school, so I went," Wade said.

When Willie and Wade arrived on campus, they soon realized that there was not much going on at the school other than academics and athletics, but they made it through together.

"That one year in school, we were roommates in school, and neither one of us had any money and he worked, he was on scholarship, and he worked in the cafeteria. And he would bring food out of the cafeteria and eat it when he could get it. And he would bring it, and we would eat that way. Also, I don't know how or where we got the clippers from, but I would cut hair, and he would line it for 50 cents and we probably made a dollar or two dollars a week, maybe that much, by cutting hair and lining it with, you have a safety razor, a single edge razor, with a double-edged razor blade. And so that's how we made it, you know, we made it through school with nothing. We never did have more than a dollar in our pocket at any time, you know. Going through that year at Alcorn and we had nothing, but we survived, we learned how to handle each other, we learned how to support each other during that time, and it wasn't the easiest thing, we didn't get through it the honest way, you know, all honesty, you know, and so that was interesting how we got through school, and how we was able to do that, you know, there wasn't no activity outside like campus kids go off campus and stuff like that. We had none of that, you know. We just, we were locked into the school, you know, but it wasn't bad," Wade said.

Wade and Willie developed a special bond that helped them navigate their new life.

"We enjoyed each other because one of the things about Willie is if he didn't like you, he's going to tell you. He's going to tell you right off the bat. And so that's what I respected about him. We could talk about each other, we could talk about each other's mama and all that stuff, but that was just us. Nobody else could do that but us. Nobody else could talk about us like us, you know," Wade said.

The nearest town was 15 miles away, and Willie didn't know anyone who had a car, so campus life was their entire life. There was one little store across the street from the school where a guy sold a few groceries, but mainly beer and moonshine whiskey. If they had a few dollars, Willie and his friends would buy some and bring it back to their dorm room to drink.

Willie got used to the routine of being a college student athlete. Being sequestered at Alcorn wasn't as glamorous as he imagined it would be, but it was certainly better than picking cotton and getting kicked in the ass by the boss man.

"You had to be at class at 8 o'clock in the morning and see at that time if you played ball and stuff, you really weren't pushed. But I got up and went, you know, and my first class was math and all of that, but I went. Then after that we'd eat at the cafeteria around four or five, and after that we went to basketball practice at six. Then you get back to the dorm about eight-thirty or nine, take a shower and go to bed, and get up the next morning to go to class," Willie said.

Willie chose to be a history major, and his freshman year he took courses in math, English, history, geography, biology, and physical education. Many of his classmates were agriculture or physical education majors.

Willie and Wade lived next door to a guy named Walter Fisher in the dormitory, and a random conversation with Fisher would lead to Willie learning more about his troubled family tree. His Mom Evie was 40 years old when he was born, but he had heard rumors that she had at least one daughter, maybe two, more than 20 years before he was born, when she was a teenager. He heard that she had given the girls away to other families, and Willie didn't know why. He asked his mom about it every so often, but she was evasive, so he didn't push. He had heard that one of the girls was adopted by a woman named Lena Lewis, and that the girl was named Evie, after his mom. One day Fisher was talking about a woman who lived next door to him, and he mentioned her name—it was Lena Lewis.

"Does she have a daughter named Evie, who is about 40?" Willie asked.

"She sure does," Fisher said.

"Can you get me her address?" Willie asked.

"I sure can," Fisher said.

Evie Lewis lived in Waterloo, Iowa and Willie wrote her a letter. The letter said that he was sorry about what had happened, but that it wasn't his fault, and he would like to have a relationship with her. Evie wrote back that she liked the family she grew up in and since their mom had deserted her, she didn't want to be bothered with connecting with his family. Willie was crushed. He would wander the streets and ask himself why did he have to have so many problems? Why couldn't he have a happy family life? His stepfather had been cruel and violent all his life. When he learned who his true father was, he couldn't live with him because his wife resented him and Robert. Now his sister told him she had a happy family life and she didn't want any part of him, so Willie began to resent his mother for giving away her daughters. If you are going to go through all the trouble of having a baby, you sure as hell ought to keep it, he thought. His mother later told him that when she was young that she had been promised a job in Memphis, but she knew she wouldn't be able to go if she had any kids. She saw it as her way out of the plantation life, but the job fell through, she was still stuck in Mississippi, and her two daughters were gone.

Willie figured that growing up as a Black person in Mississippi was hard enough; he hoped that he could at least count on his family, but that eluded him. A year after getting the rejection letter from his sister, Willie heard that Lena Lewis was dying in the hospital in Lexington, and that Evie Lewis, his sister, was there. He went to the hospital and sat in the waiting room. When he saw his sister no one had to tell him who she was. She was the spitting image of their mom. Willie just watched her walk by. There was nothing to say.

Willie's experience on the Alcorn basketball team was not what he had expected. He entered school with the mindset that this was a step toward improving his game as he continued on his quest to be a professional basketball player, but things did not go as he planned.

"Me and the coach after I got there, we didn't get along. He had his favorite players, and see, I had never rode the bench. All the way through high school, I was a starter. He played partiality, about who would play and wouldn't play and all that stuff, and then one day me and him got into an argument, well, he told me I was a hardhead and I was gonna sit beside him until he decided when I was gonna play."

Willie was the tallest player on the team at 6'8", and the next tallest was 6'6". He didn't think he was better than the other big men on the team, but he thought he was as good as them, and he wanted the chance to prove himself on the court. He tried to figure out why the coach wouldn't play him much, and if there was something about Willie that Coach Simmons didn't like, but it was a mystery.

"He very seldom would talk to me. At practice he would yell and scream sometimes, but normally he was a quiet guy."

Willie's teammates would encourage the coach to put Willie in the game, but he wouldn't. There were 12 players on the team, and Simmons preferred to only give playing time to seven of them. If you weren't one of the lucky seven, you were pretty well out of luck.

"So I made up my mind, I said well, next year I'm not comin' back. I'm going to find me another school," Willie said. He decided he needed to transfer to another school where he could get playing time and have a better relationship with the coach.

"I had a guy that I knew was at Michigan State, and I had another friend that I met through a friend of mine was at DePaul. I was intendin' to talk to them, which I did, and try to get in at one of their schools. But the thing was, you had to lay out a year, you couldn't play once you transfer. So when I found that out, I said hell with this, I'll just work in Chicago and go back to school the following year," Willie said.

After leaving Alcorn Willie did move to Chicago and this time he lived with his nephew George, his wife Gerry, and their two little kids in an apartment in the South Side. Willie went out to look for a job and wasn't as fortunate as he had been during his first stay in Chicago. He walked all day, asking businesses if they needed any help and filling out applications. He never heard back from any of them, so he worked out a deal with George and Gerry so he could stay with them. He would take care of their kids when they worked, and he would clean the apartment.

George was cheating on Gerry with another woman, and he told Willie that when his woman called on the phone, she would ask for Willie. If Gerry wasn't around, Willie would hand the phone to George. Gerry discovered their scheme and told Willie to get out. It was January and it was 10 degrees out. It didn't matter. He had to go. So Willie went two blocks away to see if he could stay with Joey, his Puerto Rican friend. Joey said sure, but Joey's dad had put him out also, and he was living in the garage. They had a little space heater in there and they put cardboard up against the garage door to try to keep the cold out.

Willie was now in survival mode. He and Joey had some other friends and together they became a band of petty thieves. One of their friends was named Chico and his father ran a Puerto Rican grocery store. Willie and his friends would get up early in the morning and follow the milkman around on his route when he left quarts of milk on stoops. They would steal the milk and sell it to Chico's dad. They would also go to the train yard and break into freight train cars, steal hams, salamis, and turkeys, and sell them to people in their neighborhood.

They made a new friend named Donny, an Italian kid, and Joey told Willie they were on their way to the big time because Donny's dad was in the Mafia. One night they all went to a truck stop to steal from tractor trailers and they each took a trailer to break into. Donny broke into a trailer containing caskets. They all asked him what the hell he was doing, because the trailer had casket company written on the side of it. What the hell are we supposed to do with caskets, they asked? They didn't even know any funeral home directors. Donny was forced to admit he couldn't read, and they all said he must have been lying about his father being in the Mafia, too. But then a few months later no one had seen Donny's father for about a week, and they noticed a putrid smell coming from Donny's father's car, which was parked in front of their apartment. Donny broke into the trunk and found his dad's corpse. He had been shot in the head three times, so they figured he probably was in the Mafia after all.

Willie started to get overwhelmed by the lifestyle and nefarious activities he was falling into. It was a descent into the maelstrom. He and his band were playing a cat and mouse game with the police, trying not to get caught, but at the same time, paying off many of the corrupt Chicago cops with bribes when they did get caught.

"I hadn't never been no hoodlum or nothing. We stole watermelons and stuff in Mississippi, but nothing compared to the shit I got involved with in Chicago. That neighborhood I lived in; everything was goin' on. Robberies, purse snatchin', house burglaries. 'Cause I know one night a dude lived down the street from us, his name was Leo, and my partner named Mac saw him buy a house full of furniture. And Leo was a drunk. They bought Leo a whole bunch of whiskey and gave it to him. He had a recliner chair, so he got drunk, went to sleep in that recliner chair, and they stole all his furniture. When he woke up the only thing he had was the recliner chair, but he didn't know who ripped him off," Willie said.

Willie was not comfortable or happy that he had fallen in with this crowd, but he felt trapped.

"I was old enough to know why some Black kids turn to crime. When your backs are to the wall, it's no limit to what a person will do. An empty stomach for a couple of days will make you try anything, and I said if it takes stealing to keep a stomach full, that's what I would do, and I didn't give a damn who in the hell it came from. I also know there was one other reason that made a Black turn to crime, because it's so hard for a Black to open a door and he is tired of being turned down. I have walked all over Chicago looking for a job. I walked so long until my shoes had holes in them when I got home, and they were good shoes when I left home. And the next day I went out again and again with cardboard in the bottom of my shoes. But the whites said they didn't need any help, and I also knew that some of them were lying to me. I would wonder what was wrong with me. I was a human. I got so fed up when I was a kid that I would wash myself for hours and hours, hoping that I would turn white. And I would also put flour on me, hoping that I would turn white."

Living in Chicago was turning into a nightmare for Willie. In Mississippi, it was clear what you could and could not do. In Chicago, you could do just about anything you wanted, as long as you didn't get caught. One night Willie walked into a tavern two blocks from where he was staying, ordered a beer, and sat down at the bar. A white woman was sitting next to him and she asked Willie if he had a match. Willie lit her cigarette and the woman started chatting with him. A redneck with a Southern accent was sitting on the other side of the woman glaring at Willie.

"Where I'm from, niggers don't talk to white women," the redneck said loud enough for everyone in the bar to hear.

"Where you from?" Willie asked.

"Mississippi."

"Really?" Willie asked.

"Yep."

Willie's mind immediately went back to Howard store and the moment that Bill Turner pulled the gun on him and threatened to blow his brains out for no reason. This was his chance to get back at Bill Turner. Willie knew it was wrong. He knew it made no sense to beat up one white man for something another man had done to you. But he couldn't stop himself; he had so much hate in him at that time.

"Well, Mississippi, how would you like to get your ass kicked?" Willie asked.

"There ain't a nigger alive who can kick my ass."

Willie got up and started to walk over to the redneck, but the bar owner told them to take it outside. When they got out to the sidewalk, the redneck turned to face Willie and put up his fists.

"Well, nigger, how do you want it? I haven't had a good fight in two days."

Willie looked at him and figured he had hell on his hands. The redneck was a big, strong-looking dude. He popped Willie with a right hook and Willie went down. The redneck wound up to kick Willie in the head, but Willie caught his foot and twisted it until he lost his balance and fell, and when he fell, he banged his head on the sidewalk. Willie jumped up and pounced on him. He started beating him in the head with his fists. One after another after another. The redneck went limp, but Willie didn't stop pummeling him.

"The bar owner pulled me off him before I killed him, but that was just what I wanted to do to him. I guess all those years I had all that hate in me against whites."

In the summer of 1962 Willie had been in Chicago for a little over a year, and he realized he had to get out of there. This was no life for him. He wasn't cut out to be a criminal. He was a basketball player. That is what he loved to do. It was time to go home and figure out which school he could get into and play basketball.

One night he was walking home with his friend Percy from a party. It was after midnight, and it was windy.

"Willie, you see that white dude coming our way?" Percy asked.

"Yeah."

"Well, I've got my little brother's toy pistol in my pocket and I'm gonna rob this dude," Percy said.

"Percy, don't do it."

"Oh, I'm doing it."

Willie crossed the street because he didn't want any part of it. When Percy got close to the guy, he pulled out the toy pistol and the man turned around and ran the other way. The man ran down an alley and Percy chased him. When they got to the other end of the alley Percy ran right into a police car. The cops busted Percy and he went to jail.

"Now if I had have helped him robbed that guy, I would've went to jail with him. But something told me, don't do it, so I didn't. I said I know I've got to leave Dodge now."

That was enough. Willie called his mom and asked her to send him some money so he could buy a train ticket and head back to Mississippi. He stayed in Joey's garage and kept out of trouble until the money arrived.

In August 1962 he left Chicago, and he wouldn't be going back.

The brothers Wade and Stanford Murry moved to Chicago around 1960 and both had successful careers for more than three decades. Wade worked in paper recycling and manufacturing, and Stanford was a member of the Chicago Fire Department. After they retired, they both moved back down south, Wade to Mississippi and Stanford to Tennessee.

Wade explained how he felt living as a Black man in the South vs. Chicago.

"I had no problem with the South. I'm here now. I have no problem with the South because people are people, and I found out that in Chicago I had more prejudice in Chicago than in the South, all my life in the South. I had to fight segregation in my job for 32 years. I had to fight to stay there to get anything out of it. So I realized that people are people, you know, and they're just prejudiced. And there's nothin' you can do about that. So I fought that, you know, just to stay in my job for 32 years. I was more comfortable down here, knowing that when I look at a white man's face what he thought about me, as opposed to when I was in Chicago and looked at a white man's face and knowing that he would cut my throat just the same," Wade said.

Stanford Murry had left Mississippi and followed the rest of his family to Chicago right after he graduated from Mileston High School. He worked for a year in Chicago before he served in the military for three years and then returned to Chicago after his service. In the late 1960s he applied to be a firefighter in the Chicago Fire Department, a department that has consistently been accused of discriminatory hiring practices. In a city whose population is split between whites, Blacks, and Hispanics, the department has long hired an overwhelming majority of white males, even well into the twenty-first century. In fact, Stanford believes he was hired in error.

"I think the reason that I got on, became a firefighter, was they looked at my name, Murry, and they thought I was Irish. And when they looked at my address, it was in an area of Chicago that was changing from white to Black. So they allowed me to get on. I really don't think it was because of ability or knowledge or whatever. I think it was something that they didn't want Blacks in the fire department," Stanford said.

Stanford became a lieutenant, which meant he supervised an apparatus, and he had five men under his command. One day in the early 1990s his engineer Bob, an Italian American, came up to him.

"Stan, you know what? I hate that O.J. Simpson," Bob said.

"Why is that, Bob?" Stanford asked.

"Well, he went and killed that lady and that other guy, who didn't even do anything. I mean, he has all this money, why did he have to go and kill her? I mean, if somebody leaves you, then you just move on," Bob said.

Stanford watched Bob get worked up and go on about how O.J. is a murderer, and he should not have gotten off just because he was famous, and he had good lawyers. When Bob finally finished Stanford looked him in the eye.

"Bob," he said.

"Yeah?"

"Who should I hate?" Stanford asked.

"Huh?"

"Who should I hate, Bob? Black folks have been put down in this country since they got here. They have been denied the right to vote, and the powers that be have usually made it impossible for them to get a decent education or a decent job. About 5,000 Black men have been lynched in this country, and none of the people who killed them were ever even prosecuted."

Bob was looking down at the ground.

"Who should I hate, Bob?"

That was the end of the conversation.

Neil Young's song "Southern Man" is a scorching diatribe against slavery and the Jim Crow South. The song was released in 1970, and it has been simultaneously revered and reviled, depending upon where you come from and your social and political leanings. A generation of young people reared on rock music in the 1970s embraced it as a shining example of rock's ability to make a profound and important statement. The tragedy of the song—despite all its brilliance—is that by focusing so fiercely on the wrongs committed in the South, it ignores what has occurred in the rest of America and tacitly implies that outside of the South, the good ole' USA is a racially tolerant and morally superior nirvana. It can inaccurately affirm many non-Southerner's smug self-confidence regarding their perceived righteousness and acceptance of others.

**8**

— · —

# I'm Uncle Sam, That's Who I Am

When Willie returned to Mississippi in the  summer of 1962, it was just as awful as he remembered it. It was hot as hell, but at least he didn't have to work in the fields anymore. He slept on the couch in the tiny apartment that his Mom and Robert had moved into in Lexington. He had to get out of Chicago, but now what? He talked to some guys he knew who were playing college basketball in Mississippi, and he was trying to figure out if he could go play at Jackson State, Delta State, or some other nearby all-Black college or university. He figured that any school could use a 6'8" big man with his skills.

In August his brother told him he had been drafted into the Army. He had already taken his physical and was due to head to Fort Jackson, South Carolina for basic training in mid-September.

"For real?" Willie laughed, "my big brother is going to be a soldier? Are they actually goin' to let you carry a gun?"

"They sure are," Robert said, "and keep laughing, funny man, because you might get drafted, too. Ain't nothin' special about you."

"Oh, shit, you're right. I'd better find out."

So Willie took a walk to see Mrs. Smith at the draft board office, which was downtown just off Courthouse Square. He was worried that Robert was going to be right, and Mrs. Smith was going to tell him he was about to get drafted.

"It was comin' up to Vietnam and the draft still was in existence at that time. And normally, if you was Black, during those days, even if you was in school, you pretty well knew you was gonna get drafted. It was gonna be a miracle to save you." Willie said.

In fact, the efficient white men of Lexington did their best to make sure as many young Black men got drafted as possible. Some of Willie's friends would be walking in town and a white guy might act really nice to them for no reason, and it would usually be someone who had never paid any attention to them in the past. "Hey, how you boys doin'? they would say with a smile. "What's your name? What plantation do you live on?  How old are you boys?" They were just gathering information to give to the draft board.

Willie walked into the draft office and saw her sitting behind an enormous solid oak desk. Every young Black man in the county was afraid of Mrs. Smith. Her hair was pulled back tight against her scalp and a pair of tortoise shell eyeglasses rested precariously on the tip of her nose. On the desk in front of her was an enormous book that contained the names of every young man in Holmes County, and the only thing more fearsome than Mrs. Smith was her book, as it seemed to have the supernatural power to foretell their future.

"Mrs. Smith," Willie said tentatively.

"Boy, what do you want?"

"My name is Willie Harris, and I came to ask, ma'am," Willie said, "I came to ask you if you can tell me if I am going to be drafted, or not."

"What month were you born, boy?" Mrs. Smith said.

"August of 1941."

Mrs. Smith stuck her chubby little pink fingers into the middle of the book and turned over more than half the pages, causing the front cover to land with a thump on the desk. She turned a few more pages, and then peered closely.

"Willie Darnell Harris. Yes, you are scheduled for a physical on September the twenty-third. You are gettin' drafted into the Army. You will get a notice in the mail soon," she said.

"Ma'am," Willie said, "I am planning on going to college in September. Do you think you can give me a deferment so I can go to school, ma'am?"

Mrs. Smith gave Willie a blank stare.

"Boy," she said," you are goin' to be drafted into the Army and you will have a physical on September the twenty-third."

Willie took that to mean the answer was no. When she turned away from him and acted like he wasn't there, he took that to mean their conversation was over, so he turned around and went home.

When he got home, he told Robert what Mrs. Smith had said.

"So what are you going to do?" Robert asked.

"Well, some of the guys I play ball with told me that they have real good basketball teams in the Air Force. Now every Wednesday the Air Force recruiter comes to Lexington. Next Wednesday I am goin' to talk to him and ask him if I can enlist in the Air Force, instead of gettin' drafted into the Army," Willie said.

"Hmmnn," Robert said.

"Why don't you go in with me? I can ask the recruiter if he will take both of us as a package deal," Willie said.

"The Air Force, huh? Okay, you ask him, and we'll see what he says," Robert said.

So the following Wednesday Willie went back downtown and saw the Air Force recruiter. On his way he was thinking that he would need to pass a physical exam before being accepted. Robert had already passed his physical for the Army, and Willie thought that if Robert could pass it, there ain't no way he would fail it, being the athlete in the family.

When he met the recruiter, he asked him about enlisting in the Air Force, and told him how Mrs. Smith said he was going to be drafted into the Army in a few weeks.

"If you haven't been sworn in yet, you can switch to the Air Force. If you come down next Wednesday, I will bring you to Jackson for your physical and written exams, and we can get it all taken care of," the recruiter said.

Then Willie told him that Robert had been drafted into the Army and asked if he could join him in the Air Force.

"Bring him along, if he wants to come," the recruiter said, "If he hasn't been sworn in yet, he can switch, too."

Willie went home and told Robert the recruiter said he would take both of them. They agreed at that time that they would go into the Air Force together as brothers. When Willie told Robert about the written test they would have to take, Robert knew there was no test he couldn't pass, being the smart one in the family.

As they got ready for the trip to Jackson the following Wednesday, they both got a little excited and scared at the same time, thinking about what could be a great adventure, or a complete disaster. Evie listened to them with a mixture of pride and sadness. She was proud that the boys were getting the hell out of Lexington and doing something meaningful, but sad that she would be losing them. They were all she had, and having recently turned 60, things seemed to get a little bit harder to do every day.

Robert and Willie gave Evie long hugs and said goodbye the next Wednesday. The recruiter drove them 60 miles south to the state's capitol city and they both had no problem passing the Air Force's physical and written exams. The Air Force had them stay at a small base outside Jackson for a few days and booked them on a flight that would leave the following Monday for Lackland Air Force Base in Texas, where they would go through basic training. The flight was the night of October 1, 1962.

While Willie and Robert were planning their future, most of the rest of Mississippi was focused on what was happening in Oxford, three hours north of Jackson, and the home of the University of Mississippi, the school lovingly known as Ole Miss by millions of Mississippi residents and alumni. The term "Ole Miss" was first applied to the school in 1896, and it quickly became synonymous with the university. The term was chosen because it evoked nostalgia for the state's white majority—as it was originally used as a sign of respect by slaves when they spoke to their plantation owner's wife.

In the late summer of 1962, a 29-year-old Air Force veteran and Mississippi native named James Howard Meredith was getting close to accomplishing an audacious goal he set more than a decade earlier: he planned to become the first Black student at the University of Mississippi.  Meredith's heritage was African American, British Canadian, Scottish and Choctaw, who were a Native American people who lived in the Southeast. But due to the color of his skin, he was nothing other than a Black man to the white folks in Mississippi. He was raised on a large farm owned by his father in Koscuisko, just 30 miles east of where Willie grew up. The Merediths and their extended family were self-sufficient, and James's father, Moses Meredith, raised them in an isolated environment. His family members were not allowed to go on white folks' property, or even visit Black folks who lived on white folks' property, and his father also guided James' actions and planted the seed of his bold mission.

"My father was the principal in everything I did before he died. Stand up. Don't give in," Meredith said.

James had served his country for nine years during the 1950s, and after leaving the Air Force in 1960, he studied for two years at historically Black Jackson State University and twice applied for admission to the University of Mississippi, his admission being denied both times. In 1961, with the help of the NAACP, he filed suit against the university, claiming he was denied admission solely because of the color of his skin.  A number of different courts agreed with Meredith's claim, and the university was ordered by the courts to admit him. One of the things standing in Meredith's way was the governor of Mississippi. Ross Barnett was elected in 1960 and was a staunch segregationist and white supremacist. He was also a Baptist Sunday school teacher who said during a gubernatorial campaign that "The Negro is different because God made him different to punish him.

His forehead slants back. His nose is different. His lips are different, and his color is sure different." He ran unopposed in that election, garnering 96 percent of the vote. The registered voters in Mississippi at the time were almost entirely white.

The flagship universities in some other southern states had integrated fairly uneventfully during the 1950s. But in 1961 a riot broke out at the University of Georgia when two Black students were admitted, ending 160 years of segregation at the school. And as in Mississippi, a federal judge had ordered the school to admit the students. At the beginning of 1962 the University of Mississippi, the University of Alabama, and the University of South Carolina were all still white only.

Toward the end of September the federal government had become involved in an attempt to enforce the court order that Meredith be admitted to the university. President John F. Kennedy sent 500 U.S. Marshals and thousands of members of the National Guard to try to maintain order in Oxford as thousands of white Mississippians had gathered on the campus to protest integration of the school. On September 30 a riot broke out as the protestors hurled rocks and bricks and fired shots at the federal troops. Two people were killed and there was significant property damage.

On the night of the riot upstate in Oxford, Willie and Robert were getting driven through the capitol city of Jackson to the airport for their flight to Texas for basic training. Willie knew what was happening upstate and he could see the anger spewing out of people down in Jackson because they didn't want any Blacks going to Ole Miss.

"I think one or two people got killed that night. And me and my brother were sitting in the backseat with these two Air Force sergeants, and they were taking us to the airport. And I never forgot, and me and my brother never said one word, and they was talkin' about killin' niggers and they oughta turn the dogs loose on those niggers, and me and my brother were sittin' there in the backseat," Willie said.

Willie breathed a sigh of relief when the car pulled into the lot of Thompson Air Field at 11 pm for the flight to San Antonio. But then he thought about being up in the sky. They would be flying commercial on Braniff International Airways and the reality of being miles up in the air in a metal tube scared the bejesus out of him. When he was working in the cotton fields as a teenager, every now and then he would hear a roar from above and look up to see a jet streaking across the sky, its puffy white tail painted on the brilliant blue tapestry. Willie would be jealous of the folks on the plane who were going anywhere other than goddam Clifton Plantation, but then he would think holy Mary Mother of God, what is keeping that plane up in the sky, and what kind of crazy person would get into one of those things and leave the earth? He was glad it wasn't him. Well tonight, it was him.

There was the plane sitting on the runway: it was a Boeing 707, one of the big boys. He took one look at it and almost soiled his boxers. Willie thought about the plane crashes he had seen on the news, like the American Airlines flight earlier that year that went down right after taking off in New York City, killing all 95 people aboard. He had never seen a plane up close, and now he could see all the little rivets holding the shiny metal panels together. What if one of those rivets pops off when we are going 500 miles an hour at six miles above the earth? And that causes the one next to it to pop off, and then another. Then what? We're screwed, that's what.

What am I doing? he thought. Kids who grow up picking cotton on plantations don't fly on jumbo jets. Yet here he was. Willie and Robert were directed toward the staircase leaning up against the plane door. Willie's legs had the jelly roll blues as he walked across the tarmac, and he ascended the steps very slowly, one at a time, until finally Robert, who was behind him, gave him a little shove in the back, laughed, and said, "Get moving, you big baby." When Willie got to the top of the stairs, he ducked his head to get under the doorway and a perky little flight attendant said, "Welcome aboard!" He had no response. He found his seat, which was next to a window. It figures. Of course, being so tall he had to bend his knees awkwardly and painfully just to wedge himself into the seat. He started to sweat a little when the plane started to roll down the runway, and then faster, and faster, and faster, until he felt the wheels jump off the ground, and his stomach was in his throat. If there was anything that made it worse, it was that the flight was at night. You can't see anything at night when you are on the ground, so how are you supposed to know where you are going when you are way up in the sky? It was madness. It was only a 90-minute flight, but it felt like 90 hours to Willie. He panicked every time every time they hit a bump of turbulence, his fingers digging into the armrests, and he knew then that people weren't meant to ride with clouds between their knees.

Somehow, miraculously, the plane eventually landed in San Antonio. It bumped on the runway a few times and then they were back on terra firma. Willie could relax a little bit, until he started thinking about the start of basic training the next day, and the fact that he had committed to doing this for the next four years. He supposed that if you are in the Air Force, they might actually want you to fly on airplanes. He hoped not.

# 9

## I'll Get Up and Fly Away

It was 2:00 a.m. when Willie and the other recruits landed in San Antonio, and a bus was waiting to take them to Lackland Air Force Base in Bexar County, just outside the city. When Willie stepped off the bus he was a little bleary, but still tingling from his first flight. The atmosphere quickly changed as he and the other airmen were met by the diminutive and pugnacious Sgt. Wilson. What the Lilliputian lacked in stature, he trebled in ferocity.

"Line up!"

Wilson saw that Willie was the biggest one of the bunch, and he walked straight to him, and stuck his nose in his chest.

The corners of Willie's mouth turned up, just a hair.

"Harris! Do you think I'm funny?"

"No, sir."

"Young man, I am your mother, I'm your father, I'm your guardian, whatever you want—I'm that. You fuck with me, I'll run up your ass sideways!"

"Yes, sir."

"I'm watchin' you, Harris. You keep your eyes straight ahead and your mouth shut."

"Yes, sir."

"I said keep your mouth shut!"

Basic training had begun. As ominous as the term is to civilians who have heard that it can be two months of hell, Willie didn't have any problem with it. He had been taking orders all his life on Clifton Plantation, whether it was from Peyton Abbot Jones or Oscar Harris. He was used to it.

The men would get up at 5 a.m. and shower, get dressed, clean their room and then go to breakfast from 6:00 to 7:00 am. Then they would spend a few hours in the classroom learning about military law, how to treat officers, and the rules of conduct for enlisted men. After that, they would spend two hours exercising on the parade ground: running, doing jumping jacks and pushups. As an athlete, the workouts were no problem for Willie. There were some over-weight guys in Flight 09 (the term for a subset of a squadron), and the ones they could get into shape, they did, and the ones they couldn't, they sent home. The officers would get right in their ear and yell at them to drop and give them 30 pushups, but they would not berate or degrade the new airmen. At night, they would retire to the barracks and either study their manual or sit in the lounge and watch TV.

The airmen in basic training did not have to do 12-mile night marches with heavy packs on their backs like they did in the Army. They were never going to be sent into battle as foot soldiers, so it wasn't necessary. Willie settled into his barracks with his room-mate James Flora, a Black guy. Unlike basic training in the Army and Marines, Lackland AFB did not have open dormitories with dozens of bunk beds. Each room had two beds, and some Black guys and white guys bunked in the same room. President Harry Truman had signed Executive Order 9981 in 1948, which decreed that all U.S. military units must desegregate and not discriminate on the basis of race, color, religion, or national origin. Much of the implementation of military desegregation would be accomplished in the early 1950s, a healthy decade before the Civil Rights Act of 1964.

A few weeks after he got to Lackland an officer addressed Flight 09. "Any of you men play basketball, either in high school or college?"

Willie raised his hand. "I did, sir."

"Come over here, Harris."

Willie walked over and the officer asked him if he played in high school or college.

"I played in high school and I played at Alcorn State, sir."

"Do you want to go out for the Flight 09 team?"

"Absolutely."

A couple of days after that, Willie again started playing the game he loved, and for the first time in his life, he was playing with and against white guys. Everything was different. He was playing ball with white guys and he was on an equal footing with them on a daily basis. He had experienced neither of those two things in the first 21 years of his life. And to his surprise, he liked it, and he got along with them.

"It was 150 degrees turnaround. I didn't trust whites. I didn't really want to be around whites. But my ambition was to play ball one day against white players. I wanted to show them, you denied me all of these years, but I can show you what I can do on the basketball court. And I enjoyed it, and after that I got to know these guys, and these guys were different than the white guys that I had dealt with in Mississippi."

Basic training ended for Willie and Robert at the end of November. Robert got assigned to Davis-Monthan Air Force Base outside Tucson, Arizona and he flew out a few days later. Willie did not immediately receive an assignment, so he moved to the grad barracks while he waited to see where he was headed.

Willie was in limbo for a few months while he waited for his orders to come in, and one night in February 1963 he was called to the orderly room and told to see Capt. Crest, who knew Willie from watching him play basketball. Willie walked into the room and sat across the desk from Capt. Crest.

"Your name is Airman Willie Harris?"

"Yes, sir."

"Well, who is Andrew Davenport?"

"Why do you ask, Captain?"

"I received a letter from the Red Cross and the letter states that your mom, Evie Harris, and Andrew Davenport's wife, Ruby Davenport, say that Andrew Davenport is your father. Is Andrew Davenport your father?"

"Yes, sir."

"Then why is your name Harris?"

"My mom is married to a man named Oscar Harris, but he isn't my father. Andrew Davenport is my father."

"Oh," Crest said. "Well, I am sorry to inform you that your father has passed away, but they want you to come home for the funeral."

Willie was stunned.

"You are dismissed until you get back from the funeral. I am sorry about your dad, but you can go call your mom and work out how you will get home."

"Thank you, sir."

When Willie called his mom he learned that Andrew was stricken with an aneurysm that had killed him, and it was most likely related to the tumor he had removed three years earlier. Willie had been worried about his dad ever since he had that operation during his senior year in high school, and now he was gone. Willie's mom also told him that Ruby had initially refused to list Robert and Willie in the obituary as Andrew's children, but some of the community matriarchs had convinced her to do the right thing, and they were both included. Willie and Robert arrived back in Howard the next day, with the Red Cross having paid for Willie's flight.

As Willie sat on the plane thinking about his Dad, he remembered the conversations they had the past few years. His dad told him that after he was through with school he should come back to help him run the farm and raise the cattle. Someday, Willie thought, maybe someday the farm and all those cattle would be his. When he thought about his future, it started with his plan to play professional basketball. If that didn't work out, he would think about moving back to Holmes County to run his dad's farm. That would be the only thing that would draw him back—the chance to own land and work with his dad. Now that dream was over. He knew with his dad gone that he would not be returning to Mississippi. Where he was headed, he had no idea, but he knew it wouldn't be back home.

The service was held at Trinity Missionary Baptist Church, a small red brick building just a mile from Clifton Plantation, and less than that from Andrew's home. Andrew's wife Ruby sat awkwardly between Robert and Willie during the service, none of them saying a word as they listened to Reverend Clay, Andrew's pastor for the past decade, talk about what a fine man he was.

After the burial, the 40 or so guests met at Andrew's house for the repast. With the help of his uncle, a carpenter, Andrew had built a beautiful new three-bedroom home on his property a few years earlier. Hampered by his health issues, he was confined to the role of directing the workers and couldn't do much of the building himself. As Willie, Robert, Evie, and the other guests sat in the living room and ate and drank and talked about what a great loss it was, Ruby asked Willie and Robert if she could speak to them in the kitchen.

When they got into the kitchen Ruby said "I didn't know he was your father."

That pissed Willie off.

"What? Everybody else knew, and I know you knew. Why do you think we spent so many nights here as kids? We had pajamas and clothes and things here. We wasn't just kids off the street, kids outta the cotton fields. There was some reason that man had us here."

"Okay," Ruby said, "I'll tell you what. When all of this is sold, whatever I'm gonna do, probate or whatsoever, I will call you and give you your share."

Robert put his hand up. "I don't want anything."

"Well, I do," Willie blurted. "I've been through too much hell and too many fistfights, and too much embarrassment. I deserve something. I want my birthright."

"Okay," Ruby said, "I'll be in touch."

Willie and Robert flew back to their bases the next day, and it was a long time before Willie heard from Ruby again.

A few days after returning to Lackland, Willie got his orders: he was being transferred to Kirtland Air Force Base in Albuquerque, New Mexico. Kirtland was a massive base that was quickly built on the site of a municipal airport in 1941 in order to support U.S. air power during World War II, and being just 80 miles south of Los Alamos, it was used as a transportation center for the Manhattan Project during the planning and construction of the atomic bombs dropped over Japan in August 1945.

As soon as he got to Kirtland, he was assigned to work in the motor pool, driving officers around, and driving trucks around the base, as needed. At that time they didn't ask the enlisted airmen what function they would like to perform, they just gave them a job. It was easy work and Willie got to talk to lots of people and make lots of friends, but his gargantuan size made it difficult for him to fit into most of the jeeps and trucks.

Also arriving at Kirtland in March 1963, fresh out of basic training, was Howard Walker, a 17-year-old white kid from Somerset, Kentucky, a city of 7,000 souls 90 minutes south of Lexington and adjacent to the Daniel Boone National Forest. Walker grew up poor and left home right after high school. Unlike Willie, he was not on the verge of getting drafted—he enlisted in the Air Force simply because he had to do something with his life. He met Willie when he was assigned to work in the motor pool.

"I was in the office and I looked down the hallway, and I saw this guy coming, dipping his head under the doorways, and I said 'Man, this is one big dude.' It was Willie," Walker said.

Willie and Walker hit it off right away and started hanging out, goofing off in the motor pool, and going downtown to party on the weekends. While they did have to follow the strict rules of military discipline while on duty, they also had a clean place to sleep, three square meals a day, and a steady income. It was a good life.

Walker's childhood was quite different from Willie's in terms of race relations. He went to school with Blacks and had many friends who were Black. Both of those things would have been unfathomable in rural Mississippi in the 1950s. When he looked at Willie he only saw a friend—an absurdly tall, gregarious, and loyal friend.

Just a few weeks after they met, they were downtown on a Saturday night, carousing in the bars and trying to pick up women, when they decided to take a shortcut through the Black section of town. They stumbled upon a house party and joined in just before a massive brawl broke out—fists were flying and a few gunshots rang out. Willie got clocked in the head and when he landed on the ground he was near a two-by-four. He picked it up and started swinging it to clear a path so he and Walker could get the hell out of there.

"Willie was battin' them off with the board. He was wearin' some heads out with that," Walker said.

A few months after he got to Kirtland, Willie met a man who would be his other best friend in the service. Chet Atkins was from Biloxi, Mississippi, down on the Gulf of Mexico. Willie, Howard, and Chet all worked in the motor pool and became tight during their service and beyond.

While Willie was enjoying making friends with white guys and being treated as an equal in the military, it wasn't all sunshine and butterflies. Human nature being what it is, and American culture being what it is, there were some racist white airmen who didn't appreciate serving alongside Blacks. Willie would talk to Walker and Atkins and they would tell him which guys were saying things about the Blacks, so Willie knew who to avoid. As much as Willie generally distrusted whites when he entered the service, perhaps it was his affable and friendly nature that made it easier for him to befriend white guys than it was for some of the other Black airmen, many of whom only made friends with other Blacks. Overall, the dynamic between Blacks and whites was exponentially healthier than anything he had experienced on the plantation or in Chicago. The racist whites, at least the overtly racist whites, were the minority, and there weren't any major race-related fights or other issues.

Robert's first experience working with whites at his base in Tucson was less pleasant. His first assignment was in a small department that consisted of only white guys. On his first day his supervisor approached and bluntly told him what he thought about him.

"I don't like you, Harris," he said.

"Why not? You don't even know me," Robert said.

"I don't like you because you're the wrong fuckin' color," he said.

"I don't give a fuck what you think about my color, just don't mess with me," Robert shot back.

Though he was generally more mild-mannered than Willie, Robert knew when he had to speak out.

"So I made a stand at that point and I had an old white guy from Alabama, and I had two other white guys from Alabama that I worked with. They were civilians, I was military, they were civilians. Those guys took care of me for about a year until I got to the point where I knew everything, and I could take care of myself. And after that, I didn't have any more problems because I knew the system. I know how to deal with the system, and the thing were, when you go into it you learn everything about the regulations and all that, so you are smarter than the rest of the people there, and it paid off. So I had a good time."

Having played on a squadron team at Lackland, Willie had his eye on playing for the base team at Kirtland. The base teams would fly to play other bases and play scrimmages against Division 1 college teams. It was kind of a big deal. Several months after getting to his new base, he went to see Sgt. Williams at the gym.

"Sgt. Williams, I am Willie Harris, I work in the motor pool and I would like to try out for the base basketball team."

"Where did you play ball?"

"I played in high school in Mississippi and I played one year at Alcorn State."

"What can you do, Harris, can you dunk a ball?"

Willie couldn't believe he asked him that. "Of course I can dunk a ball. I can dunk it any which way you want a ball dunked, sir."

"Okay, then come out to practice tomorrow at 4:00."

As soon as Sgt. Williams saw what Willie could do on the basketball court, he put him on the team. The problem was that Sgt. Malloy, who ran the motor pool, didn't want Willie going over to basketball practice every afternoon. Willie's shift in the motor pool ended at 5:00 pm each day, and after the first few days of practice Sgt. Malloy told him he couldn't leave work early for practice anymore. So about a week after making the team, Willie was in the gym and Major Cosner, Sgt. Williams' superior officer, asked him why he hadn't been at practice.

"I want to come, Major, but Sgt. Malloy won't let me."

"Well, goddammit," Cosner said, "I'll fix that. Do you want to get out of the motor pool and come work in the gym?"

"I would love it, sir."

Major Cosner called the base headquarters, had them draw up transfer papers, and had Willie transferred right away to Special Services, which meant he worked for the athletic department in the gym. From then on, Willie didn't have to wear a uniform when he went to work. He wore a cap emblazoned with KAFB, a grey shirt with KAFB across his chest, and khaki pants. His primary duties:

administer physical fitness exams to airmen, keep the gym in order, and play basketball. It was one of the better jobs on the base, and he got to know just about everyone, including Major Robert Henry Lawrence, Jr., an African American pilot and scientist who would go on to become the first African American astronaut in 1967. Major Lawrence would come to the gym and Willie would administer his fitness exam. Major Lawrence never made it into space, however, because six months after joining the space program he was killed during a training flight at Edwards Air Force Base in California.

One Friday in late October Willie cashed his paycheck and when he returned to the barracks, the guys were playing dice. Willie went all in, and as often happened when he gambled back on the plantation, he lost almost all his money. Two hours after cashing his paycheck, he had one dollar in his pocket.

"Willie, what are you gonna do tonight?" his friend Jackson asked.

"Well, I got no damn money, what the hell am I gonna do?"

"C'mon, man. Don't tell me this town ain't got no heart. Sometimes you just gotta poke around. Why don't we go check out the American Legion hall downtown?"

"Any Blacks go there?" Willie asked, knowing that there were only a few places downtown where Blacks could go and not have any problems.

"I think Blacks and whites go there," Jackson said.

"How much do they charge to get in?"

"I think it's free," Jackson said.

"Alright. Let's go."

When Willie and Jackson walked into the hall, the Freddy Williams Band was playing the blues, and Marlboro smoke was wafting up from the tables. Jackson went to the bar to get a drink, and Willie surveyed the scene. A few airmen were playing pool, some other guys were throwing darts, and in the back corner he saw two women sitting at a table, laughing. One was Black, and one was white.

What the hell, Willie thought, it's worth a shot, so he walked over to the table, said hello, and sat down next to the Black woman. She introduced herself as Mamie, and as soon as they started chatting, her boyfriend walked into the bar and stood in front of the table. Willie looked up at him, got up to leave, and said "Okay, I guess I will see you all later."

"No, stay, Willie," Mamie said, "You can get to know my friend Maureen."

Willie looked down at Maureen. She had brilliant red hair, ivory white skin, and luscious blue eyes.

"Hi," Willie said.

"Hi there, Willie, have a seat," Maureen said, patting the chair next to her.

Willie sat down. Slowly. Carefully. Reluctantly. He had never really had a meaningful conversation with a white woman before, certainly not in a bar. And frankly, he really wasn't interested in talking to a white woman. Ever since he was a little boy, his mom had told him that messin' with white women could only end up with you getting a beating, or hanging in a tree. But what the hell, he wasn't in Mississippi. He was in Albuquerque. What's the worst that could happen?

Maureen asked Willie how tall he was, and he told her. She asked if he played basketball, and he said yes. She asked if he was in the Air Force, and he said yes, and he noticed her accent. It was not something he had heard before. He knew right away she was not like other girls.

"Excuse me for asking, Maureen, but where are you from?"

"Why, do you think I talk funny?" she said," I'm just a girl from Birmingham."

"Well, I met a couple of people from Birmingham, and none of them sound like you."

"That's because I'm from Birmingham in England, you silly. The real Birmingham."

"Oh, okay," Willie laughed, "maybe tomorrow afternoon I could have a spot of tea with the queen."

They kept talking, and it felt natural and easy. He was happy to sit there and talk, and he was even happier that Maureen never asked him if he wanted to dance. As good as Freddy Williams sounded, Willie did not like to dance. But he did get a little nervous every time he fingered that solitary George Washington in the pocket of his khaki pants.

"Maureen, would you like a drink?" he finally asked.

Willie was normally not a praying man, but he did say a little prayer that she would not ask for a vodka drink, 'cause if she did, he was going straight out the front door. A dollar would not cover that.

"Yes, I'll have a Coke. Thank you."

A Coke was 50 cents.

As Willie got up to get the Coke, she gently held his forearm.

"And Willie, tell him to put a cherry in it," she smiled.

"Yes, ma'am. I will."

Willie went up to the bar and found Jackson leaning against it.

"Willie, whaddya think about that white chick with the red hair?" Jackson asked.

"Well, there ain't nothin' wrong with the way she moves," Willie said out of the side of his mouth. But he wasn't thinking about her body—he was thinking about how good he felt talking to Maureen. Oddly good. Astonishingly good. Frighteningly good.

He returned with Maureen's Coke and they kept talking. For hours. They actually closed the joint at 2 a.m. and Willie and Jackson dropped off Maureen at her house, just a few blocks from the base. He had her phone number.

Willie and Maureen started seeing each other a couple of times a week, and when they didn't see each other, they would talk on the phone. She would call him on the common phone in the barracks and they would talk about anything and everything. Willie told her about life on the plantation, living under the thumb and the boot of Peyton

Abbott Jones. He told her about his dreams of getting out of that life and doing something special. And he talked about the thing that hurt him the most—growing up with his dad living just a mile from him, but not having his parents together. He told her how sad he was when he saw all the other kids on the plantation playing with their dads, and how angry it made him when he was teased about it.

"I would never walk out on a child of mine," he vowed.

Maureen had two small children when they met, a girl and boy, ages one and three. Maureen never said anything about the father, and Willie never asked.

The more time they spent together, and the closer they got, the more Willie thought about how this would never happen in Mississippi. If a white girl was found dating a Black man, most fathers would probably kill the Black man first and then he might think about killing his daughter, too, as he would be so embarrassed and repulsed. So what was it about Maureen that made it seem so natural for her to date him? Growing up in England, Maureen and her friends were not indoctrinated from an early age to believe that Blacks were inferior. She was exposed to American racism, however, during World War II, when she was a young girl and she would hear about what the Americans told the English girls.

"The American white GIs said don't fool with the Black dudes, 'cause they like monkeys—their tail comes out after the sun go down. And when they would see a Black GI on the street, there in England, they would look for his tail if it was at night," Willie said.

Surprisingly, none of the white guys at the base seemed to care that Willie was dating a white woman. At least none spoke openly about it or confronted him, but maybe that was because he was 6'8". His friend Walker would sure tease him about it, though.

"Goddam, Willie, you're from Mississippi, and you're dating a white woman. Are you crazy?"

"I sure am. How about you, you ever dated a Black woman?" Willie retorted.

"Actually, I have," Walker began. "In my town of Somerset, Kentucky the railroad tracks run right through the center of downtown. We live on one side of the tracks, and all the Blacks live on the other side. Well, my dad, you see, he would cross the tracks and go see this Black woman. One night when I was in high school, my mom had had a few glasses of bourbon, and she told me 'Go over there and get your father from that bitch's house.' So I went over there to get my dad, but when the door opened, it was the woman's daughter. She grabbed my hand and pulled me in. I spent damn near the rest of that summer over there with my dad."

As the end of 1963 approached, Willie looked around and almost couldn't believe his new life. He was playing ball for his base team in the Air Force; he had a good job working in the athletic department; his two best friends were a hillbilly from Kentucky and a white guy from Mississippi; and he was dating a white woman. A little over a year ago he was sleeping in cars and freezing cold garages in Chicago, running with a bunch of hooligans, and a couple of years before that he was picking cotton on Clifton Plantation, dreaming of something better—anything, it seemed, would have been better. If only his mama could see him now.

It was as if the clouds had parted and a warm, nourishing sun was shining gently on his face. This was not the brutally hot Mississippi sun that smothered him as he worked from can to can't in the fields, telling him to keep his head down, get the job done, and know your place, because you ain't nothing but a poor Black boy anyway and won't amount to anything, so don't bother trying. No, this was a sun that made him hopeful when he saw it over the horizon in the morning. This sun made him think that there are good white people in the world and he could make something special out of his life if only given a chance, and having a chance is the only thing he had ever wanted.

But if Willie had a crystal ball and could see everything that would happen to him during his service in the Air Force, he probably would have run as fast and as far away as he could—while he still had the legs to carry him.

# 10

## A Bad Break

Willie and Maureen went out to dinner the night before Christmas Eve in 1963, and it was almost 2 a.m. when Maureen dropped him off at the base. The temperature in the desert had plunged down into the 20s after sundown and it was windy as Willie walked back to his barracks. As soon as he got inside, he lay down in the extra-long bed the Air Force had issued him, and was asleep in seconds, so happy to be where those chilly winds don't blow.

About a half hour later there was a knock at the door. Willie's roommate James got up and opened it, and the visitor was a very large Black man. He was 6'4", wore a dark green military coat, and his name was Air Force Master Sgt. David Thomas. He was stationed at a base in Alaska, but he had just returned to Albuquerque for the holiday break. He had a determined look on his face.

"Is Harris your roommate?" Thomas asked coolly.

James noticed that Thomas was holding a pistol in his right hand, down by his thigh, pointed at the ground.

"Whaddya mean?"

"There are two Harrises in these barracks," Thomas replied. "I want the long one."

Willie had a few drinks at dinner and was a little bleary as he woke up and saw Thomas brush past James into their room. Thomas looked at Willie's extra-long bed and knew he had found his man. He walked over to Willie and tapped him on the shoulder.

"Get up."

"What?" Willie asked, not sure if he was dreaming.

"Get your ass up," Thomas said, "and while you're at it, tell me why you're messin' with Maureen."

Willie saw the gun. He was now fully awake.

"I don't know any Maureen," he said.

"Really?" Thomas asked.

"Really," Willie replied.

"Then tell me something, Harris, why do you have Maureen's picture on your nightstand?"

Willie looked at the picture of Maureen. Then he looked at the gun. Busted.

"Oh, shit," he muttered.

"Oh, shit is right, you sonofabitch. Now get up. You wanna mess with my wife? We're goin' for a walk in the parking lot."

Willie unfurled his blanket and got up slowly. He was very confused, and he only knew one thing for sure: he was not going for a walk in no damn parking lot.

Trying to think of any way to stall, he asked Thomas if he could have a cigarette.

"Go ahead, because it will probably be your last one," Thomas said.

Willie grabbed a pack of Marlboros off his nightstand, slid out a cigarette, and held it between his lips.

"Got a light?" he asked Thomas.

When Thomas started to reach into his pocket for some matches, he moved his pistol to his left hand to free up his right hand, and Willie seized his opportunity. He grabbed the pistol and all four of their hands fought for it. Willie's roommate took off down the hall to tell the Air Police what was going on.

Soon after they started fighting for the gun, Willie was able to yank it from Thomas, and before things got any worse, four or five APs showed up. They took the pistol and told Thomas he had to leave, so they walked him out to his car and found a shotgun in it, so they took that, too.

"The next day I had to go to see the base commander. Rules and regulations in the military said you didn't fool with another GI's wife. The reason I escaped Article 15 of being court-martialed is because I played basketball. But Christmas Eve of '63, and Christmas Day, and the day after Christmas Day, I spent in the stockade. I wasn't locked up, but they put me and my bed over there 'cause they didn't want him to come back, or whatsoever, and something go wrong," Willie said.

As soon as Willie got back to his barracks, he called Maureen.

"What the hell, Maureen?"

"I'm sorry, I'm sorry," she said.

"Why didn't you tell me you were married? I never, never would have gotten involved with you if I had known that."

'Oh, don't worry about him. We don't get along. I'm going to divorce him, and I was just waitin' for somebody to come along who I like, and I found you. I love you, Willie."

"Oh, jeez. I don't know. I am going to have to think about it," he said.

Willie thought about it for a few days, but he stayed with Maureen. She did file for divorce, and when she went to a lawyer to sign the divorce papers, Willie went with her. He was not going to get caught up in any more shenanigans.

After the fiasco with Maureen's husband faded, Willie was able to concentrate on basketball. His first season on the Kirtland base team was starting to heat up. Having played on his squadron team at Lackland AFB, playing for the base team was multiple steps up. While a squadron cobbled together a team from 60-70 airmen, the base team chose the best players out of the thousands of airmen stationed there. The gulf in talent was like the difference between a trickling stream and the mighty Mississippi River. And the players were treated quite well. The Air Force would fly them on weekends to play games against base teams in Arizona, Texas, Colorado, and Florida. It was part of a thriving athletic culture that included football, basketball, and baseball teams, as well as boxing and other sports. Attending these contests was the primary recreational activity for the airmen at bases all over the western and southern U.S.

Playing on the Kirtland team challenged Willie, made him a better player, and helped wash away the bad experience he had playing at Alcorn.

"Men could understand each other. In college you have men dealing with young men or boys; in the Air Force you got better respect because you had men dealing with men," Willie said.

The level of competition was even higher than when Willie played at Alcorn. Many of his teammates and opponents played college basketball at top programs, and some went on to play professionally.

"When I really put my skill together was in the Air Force, 'cause you had guys in the Air Force who could play pro, but there were only 16 pro teams then. And there weren't enough teams for the players, so a lot of the smart guys that played college and all of that, instead of going into the Army for Vietnam, they went to the Air Force," Willie said.

The more intense competition required Willie to sharpen his game. He worked to become a terror on the boards, pulling down 12-15 rebounds a game, and his m.o. was not to lay it back in off the offensive glass, but to slam it home with a thunderous dunk. At the same time, he had finesse and could elevate above the opposing center to sink mid-range jump shots with a diamond cutter's touch. He was an all-around player.

He had to be at his best in order to compete because the level of play was very high. Willie particularly relished his battles with one enormous white dude. Dan Lotz was 6'7", and he outweighed Willie by 30 pounds. Lotz played for Holloman Air Force Base in New Mexico, and before that, he had played for the University of North Carolina at Chapel Hill. In the 1957 NCAA tournament final, Lotz was matched up against Kansas Jayhawks center Wilt Chamberlain, the man who would become the most dominant player in the history of basketball, and Lotz beat him, helping the Tar Heels complete an undefeated season and secure their first national championship.

Holloman and Kirtland were just a 3-hour bus ride from each other, and they were natural rivals, playing each other four times a year. Every time they played it was a close, hotly contested battle. Willie and Dan did a lot of trash talking, with most of it being done by Willie.

"Dan was a captain and I was a two-striper—but in sports, you know, we were equal. And I would tell him, 'You know something, Dan, I got a whoopin' for your white ass tonight.' He would just laugh. He'd say 'Okay, Harris, let's see what you've got.'"

Lotz would go on to become a dentist after the service and marry Billy Graham's daughter Anne. Though massive, he was also nimble. He could jump, he could box you out, and if you weren't careful, he could block your shot. Dan got the best of Willie the first few times they played.

"If you come in here today, Harris, you're gonna get hurt," Dan would say.

"Well, I guess you are gonna have to hurt me, 'cause here I come."

Willie had to learn how to adapt his game to play against Dan. He became more patient and told his point guard Remaldo to get him the ball down low. By working in the paint, Willie was able to get Dan into foul trouble. It was very gratifying for Willie to finally be able to play against a top-flight white big man, and beat him. Sometimes.

Willie's basketball life was very satisfying. He was playing well, and being in the Air Force made him feel like he was part of something special.

"Guys then that had any type of schoolin' or anything, they went to the Air Force. They didn't want no parts of the Army. 'Cause they would say the Air Force was the elite of the military, and the Marines and the Army was mostly, you know, jackasses."

In February 1964 the Kirtland team was flown to Cocoa Beach, Florida to play Patrick Air Force Base. In the second half Willie and two guards were running a 3-on-1 fast break. Rather than laying it in, one of the guards passed it off to Willie, who was flying down the center lane. But the pass was late, and Willie was too far under the basket, so he spun and did a reverse dunk, and as he did so, the defender undercut him and flipped Willie in the air. He came crashing down on the hardwood, landing on both knees. He had been hurt before, but this was intense pain like no other. The doctors in Florida examined him and told him to go to the infirmary when he got back to his base in New Mexico. Something didn't feel right. He was more than just a little nervous from the fall.

The doctors at Kirtland took a look at him and said that if his knees kept bothering him, he should come back the day before his games and they would give him something to ease the pain. So the following Thursday Willie went back to the infirmary, as he was in a lot of pain, and he had games on Friday and Saturday. The Air Force doctor took out a long needle and injected both knees with cortisone. Willie felt better right away, and this became a routine. His games were usually on Fridays and Saturdays, so on Thursdays he would go to the infirmary to get his shots. Every week.

As summer approached Willie was spending more and more time with Maureen. One day in June she had a cheeky grin on her face when she asked him if he thought he would become a father someday.

"I'm sure I probably will, someday," he said.

"Guess what, Willie?"

"What?" he said.

"Someday will be sooner than you think," she smiled, "I'm due in February. You're going to be a daddy."

"What?"

"It's true," she said, patting her stomach.

"Why did you do this?" he blurted.

She was startled by his outburst. "Because I love you, and I want to be with you, and remember when you told me you would never walk out on your child. Remember that?"

"Yes, I remember," he said.

"So aren't you excited? Now you can give your little boy or girl all the things your dad couldn't give you," she said.

"I guess I'm excited. I don't know. This is a lot to deal with," he said, feeling dazed and confused.

"So what are you gonna do?" she asked, now near tears.

"I'm going to have to think about it."

Willie went back to the base and fell into a funk for a couple of days. What should I do, he thought? I'm 22 years old. My whole life is ahead of me, waiting to be enjoyed. I don't know what my life will bring, but it sure looks a lot more promising now than it did a couple of years ago when I was picking cotton. I know I don't want to get married, not now. But I do not want my child being raised like I was, by some other man who doesn't care about the child and treats him or her like garbage. That is the one thing I cannot bear. Maybe I should marry Maureen. I don't know. This is heavy. I need to call my mom.

"Hi, Mom," Willie said.

"Hi, baby, how you doin'?" Evie replied.

"I'm okay. I have some news for you."

"What is it, child?"

Willie paused, and had to dig deep to find a little courage. "I'm goin' to get married, Ma."

"Married? I didn't even know you had a girlfriend," Evie said, aghast.

"I told you, Ma, that I was seein' a girl named Maureen."

"Why you wanna get married? Where is this Maureen from?"

"She's from England."

"England? I didn't know there were any Black people in England," Evie said.

Willie chuckled. "I don't know how many Black people are in England, Ma, but she's not Black."

"Not Black? Then what is she?" Evie asked, stupefied.

"She's white."

"Oh, no, no, no, no, no, no, son. You can't do that! Are you crazy? Is this my child I am talking to?" Evie said.

"Calm down, Ma."

"Why do you wanna get married?"

"She's going to have a baby, Ma."

"Oh," Evie said, softening, "and you're the father?"

"And I'm the father," Willie said.

"How did this happen, son?"

"I think you know how it happened, Ma."

"Is this really what you want to do? Get married? You're so young... and she's white. Holy mother of God," Evie mused.

"Not really," Willie said, hesitating, "actually, no, I don't want to get married, but what I am going to do about the child? I don't want my child to be raised by another man. Like I was," he said, letting that hang there.

Willie and his mom decided to talk about it some more. Evie suggested that perhaps Willie could just live with Maureen and raise the child, but then they decided that really wouldn't work. He would do the right thing and marry Maureen. He went home to Mississippi in September to talk to his mom and make the final plans. The plan was set. Willie and Maureen would be wed on Saturday, October 31, 1964. Halloween. The ceremony would take place at the preacher's house just a block from Maureen's in Albuquerque. They actually could not have legally married in Mississippi at the time, or in any of 16 other states. Marriage between people of two different races—known as miscegenation—was a crime. In Mississippi, it was banned immediately after the South lost the Civil War in 1865 with the enactment of the Black Codes:

> [I]t shall not be lawful for any freedman, free negro or mulatto to intermarry with any white person; nor for any person to intermarry with any freedman, free negro or mulatto; and any person who shall so intermarry shall be deemed guilty of felony, and on conviction thereof shall be confined in the State penitentiary for life.

A life sentence, for getting married. Southern legislators who created the laws, and Southern judges who upheld the laws during the Jim Crow era, leaned on a ridiculous and irrelevant religious argument for their rationale: since Almighty God created different races of humans, that shows he did not intend for them to mix, they claimed.

The outrage expressed by some Southern lawmakers as they tried to prevent any Blacks from marrying any whites indicates that they thought it was one of the most important, if not the most important, issues facing the country. In 1912 a bill was presented in the United States House of Representatives which called for a nationwide ban on marriage between a Caucasian and any person who contains any African American ancestry. Seaborn Roddenberry, the Democrat from Georgia who sponsored the bill, was incensed by the marriage of Black heavyweight boxing champion Jack Johnson to a white woman. This is the language he used on the floor of Congress when introducing the bill:

> No brutality, no infamy, no degradation in all the years of southern slavery, possessed such villainous character and such atrocious qualities as the provision of the laws

> of Illinois, Massachusetts, and other states which allow
> the marriage of the negro, Jack Johnson, to a woman
> of Caucasian strain... Intermarriage between whites and
> blacks is repulsive and averse to every sentiment of pure
> American spirit... Let us uproot and exterminate now
> this debasing, ultra-demoralizing, un-American and in-
> human leprosy.

What Roddenberry is saying is that if a man and woman love each other, and they happen to be of different races, then allowing them to marry is worse than the institution of slavery itself. The hysterical aversion to marriage between Blacks and whites was likely motivated by two goals: to prevent mixed race couples from marrying and begetting mixed race children; and to prevent Black men from commingling with white women, particularly Southern white women. One can only deduce that the latter was the primary goal of proponents of anti-miscegenation laws, in light of the fact that mixed race children had been proliferating throughout the South for hundreds of years due to the rape of female slaves by their owners or other white men in positions of power. And then, of course, because the children produced by such assaults had one Black parent, they would normally be enslaved by their own fathers. What the duly elected Representative from Georgia was saying when he proposed a nationwide ban on mixed race marriages is that they are far worse than rape, enslaving your own children, whipping people to the point of death, selling people and splitting up their families, prohibiting people from learning how to read and write, or providing them with any of the rights and freedoms trumpeted in the Declaration of Independence and guaranteed to all Americans in the U.S. Constitution.

Anti-miscegenation laws such as the one stipulated in the Mississippi Black Codes were not deemed unconstitutional until the U.S. Supreme Court *Loving v. Virginia* decision in 1967. No state could enforce a law banning interracial marriage after that decision, but

Mississippi did not repeal its law banning marriage between whites and Blacks until a 1987 referendum was held, and the vote by the citizens of Mississippi was 52% to repeal the law, and 48% to keep it in place, even though it could not be enforced. The South will rise again, apparently—at least in the minds of the 48% who voted against repealing the law.

Willie and Maureen's wedding was very simple. His mother couldn't afford the trip to attend, and his best man was Sgt. Williams from the gym. After the ceremony, they had a little party with some of Willie's basketball teammates and GI buddies back at Maureen's house. Even though Willie wasn't a big drinker at the time, he got so hammered that night that he didn't wake up until late Sunday afternoon.

Right after Willie got married, he moved off base and lived with Maureen and her kids in her house. She was five months pregnant and really starting to show. He would walk to work every day at the gym, stopping first at the mess hall for breakfast. Every time he walked in to get his breakfast he saw the server Milton runnin' his mouth and carrying on. The man wasn't but five and a half feet tall, but he was always cussin' and going on about something or other. Willie found him to be an annoying little twit, and wished he would just serve the damn food and keep his mouth shut.

Now that Willie lived off base, he had to pay for his breakfast. He paid the cashier 30 cents and got in line. He was behind three GIs who were friends with Milton, and they were laughing with him and holding up the line. Willie watched closely as Milton gave them each three pancakes and heaped piles of bacon and sausage on their plates. When Willie's turn came, Milton did not speak as he put two pancakes and two slices of bacon on his plate.

"What's this?" Willie asked.

"That's your breakfast," Milton said.

Willie stared down at him. "No, I want what you gave your friends. Gimme another pancake and more bacon."

"Go fuck yourself, Harris."

That was it. Willie stormed around the serving station and grabbed Milton. The top of his head barely reached Willie's chest, so he lifted him up and pinned him against the wall so he could look him straight in the eyes.

"How many pancakes am I gonna get?" he roared.

"Two," Milton said, struggling to get the words out.

Willie was about to clock Milton when Sgt. Jed Adams, the officer who ran the mess hall, came running around the corner.

"Harris! Put that man down." Adams yelled.

"Put this man down?" Willie asked.

"Yes, put that man down!"

"Okay, I'll put him down," Willie said, and he slammed Milton down on the ground. The little guy lay there crumpled, as if Pinocchio had just been dropped by Geppetto.

"That's it," Adams said, "you are getting written up for this."

This was now the second time Willie faced potential military discipline. The first time he had been sleeping with a fellow GI's wife, but this time he was just hangry. Most of the time, Willie was an easygoing gentle giant, but if you messed with his breakfast, that was a recipe for disaster.

"He wasn't going to treat me like that and talk to me like that, especially since I was paying for my breakfast. Adams wanted to put me in the stockade 'cause of what I did to the dude. They wanted to give me an Article 15 court martial and take a stripe from me. Major Cosner and my squadron commander said no," Willie said.

So for the second time, Willie's status as a premiere basketball player kept him out of trouble. Sometimes it helps to have high friends in places.

That fall Willie began his second season on the base team, having established himself as their best player. Hubert "Peppy" Callahan joined the squad as a player/coach. A native of Long Island, NY, Peppy had just finished playing for Coach Dean Smith on the UNC Tar Heels, where he was a teammate of future NBA legends Billy Cunningham and Larry Brown. Callahan would spend 26 years in the Air Force, flying hundreds of combat missions during the Vietnam War as a Master Navigator, eventually earning the rank of Colonel. The base team was a mix of players from different backgrounds. Most of his teammates were Black, but there were two white players and one Hispanic, Ignacio Lopez from El Paso, Texas. Willie appreciated the way Peppy handled the team, telling them they are all men here, all equal, and all working toward the same goal.

The season would begin with scrimmages against the University of New Mexico varsity team to help them get tuned up, and then on to the battles with the other base teams in the Air Force Systems Command: Edwards, Brooks, Eglin, Holloman, Patrick, and more. Willie enjoyed the competition, the camaraderie, and traveling to play at different bases. He was even starting to get over his fear of flying. But his knees kept getting worse. He was going to the infirmary at the end of every week to get his knees shot up, and then playing through the pain. It was mind over matter.

The progression of the 1964-65 season also coincided with the last few months of Maureen's pregnancy. She was due the second week of February, and as the date approached, Willie had a game scheduled in Florida. She told Willie to fly to his game. It was the Air Force Systems Command tournament that was held at the end of every season, so Maureen knew it was important. She would be fine. That made Major Cosner very happy, and he instructed Sgt. Williams to call Maureen every day to see how she was doing. The team flew out the morning of Saturday, February 13, and Maureen went into labor a few hours later. She went to the military hospital on the Kirtland base and gave birth that night to a healthy baby boy, Darnell Harris. They had given him Willie's middle name.

As Willie prepared for another basketball season in the fall of 1965, his knees continued to deteriorate. Not only did they hurt, but they were now swelling on a regular basis, especially when he played ball or ran. He went to see an orthopedic specialist who told him that he had stressed ligaments and his recommendation was that he give his knees a rest and stop playing ball.

Willie went to talk it over with Major Cosner. He told the major that he was in a lot of pain and wasn't sure if he could keep playing, or if playing was even a good idea.

The major sighed and looked at Willie with a slight paternalistic grin that seemed to say: "Listen to me, boy, I know what is good for you."

He put his hand on Willie's shoulder and said softly "But Willie, if you don't play, we don't win." There it was. The quid pro quo. We took care of you. Gave you a cushy job in the gym. Made sure you never had to work in the kitchen like everyone else. Got you out of trouble when you got into fights. Made sure you never got sent to Vietnam. You owe us. Now get your ass out on the court and play ball, because that is what you are good at.

Willie sat there and didn't know what to say, and he just kept getting the shots every week so he could keep playing ball.

In early January of 1966 he got hurt during a game. He was coming down with a rebound and someone stepped on his foot, causing a stress fracture in his ankle. He couldn't play for several weeks and at about the same time, an order came from headquarters that he was being transferred and he was told to go see Major Cosner. Willie knew that there was an opening in an athletic department at one of the bases in Vietnam, and he was worried he was going to be sent there. But when he got to Major Cosner's office, he told him that he was being transferred to the Los Angeles Air Force Station in El Segundo, California, just south of LA. The major told Willie that if he didn't want to go, he could keep him at Kirtland for the rest of his scheduled enlistment, which would end in October of that year. Willie didn't know anyone in California, so he said yes, please keep me at Kirtland. But when he got home and told Maureen about it, she started crying and said she wanted to go to California. She had an English friend in LA, and New Mexico was boring.

So Willie went back to the major's office.

"Actually, major, the wife wants to go to California, and she is giving me all kinds of hell about it," Willie said.

"Well," the major said, "you're not playing ball anyway right now, do you just want to go?"

"Yes, sir," Willie said, and the major processed the transfer paperwork.

After three years in New Mexico, Willie was about to move on. When he enlisted in the Air Force in September 1962, he was a 21-year-old young man whose two main goals were to play basketball and avoid getting drafted into the Army. Almost all of his life experiences up that point were Black and white, whether it was toiling as a sharecropper on Clifton Plantation, attending all-Black Alcorn State University, or living a precarious life on the south side of Chicago, the baddest part of town. Despite his outgoing personality and easy smile, he had been angry inside about the way he and other Blacks are treated on a daily basis. Ironically, it was in the Air Force that his perceptions about race and the potential for racial harmony, to some degree, changed. He befriended white guys, married a white woman, and thrived in an integrated culture. While he was undergoing a metamorphosis in, of all places, the United States military, the turmoil and tumult of the civil rights movement was exploding around the country: the March on Washington and Martin

Luther King's "I Have a Dream" speech; the 16^th Street Baptist Church bombing in Birmingham; the murder of three civil rights workers in Philadelphia, Mississippi during the Freedom Summer of 1964; Bloody Sunday in Selma; the Civil Rights Act of 1964 and the Voting Rights Act of 1965; the Watts Riots; and the assassination of Malcolm X. All of these incidents occurred while Willie was tucked away in the insulated cocoon of the United States Air Force.

"I wonder would I be alive today if I hadn't been in the Air Force, doin' all of the sit-ins in Mississippi and Freedom Riders and all of that, 'cause I sure would have been involved with it. But in the military you couldn't get involved with that," Willie said.

Another question is how would Willie have approached the struggle? Even though the insistence on non-violent direct action espoused by Martin Luther King, Jr. led to the greatest successes of the movement, did Willie have the patience for that? Willie is the kind of person who likely could have participated in a non-violent lunch counter sit-in for about 10 minutes, getting spat on, verbally abused, and punched and pulled before he would say enough of this crap, and start kicking ass. Given his temperament, would he have been successfully wooed by the more militant approach of Malcolm X, which demanded rights and respect for Black people, and sought to gain those rights by any means necessary?

"I had so much hate, and had been misused and abused, and all of that. 'Cause I saw so much with Sheriff Dick Byrd, how I would see people get kicked, slapped, and all of that, and you just have to stand there and take it. Yeah, I probably would have taken the Malcolm X way," Willie said.

# 11

## THE GOLDEN ROAD

When Willie was transferred to the Air Force base in El Segundo, California in February 1966, there was no base housing, so he and Maureen had to find a place to live with their kids. Little Darnell had just celebrated his first birthday, and Maureen's children from her first marriage, Sheree and Brian, were four and six. El Segundo is a small city that sits on the south end of LAX Airport, and they started looking for a place to rent in Inglewood, a few miles east of the base. At the time, Inglewood was predominantly white and every time they went to look for a place to rent, they struck out.

In the office at the base one day, a sergeant, a white guy, asked Willie if he found a place to live yet.

"Nope. Still living in a motel. Every time me and the wife go to look at a place, they say it ain't available."

"It ain't my business, but Willie, let your wife go, you don't go," the sergeant said.

"You think so?"

"Yes, I think so."

So Willie had Maureen go look for a place on her own, and two hours later she was back with a signed lease in her hand. She found a cute little two-bedroom house in a quiet neighborhood on 105th St. in Inglewood. They moved out of the motel on Friday night and into their new home. On Saturday morning, Willie got up, looked out his front window, and saw four white guys standing on the sidewalk in front of the house, chatting. He went outside and walked over to them. He knew what they were thinking.

"Good mornin'," he said.

Silence.

"My name is Willie Harris. I'm in the United States Air Force. I don't want no problems out of anyone. I don't bother anyone. But if you throw a brick through my window or whatsoever, I will fight back."

The men stared at Willie, and only one of them spoke.

"Nice to meet you, Willie," he said, stepping forward and shaking his hand.

From then on, Willie had no problems in Inglewood. He was the only Black person in the neighborhood, but no one bothered him, and he even made a few friends. A couple of the guys down the street would come over to the house and play a little poker.

While being married to a white woman in Mississippi would have been unthinkable for Willie in the 1960s, it also wasn't easy living as a mixed-race couple in California either. It may have been one of the most liberal states in the union, but everything is relative, and changing hearts and minds can take decades. One day Willie and Maureen got a bite to eat in a café, and when they came out, two Black women were standing on the sidewalk. They looked at Willie—tall, dark, and handsome. Very tall. Very dark. Very handsome. They assessed Maureen, looked her up and down, then down and up, then sideways.

"Look at that fuckin' cracker," one of them said.

"Mmm-hmm."

Maureen looked confused, and Willie just grinned to himself.

When they got in their car, a 1963 Ford Galaxie 500XL, Maureen asked "What's a cracker?"

"It's a saltine."

Later, when she learned the meaning, she slapped Willie in the arm.

"You liar!"

Willie just laughed. There was nothing left to do but smile, smile, smile.

Willie, Maureen, and the kids settled into a quiet, normal life in the LA suburbs. Maureen got a job at a Max Factor cosmetics distribution center, working the second shift on the assembly line, shipping out orders. Willie continued doing the same work at the air base that he had been doing back in New Mexico, administering physical fitness exams to all the airmen. On the Tuesday of your birthday week, you went to see Willie to take your exam. The rest of the time he helped run the athletic department. He would answer the phone in the gym, make sure the boiler room was functioning properly and kept clean, and work on the fields. The base had softball and baseball diamonds, and Willie learned how to properly line and prepare the fields. At night, he would go keep score at the ballgames.

Willie was scheduled to be discharged from the Air Force on October 1, 1966, but he stayed on because as he got closer to leaving the service, he realized how bad his knees were getting, he thought about how much pain he was in, and he knew it was all because he had sacrificed his body to help his base basketball team win games.

"They used me. They crippled me. And I wasn't going to accept just walking out like a dog with my tail tucked between my legs without fightin' back."

Willie petitioned the Air Force for a retirement due to his disability. He was sent to March Air Force Base in Riverside, a couple of hours east of L.A., to be examined by a team of orthopedic specialists. After assessing him, the doctors there said that if he was going to receive a retirement, he would need to be go before a medical board at Kelly Air Force Base in San Antonio, and they could issue a ruling. So he flew to Texas, was seen by the board and they decided that he qualified for a medical disability. He would receive a small monthly stipend for the rest of his life, plus have medical privileges at the base hospital and the VA. The stipend wasn't a lot of money, but it was an admission by the Air Force that his injury was caused by his service, even if that service was playing basketball. Willie felt pretty good when he flew back to El Segundo, and then he was called to the base commander's office.

"Airman Harris, I have some bad news for you," the base commander said.

"What is it, sir?" Willie asked.

"The Air Force has revoked your disability retirement."

"What? Why?"

"It doesn't say exactly, just that the determination has been made that you will now be discharged with a physical disability, but you will receive a one-time severance payment, and are being awarded privileges to access care in the VA medical system," the commander said.

Son of a bitch. Just when Willie thought the Air Force would do the right thing and take care of him a little bit, they took that away.

Willie kept fighting, but the Air Force wouldn't budge. On February 10, 1967 Airman Second Class Willie D. Harris was honorably discharged from the United States Air Force. His discharge papers stated he was "physically disqualified for the performance of active duty." His DD 214, the document provided to all members of the U.S. military when they leave the service, stated he had a "Physical disability with entitlement to receive disability severance pay."

The Air Force handed Willie a severance check for $2,200 and said: Get out, and thank you for your service.

Now a civilian, he started looking for a job, figuring he could use the skills and experience he gained in the base athletic department. He applied to be a groundskeeper at Dodger Stadium. He applied to work all kinds of jobs in the athletic departments at UCLA and USC. He applied anywhere else he could find where people were needed to maintain athletic facilities. Everywhere he applied, the answer was the same. The human resources office would ask to see his DD 214 and when they saw the words "physical disability," that was it. They said we're sorry, we can't hire you, but thank you for your service.

Frustrated, and needing to earn income to support his family until he could find something better, Willie accepted a temporary job as a security guard at the Watts Skills Center, a vocational school not too far from Inglewood.

When Willie had some free time, he would go to see the horses run at Hollywood Park. He would stand down by the finish line and one day in June a guy looked up at Willie and asked a common question: do you play basketball? The man's name was C.D. Williams and he told Willie about a summer basketball league and asked if he wanted to join. Willie thought about how bad his knees were feeling, but there was nothing he loved more than playing ball—and he always had his knee braces to get him through. "Sure," he said.

Willie started playing in the league on weekends and weeknights in local gyms, and he was amazed when he was playing with ABA and NBA players, including Connie Hawkins, Hambone Williams, and Walt Hazzard. He was playing well and doing a good job hiding the fact that his knees were killing him. Willie didn't know that professional scouts would attend the games, but they were there, and they were watching him. In July he received a letter from Bob Bass, head coach of the Denver Rockets of the newly formed American Basketball Association. Coach Bass told Willie in the letter that he wanted him to come out to their rookie tryout camp which was being held that month just outside LA.

Willie was excited and nervous when he went to the tryout. Excited that he finally had a chance to make a pro team, but nervous that his knees would betray him—and they did. He battled for two days but couldn't finish the second day of the tryout. His knees gave out, and he was done. His dream of playing pro ball was over.

He went back to work at Watts Skills Center, and one day he was approached by one of the female teachers he had become friendly with named Roy Cash.

"Hey, Seven," Roy said one Friday. She called Willie Seven because she thought he was 7 feet tall. "Do you want to go to a party tonight?"

"Does a bear shit in the woods?" Willie asked. "Of course I want to go. I'll bring my wife."

Willie and Maureen arranged for the teenage girl who lived next door to babysit the kids and drove to the house party in Covina. When they arrived Roy introduced Willie to her first cousin Archie, a feisty young woman who grew up in Grambling, Louisiana, three hours west of Willie's home in Mississippi, on the other side of the big river.

Willie got to know Archie a bit, and one day they were talking, and for no particular reason, Archie mentioned her friend Calvin Brown.

"Willie, do you ever watch *I Spy*?" she asked, referring to the groundbreaking 1965-68 secret agent drama starring Robert Culp and Bill Cosby. It was the first American television drama to feature a Black man in a leading role.

"Sure."

"Well, my homeboy from Grambling, Cal Brown, does stunts and doubles for Bill Cosby. Would you like to meet him?"

"Absolutely."

Calvin Brown and Archie had been friends growing up in Grambling, and they kept in touch after they moved to the LA area in the late 1950s. Calvin had graduated from Grambling State University in 1957 with a bachelor's degree in business. When he got to LA, he applied for work as a bookkeeper at UPS and all the banks in the Black neighborhoods south of the city. The answer was the same everywhere he went—he was told he was "overqualified" for the job. So Calvin fell back on something he had been doing since he was 13 years old: delivering mail. He had a letter of recommendation from the post office in Grambling and landed a job as a mail carrier in a few days. Soon after that, he started working as an extra in films to supplement his income.

In 1962 he was working as an extra during the filming of *Drums of Africa*, which starred Frankie Avalon and Mariette Hartley, when the director took one look at him and said, "You're my chief," referring to the uncredited character of African Chief in the movie. Even though he was playing the chief, he was still classified as an extra, and the standard pay was $11.15 a day. There is a scene in the film that involves a slave trader, portrayed by Lloyd Bochner, chasing a potential slave who climbs up a tree. Bochner's character tells him you are no good to me up in that tree, so if you don't come down, I'll shoot you.

At this point the director said, "We need someone to fall out of the tree."

He looked at all the Black men on the set who were working as extras and they all looked at each other. No one moved.

"The person who falls out of that tree, I'm going to pay you a hundred ___."

"Before he got 'dollars' out, I was up the tree," said Calvin, who played multiple sports growing up and was very athletic. "I'd been fallin' out of trees in Louisiana for free."

Calvin fell out of the tree and the director said that was a good fall, but we need you to do it again. Don't worry, he said, every time you fall out of the tree, I'll give you $100.

"I fell out of that tree six times that day, and they paid me $600 in $100 bills. I had never had that kind of money."

Now flush with cash, Calvin was able to take about one-third of his earnings and pay the membership fees for the Screen Actors Guild, American Federation of Television and Radio Artists, and the Screen Extras Guild, all in the same day. He got his SAG card, went home with a big smile on his face and told his wife he was through working at the post office.

"Are you crazy! That's a good-paying job!" she screamed.

This will be better, he told her. For the next few years he did a few stunts, but mostly continued to work as an extra. Then in 1965 he was working as an extra on *Gomer Pyle, U.S.M.C.*, when the legendary actor, director, and producer Sheldon Leonard approached him. Leonard told him that he was starting a new show called *I Spy*, starring an unknown Black actor named Bill Cosby. Leonard told

Calvin that he looked like Cosby, and if he could do stunts, he had a job for him as a stuntman.

"Sheldon was an ideal person. He was a jewel. He went out on a limb when he first hired Cosby as the leading man in a dramatic TV series. He went out on a limb when they hired me to be the stunt double. In the pilot, Cosby was doubled by a white guy that was painted down. Cosby told Sheldon that would never happen again if the show went. So the show went," Calvin said.

The painting down of white stuntmen to double Black actors had been going on for years in Hollywood. It was primarily done on movie sets, because up until the mid-1960s there was almost never a need for it in television productions, since there weren't any Black actors playing significant roles on television shows. The practice was straightforward: apply blackface to a white stuntman so he could double a Black actor. Painting down had its roots in a classic stew of racism, economics, and cronyism, but racism was the primary factor. Producers and directors hand off the duties of planning stunts and hiring stunt men and women to a stunt coordinator, also known as a second unit director. In the 1960s almost all the stunt coordinators in Hollywood belonged to the Stuntmen's Association of Motion Pictures. They were all white. They would only hire stuntmen who belonged to their association, all of whom were white. It was virtually impossible for a Black man to join the association, because their by-laws were intended to keep it a closed group, and membership was by invitation only. Under their by-laws, a stuntman had to earn at least $10,000 a year doing only stunts and was forbidden from working even one day as an extra. For Blacks, especially since Calvin Brown was the only working Black stuntman throughout most of the 1960s, that was simply impossible.

Perhaps some directors and producers felt uneasy seeing a white stuntman getting painted down to double Sidney Poitier or Harry Belafonte. Perhaps the makeup artist applying blackface to a white stuntman who was doubling Sidney or Harry felt this was wrong.

But if the director asked why don't we use a Black stuntman for this job, the stunt coordinator would just say that there aren't any Black stuntmen. And the show must go on.

Following the success of *I Spy* in 1965, Greg Morris became the second Black actor cast in a significant role in a television drama when *Mission: Impossible* was created in 1966. Calvin Brown now found himself with two jobs, doubling Greg Morris and Bill Cosby. *I Spy* was shot in exotic locations across the globe, and Calvin worked in China, Japan, Spain, and Italy. Sheldon Leonard paid Calvin to take judo and karate classes so scenes which included martial arts would look more believable. On some days, he would go to three or four different studios to do stunts. Calvin was 6'2", and if he needed to double a shorter actor, they would dig a hole and he would stand in it. Whatever needed to be done, he would do it. Things were going well for Calvin, but he was the only Black stuntman working with any regularity, and his success would not have been possible if Sheldon Leonard and Bill Cosby were not standing behind him and making sure he was treated fairly. In one incident, Calvin learned that white stuntmen working with him on a scene were paid twice as much as him. When he told Sheldon Leonard, the stunt coordinator was fired, and Calvin received equal pay.

Having one working Black stuntman to serve the American motion picture industry was not sustainable. The civil rights movement was exploding across the country. It may have taken several hundred years, but Americans were confronting the racial, gender and social inequities that were part of the bedrock of their society. More roles were opening up for Black actors who needed stunt doubles. However, with the dominant stuntmen's association effectively closed to Blacks, there was nothing for aspiring Black stuntmen to do but start their own organization. Calvin knew Eddie Smith, and Eddie had been around Hollywood since the mid-1950s, working as an extra and a freelance TV news cameraman. Eddie started to think about creating a Black stuntmen's group in 1963 when he saw white stuntman Loren Janes getting painted down on the set of *It's a Mad, Mad, Mad, Mad World*. Janes was doubling the Black actor Eddie "Rochester" Anderson in the film. When Eddie questioned Director Stanley Kramer about it, Kramer told him there were no Black stuntmen, so they had no choice. This was the spark. Eddie thought that if they could train Black guys to do stunts, then the studios would have to hire them and stop painting down white stuntmen. He knew they had to train themselves, because no one was going to do it for them. In 1967 Eddie gathered a group of Buffalo Soldiers to be the core of a new Black stuntmen's group. The Buffalo Soldiers were a group of young Black men who rode horses in parades to honor the original Buffalo Soldiers, the 10th Cavalry Regiment of the U.S. Army, which was formed in 1866 at Fort Leavenworth, Kansas. They fought in the American Indian Wars in the 19th century and were not completely disbanded until 1951 when the U.S. military was finally integrated.

Eddie decided to train the Buffalo Soldiers because they were young and athletic, and already had the ability to ride horses, all of which made them good candidates to be stuntmen. They started training in Athens Park, just west of Compton, on Wednesday nights in the summer of 1967. Calvin would often lead the training sessions along with Buffalo Soldier Ernie Robinson. Ernie had recently been discharged from the U.S. Army and he infused the group with military discipline and showed them fighting techniques. There were about two dozen men in the original group, as well as two women, Evelyn Cuffee and Marie Louise Johnson.

It was right around this time that Archie introduced Willie to Calvin Brown. They chatted about life in Mississippi and Louisiana and Calvin told Willie about the stunt group they were forming, and he asked Willie if he would like to work out with them at the park.

Here was Willie, 27 years old and fresh out of the military with busted knees, a wife and three kids at home, and no viable career path on the horizon. A tremendous athlete just a few years ago, his damaged knees now made him a less than ideal candidate to be a stuntman. But he heard his mom's words in his head, always. "Son, don't be like me. Don't put yourself in a position where you need to be takin' handouts. Do something with your life and make me proud." He thought about Peyton Abbott Jones, Bill Turner, and Sheriff Dick Byrd, and he remembered the face of every other man who had treated him like a piece of garbage. Well, goddammit, he thought, if I'm going to be somebody, I need to give this a shot.

It could be an illusion, but he might as well try, so he decided to go for it.

"I'll be at the park this Wednesday night," Willie said.

Calvin Brown led the training at Athens Park.

"I trained them to fall off the bleachers. We did fight scenes. We did tumblin' and wrestlin', anything that entailed basic stunts," Calvin said. They would find old mattresses and fall off the top of the baseball backstop onto them. They would rent old cars and practice doing 180s and donuts, until the car rental agencies figured out what they were doing and stopped renting to them. And every Wednesday, they would see unmarked cars sitting across the street. They learned these were plainclothes police officers, keeping an eye on them, fearful they may be a group of Black Panthers. They weren't militant; they were just a bunch of guys trying to train themselves so they could work in Hollywood.

Eddie Smith was an accomplished stuntman and actor and would eventually tally scores of credits in major films, but his greatest contribution to the movement to open up Hollywood to Blacks was as a leader and fighter. He founded this group, which soon became known as the Black Stuntmen's Association (BSA). He was the glue that kept them together. He motivated them to stick with it, even though they were really chasing a dream. They all had jobs and families to worry about, and there was no certainty this stuntman training would ever pay off. After they were trained, he fought hard to get them jobs. He was known as a highly skilled negotiator who could talk his way through any situation, even the time he got caught cheating while playing poker with some white stuntmen. They held him upside down by his ankles, but he used his impressive oratorical skills to navigate his way out of that quagmire, avoiding any bodily harm.

Calvin continued to train them into 1968, even when he shattered his leg doing a stunt while doubling Jim Brown in *The Split*. This put him in a cast for two years. He would come to the park and lead the training, while keeping a bucket of plaster of Paris in the trunk of his car so he could repair his cast when it cracked.

Willie kept working out with the BSA in 1968, but he had not yet worked as a stuntman because he didn't have a Screen Actors Guild card, which was a basic requirement to do stunts. They were not easy to get—not only did they cost several hundred dollars for the registration fee, but you had to have someone in the industry refer you. Then one day in the early spring of 1969 he drove up to North Hollywood to drop a friend off. On the way home he couldn't find the freeway and got lost. Seeing a bunch of lights set up on a street he thought to himself, well, what is this? I'll check this out and see if anyone can give me directions.

Willie parked his car and as he walked toward the lights, he discovered it was a movie being shot on location. He stood there watching when a tall guy with straight black hair walked up to him.

"Hey, how you doin'?"

I'm doin' pretty good," Willie said, "but I would be better if I could find my way back to the freeway."

"Oh, I can help you with that. How tall are you, man?'

"Six-eight," Willie said.

"Do you play basketball?"

"I used to, but I busted up my knees in the Air Force, and it ain't the same. Can't play no more, unless I fake it."

"Oh, that's awful, so what do you do now?"

"I've been working out with some guys and we're tryin' to break into the motion picture industry as stuntmen, but I need a producer to write a sponsor letter for me so I can get a Screen Actors Guild card," Willie said.

"Really," the man said, as he looked up at Willie. The man was Elliott Gould, and he was in the middle of filming *Bob and Carol and Ted and Alice*, with his co-stars Natalie Wood, Robert Culp, and Dyan Cannon. He liked Willie right away. Something about him. Just took a shine to him.

"What are you doing tomorrow?" Elliott asked.

"Nothin'."

"Okay, how about this. Do you know where Bronson and Sunset is?"

"Right there near Channel 5?" Willie asked.

"Yes. Columbus Studios is there. Come to the gate at noon tomorrow. I will leave a pass for you to get in. I'm going to get Robert Altman to write a letter for you to take to the Screen Actors Guild so you can get your card."

Willie was astounded.

"Thank you. I'll be there."

Excited, Willie found the freeway and headed home. When he arrived at the studio the next morning, sure enough, Elliott had left a pass for him. He found Elliott on the set where they were working and Elliott gave him $25, suggested he go have some lunch and come back at 2:00 when the letter would be ready. Willie came back, got the letter, and walked the half mile down Sunset Boulevard to the Screen Actors Guild office. He went in to fill out the application and get his card, but there was a problem. The fee to join was $236. Willie didn't have anything close to that kind of money. He walked back to the studio to find Elliott.

"Hey, Willie, did you get the card?" Elliott asked.

"No, I filled out the application, but the fee is $236. I ain't tryin' to hustle nobody Elliott, but I ain't got that kind of money."

"No, it's fine. Listen, I don't have any extra money on me now, but come back tomorrow."

"Thank you," Willie said, shaking his hand.

So Willie went back the next day, Elliott gave him the money needed to join, and he got his SAG card. He looked at that card and thought, my oh my, I am a long way from the cotton fields in Mississippi. To think about the generosity of that man, who he just randomly met on the street, it blew Willie away.

Years later, Elliott matter-of-factly recalled his reaction when he met Willie.

"I was taken with his misfortune of having blown his knees out, and we talked, and I felt for him, and felt he was instinctively worthy to be helped and so we were able to help Willie. I was privileged to be able to be there at the right time to help him."

Elliott's philosophy was simple: you see someone in need, and you help them, if you can.

"I believe in loyalty, and I also believe that for those of us that are still here it's really significant and valuable and important to be there for one another, and Willie gave me an opportunity to be there for him, and he never forgot."

Willie's first job as a stuntman was portraying a boxer on *The Bill Cosby Show*. He was on his way.

# 12

— · —

## KNOCKIN' DOWN THE DOOR

Sometimes it takes just one person with a bold idea to start a movement. The idea for the Black Stuntmen's Association was conceived by Mr. Eddie Smith in 1963 when he saw a white stuntman get blackface put on him so he could double a Black actor. That stuck with Eddie, and over the next several years he stewed over what he could do about it.

The people who knew Eddie Smith best called him charismatic, a hustler, a mouth, a jack of all trades, a crook, kind of a funny creature, and very crafty. He was all that, and more. Though he stood just 5'6", he had an enormous personality and the combustible magnetism of Kevin Hart. When he first complained about the paint-down of a white stuntman in 1963, it was a different world. The civil rights movement was progressing rapidly, but it was focused on hope and raising awareness of the plight of African Americans and exposing all the ways they had been treated unfairly in this country since their arrival more than three centuries earlier. Fast forward to 1967 and a lot had changed. Federal laws had been passed to protect the rights of all Americans, regardless of race, sex, or other characteristics. In 1965, the neighborhood of Watts, just 20 miles south of Hollywood, had imploded in violence to protest police brutality and discrimination against Blacks. The counterculture in the U.S. was growing exponentially, and protests against the Vietnam War were dovetailing with demands for civil rights for racial minorities and equality for women.

When Eddie would run around Hollywood studios in the mid-60s complaining about the lack of Blacks working on movie and television productions, he was a lone wolf crying in the wilderness. By 1967, he knew it was time to seize the day, and he knew if he wanted to be successful in integrating Hollywood, he would need some backup. Enter the Buffalo Soldiers. He befriended this group of African American equestrians who practiced their riding and military drills on Sundays in Griffith Park, just northeast of Hollywood, and he convinced almost two dozen of the Buffalo Soldiers to join the new stunt group he was putting together. Eddie had connections in Hollywood, and if they worked hard to get properly trained, he could get them jobs in the movie and TV business. On top of that, who wouldn't want to be part of a group with the ridiculously cool name of The Black Stuntmen's Association?

By 1967 Eddie was in his early forties, and the men he recruited to join the group were almost all in their twenties. Eddie wasn't really a father figure to them, but more of an obnoxious big brother who had done a lot and seen a lot, and there was an awful lot he could teach them. Alex Brown, one of the Buffalo Soldiers who joined the BSA when it was founded, became close to Eddie, and understood what motivated him to enlist the Buffalo Soldiers.

"When we got together, being a little younger, a little more spirted, he had some support in trying to get what he had been wanting to do all the time. So when that happened, it was for sure he had a little strength, a little backing, and a little more support," Alex Brown said.

Eddie didn't stop building the BSA with the Buffalo Soldiers. While more than half the original members were Buffalo Soldiers, he reached out to others in his diverse circle of friends and acquaintances to bolster the group. He recruited Henry Graddy, a friend of his since the late '50s who Eddie met when he would go to the roller-skating rink where Henry worked as the DJ spinning records for the skaters. Eddie would do his best to schmooze the young ladies who came to the rink, and the two became friends. Then one day

Eddie saw 13-year-old William Upton in the park doing back flips. He went up to him, got to know him and his mother, and told them he was going to make him a stunt performer in the movies. A few years later when Upton worked his first movie in 1970, *Halls of Anger,* he was the youngest stunt man or woman in Hollywood at the time.

Shortly after the fledgling group started practicing in Athens Park, Willie had his fortuitous meeting with Calvin Brown and was invited to join them. When they warmly accepted him into their circle, he knew he had finally found his people. The taste of his recently ended basketball career was still bitter on his tongue. He thought about how the Air Force had abused his body. He thought about how much abuse he saw and endured in the South. These guys were fighting for jobs for Black people who were shut out in Hollywood. This was important. This was special. This felt familiar. He did not hesitate, and he embraced the mission wholeheartedly.

From the beginning, Eddie made it clear that they needed to be competent in order to be successful. They weren't just jumping off bleachers onto mattresses, learning how to do tricks in cars and motorcycles, and throwing fake punches at each other because it was fun. They had a goal: to break down the door that was preventing Blacks from working in any significant numbers in Hollywood productions, particularly in the area of stunt work. To do that, they had to know what the hell they were doing. As Black men in America in the 1960s, they understood they usually had to be better than a white guy at something in order to even have a chance.

"If you walked into Hollywood, being Black, and didn't know what you were doing, that would be the first job, and the last job," Willie said.

The group quickly formed an executive committee. Ernie Robinson was named its first president. He had recently been discharged from the U.S. Army and had a zeal for discipline. He used his military background to lead the training sessions at Athens Park, along with Calvin Brown. S. J. McGee was the treasurer, Alex Brown was the secretary, and Henry Kingi was the business manager. Eddie Smith wasn't interested in an official title, as he preferred to be the mover and the shaker, pulling strings behind the scenes, making shit happen. He was well-known around Hollywood, and producers knew they could go to him when they needed Black people for extras or other roles.

"Eddie had been in the business for a long time before most of us, so he kind of knew the ins and outs. And Eddie had advanced himself to a lot of the studios and casting agencies. And they'd say if you need somebody, call Eddie Smith. People in the studios didn't know how to get Black people, so Eddie Smith was the one who got 'em. And the more he got, the more power he got," Alex Brown said.

Eddie knew how to motivate the group, telling them about how white stuntmen were having blackface put on them so they could double Black actors.

"Eddie Smith was pretty crafty, very crafty. When the word got out that whites were being painted down, once we found that out, that's when we started training really hard," said Doug Lawrence, a Buffalo Solider and original BSA member.

After the training sessions in the park, the group would go to Eddie's or someone else's house for strategy meetings. The topics would always be twofold: what jobs are available, and which member of the group was best suited for a particular job.

"Our motto was, if you can't do the job, don't take it. We didn't want to look bad. We were very aware of the fact that we didn't want to get a bad reputation about not being able to do the job. Don't send somebody out there because he's Black. You need to be Black and good," Alex Brown said.

As exciting as it was to think about working in the movie industry, the BSA leaders made it clear that it would not be an easy road. After they overcame the discrimination and racism permeating the studios, they needed to actually do the work of a stuntman. That meant they could expect to get hurt. Broken fingers, dislocated shoulders, concussions, cracked kneecaps: those were all just fringe benefits of being a stunt performer. The really bad injuries included breaking your back or having your leg crushed and broken in multiple places. They called it "hittin' the ground." If you couldn't handle hittin' the ground and getting hurt, then you weren't cut out to be a stuntman. Go do something else like sell insurance or work in real estate. This wasn't for you.

When it came to trying to secure jobs, someone would go to the studios and get the call sheets. They would discuss what the studios were looking for, and what jobs they might have a shot at getting, whether it was stunt work or something else. Eddie would often encourage them to go stand in line to be considered for extra work. It only paid about 20% of the daily base pay for a stunt performer, but it was important to be seen, and to be on sets, in case other opportunities came up. As a Black man, you weren't going to walk into a studio and have them just hand you a job as a stuntman. In fact, it was just the opposite. You always had to be hustling, just as Eddie Smith had done for the past decade.

Extra work was fine in order to make a little money and stay active on the studio lots, but it wasn't the ultimate goal. When they were well-trained, Eddie started making more noise about stunt work.

"Eddie knew some of the executives at Fox, Universal, and all of that, and he would go in and raise hell with them," 'Willie said, "and they were sayin' that the white stunt guys were sayin' that we weren't ready for it, that we didn't know what we were doin'. So Eddie would tell them, 'Hey, why don't you test us and see what we can do?'"

The BSA also joined the local NAACP chapter to show the studios they were serious.

"We joined the Beverly Hills Hollywood branch of the NAACP, collectively as a group, and Eddie suggested that. He said we need to have us a hammer, so when we go in these offices we can tell people we are members of the NAACP, and if we don't get some Black people jobs, we are going to have the people come out and march," Alex Brown said.

BSA members did not get much work doing stunts in the first couple of years after the group was founded. Ernie Robinson did stunts in the 1968 film *Planet of the Apes,* and Calvin Brown doubled Jim Brown in the 1968 film *The Split*, during which Calvin suffered a devastating leg injury that sidelined him for two years. Doug Lawrence started out as an extra on the film *M*A*S*H* in the summer of 1969, and he was asked to do stunt work during the filming, earning him his Screen Actors Guild card and launching him on a successful career as a stuntman for the next twenty years, mostly in television. Lawrence had met the Buffalo Soldiers when he saw them practicing in the park, which was just a mile from his home. He came to stunt work with transferable skills: he had rode motorcycles and horses back in his native New Jersey, he could scuba dive, and had learned martial arts while serving his country in the U.S. Navy, as he had enlisted the day after his high school graduation in 1958. He had come to Los Angeles in 1965, accepting a job transfer from the New York office of the Great American Insurance Company, where he had worked as a private detective for three years. When he got to LA and walked into the office and they saw the color of his skin, they told him he was "overqualified."

"The only thing black in the office was a telephone," Lawrence said.

Like many members of the BSA, he had suffered discrimination in the workplace or while trying to find a job, and he saw the opportunity to work as a stuntman as a godsend.

"Those of us that were in the Buffalo Soldiers, it was a piece of cake. Once Eddie came and approached us as a group, and explained to us what he was attempting to do, it was automatic. Here's a bunch of young Black guys, all of us are athletic to a certain degree, and who didn't want to work in the movie industry?" Lawrence said.

Overall, though, Lawrence was one of the fortunate ones, as most BSA members rarely got work doing stunts in the late 1960s and at the start of the next decade, and they had to stay focused on the goal, and keep the faith that things would open up eventually.

One highlight for many of the BSA members who were also Buffalo Soldiers was their inclusion in the 1969 film *Hello Dolly*, which starred Barbra Streisand and was directed by Gene Kelly. The romantic comedy musical includes a grandiose parade with the Buffalo Soldiers riding on horseback, but they were in the film as extras, not stuntmen.

In the fall of 1969, Twentieth Century Fox was producing the film *The Great White Hope*, starring James Earl Jones. The story was inspired by the life of Jack Johnson, the first Black world heavyweight boxing champion, who reigned from 1908-1915. The title comes from the intense desire on the part of white racists in America to find a white boxer who could beat Johnson, thus proving that whites were superior to Blacks, and return things to their alleged natural order. The problem for the white racists' racial superiority theory was that Johnson was the best fighter in the world during his prime, and he couldn't be beaten.

Eddie Smith was on the set for the film and noticed that just about everyone working behind the camera was white, and he got mad. At that moment, he wasn't focused on stunt performers, but the entire crew. He told Alex Brown they were going to go talk to the producer.

"Hi Eddie, how are you doing? What can I do for you?" the producer asked.

"I'm okay, but I was better before I took a look at the crew for this movie," Eddie said.

"What do you mean?"

"What I mean," Eddie said, trying to stay under control, "is this is a movie *about* racism, and when I look around all I see are white make-up people, white cameramen, white set decorators, white wardrobe techs, and white everything else. That crew is whiter than a cotton field in October. Even the catering people are white! Are you sensing the same supreme irony of this situation that I am?" Eddie bellowed.

"Okay, okay, calm down, and have a seat," the producer said, as he pulled out a cigar and carefully lit it, taking time to think about his response.

"Well?" Eddie said.

"Okay, Eddie, you have a point, so here is what I am going to do. In the next couple of months, we are going to be filming on location in Spain, in Barcelona.  I will send five Black people to work on the crew, entry-level jobs. They don't need a lot of experience. We'll train them. One in men's wardrobe, one in women's wardrobe, a set decorator, and two other people. Can you find me 5 people who are willing to go to Spain for 2 months?" the producer asked.

"That will not be a problem at all," Eddie said.

"Great. Get back to me by next week when you have those five people lined up," the producer said.

"Thank you. I will get back to you by the end of this week, and it is a pleasure doing business with you, sir," Eddie said, and as he and Alex got up to leave, he added, "Oh, and I'll take one of those cigars for the road, if you don't mind."

When they were outside the producer's office, Alex was jumping up and down, he was so excited about the victory.

"Well, bro," Eddie said, "looking him in the eye and smiling, "do you want to go to Spain for two months and work in men's wardrobe?"

Oh, shit, Alex thought, he hadn't considered that. He didn't have any interest in working in wardrobe, but if you are going to make a lot of noise, you need to be willing to perform when called upon. So he went, and Eddie went, too.

"So we did that, and that's when it kind of opened up. He not only fought for people in front of the camera, he'd fight for people behind the camera. A lot of people didn't realize that was the beginning of all those trainee programs, when we would begin to have people come behind the camera doing things. I had to learn to pin and measure and everything else before I could go on the set. Hanging clothes up, and women had to do the same things. The one in set decoration had to learn how to move furniture around. But when we came back, that's when the programs started for the people behind the camera," Alex Brown said.

One person who benefitted from a trainee program was Bernadine Anderson. A feisty, no-nonsense young Black woman from New York City, Bernadine moved to Los Angeles in 1965 after having studied art and psychology at NYU. She didn't go to Hollywood as some starry-eyed dreamer who believed she was destined to see her name in lights. She was a pragmatic single mother with two children to support, and she was interested in a career as a makeup artist. She had an art background and was also that girl who did the makeup for all her friends for proms, bar mitzvahs, and weddings.

Anderson had a friend who worked in human resources at Warner Brothers Studios, and she asked him in 1965 if he could help her get a job. He tried, but nothing was available, and he let her know he would keep her in mind if something opened up, but she didn't hear from him for a while. So she started knocking on doors, but everywhere she applied for a job as a makeup artist, she hit a brick wall. She stayed in the business by doing extra work, and she even got a few speaking parts in productions, earning her a Screen Actors Guild card. But her goal remained the same: she wanted to land a stable job as a makeup artist to support her family. Bernadine noticed some other people were in the same situation as her. She looked around the sets, and most of the Black people she saw who had steady jobs were janitors. So she talked to a lawyer and was prepared to file a class action lawsuit against the studios for discriminatory hiring practices. But then in 1968, there was a small breakthrough. Her friend in human resources called and said there were openings for makeup artist apprentices. It wasn't a union job, but it could be a path into the union. She jumped on it.

It wasn't surprising that there were jobs available at that moment for apprentices, as the first production she worked on was *Planet of the Apes*. It took an army of makeup artists to work on the actors and extras in the film. It was the perfect boot camp for her, and she was assigned to work on the extras.

"It takes hours to apply this stuff. Eight hours to put on the makeup and four hours to take it off. Nowadays they just have suits they zip them up into, and they're on their way. But we built faces," Anderson said.

Anderson worked as an apprentice on a variety of films and television productions from 1968-1971. She got to know Willie when they both worked on an episode of the television series *The Name of the Game* in 1969. Seeing other Blacks working on a set was a rarity, so they usually got to know each other and looked out for one another. Willie told her about the struggle the BSA was waging, trying to break through in Hollywood, and she could certainly identify with that.

Then in 1971 Anderson got the news that she was being accepted into the union, the Make-Up Artists and Hair Stylists Guild Local 706. Normally, an apprentice being granted union membership is a routine occurrence. But in Anderson's case, this was a very big deal. Not only was she the first Black person admitted to the union, she was also the first female. Of the approximately 200 union members at the time, all of them were white males. She immediately became a pioneer on two fronts.

Her next big break came when she became Jane Fonda's personal makeup artist, and she worked on all her films for eight years, including *Nine to Five, The China Syndrome,* and *The Electric Horseman.*

"(Fonda) requested a female minority to be her makeup artist. I was the only one, so that's how I got the job," Anderson said.

It has been a long, hard struggle for minorities and women to make inroads in white male-dominated Hollywood. One example: Jane Fonda appeared in 47 films over 58 years from 1960 to 2018. In every single one of those films, the director was male, and in 45 out of 47 films, he was a white male.

Anderson's career continued to advance during the 1970s and by the 80s she was working as the head of makeup on some movies, including *A Soldier's Story* and *Coming to America,* where she was responsible for directing all the makeup artists and hair stylists on the production.

Despite her success, it was never easy. Throughout her career she saw—and experienced firsthand—the dark side of Hollywood productions, where sexism and racism were prevalent.

A woman walking around a Hollywood set would routinely be hunted down by a lecherous producer seeking sexual favors. Anderson was a professional makeup artist, and she was very pragmatic about these encounters.

"My thing was: that's two jobs. If you're paying me for two jobs, then I'll do two jobs, but if you're only paying me for one, then you only get one job," she said with a chuckle.

She also had the occasional blunt reminder that some people considered her, and everyone who looked like her, to be beneath them, well beneath them.

"A couple of times, by a couple of different people, I was said exactly this to my face: 'I will not let a nigger touch me.' And I said, 'Well if you find a nigger, let me know,'" Anderson said.

These were high-profile actors saying this to her, and it had happened when she was the head of makeup on a production. She refused to work on them, and the producers incurred an extra cost to appease the actor's racism.

"I told the first assistant (director) that I could not work on these people. They had to hire somebody to come in, as an extra makeup artist to do them, because they already told me I can't touch them. I was the head of makeup on the show, and I had to hire somebody to come in and do them," Anderson said.

She also saw the paint-down of white stuntmen to double Black actors. In at least one case, she was told to apply the makeup to a white stuntman herself. As a young makeup artist, she did not have any leverage, and if she wanted to keep her job, she had to do what she was told to do, so she did it. The makeup colors used were Dark Egyptian or Light Egyptian, depending on the skin tone they were striving to replicate.

After Anderson got into the union, she was not followed by a mighty stream of women and minorities. As with other professional areas of Hollywood, it seemed as if once there were just a couple of people included who were diverse—amongst a sea of white males—the powers that be figured they could go back to business as usual, having done their part. For Anderson, she tried to do what she could to help integrate the business with others like her, hiring and referring women and minorities.

"If you can bring a few people in when you come in, on your coattails, then you've done something, because it is a business of nepotism," Anderson said.

The word nepotism has its source in the Latin word *nepos*, which means nephew. The word was initially used to refer to the way popes in the Catholic Church during the Middle Ages would bestow the title of cardinal on their nephews, as well as give them land and large sums of the Church's money. Of course, being popes in the Middle Ages, these "nephews" were often actually the pope's illegitimate children, but that is another story. Much like these scandalous popes, the white men who dominated the stunt business were very concerned about keeping the work and flow of money all in the family, even if that meant putting blackface on a white stuntman so he could double a Black actor, or putting a wig on him so he could double a woman.

"In the stunt business, you have nepotism. You have people whose father and grandfather worked in this business. And they wanted to keep it that way, they didn't want other people coming in. They felt you were taking money away from them that they could have given to somebody in their family," Upton said.

The BSA started their fight in Hollywood at a time when the movie industry was in transition. The Western genre was dominant in both feature films and television in the 1960s, with the studios churning out an average of 30 Western movies per year throughout the decade, with stars such as John Wayne, Glenn Ford, and Clint Eastwood. While the industry would migrate to other genres in the 1970s, the proliferation of Westerns in the 1960s had created an infrastructure of stuntmen who were skilled on horses, and cowboys who had become stuntmen practically controlled the Hollywood stunt world. It was their well-fortified castle, and they were not interested in letting anyone cross the moat.

"None of us were really cowboys, and during that time, cowboys almost ran the business. You know, the wranglers, they would be stuntmen, and they would hire their sons, and they would hire their son's sons, and in-laws. I mean generations of stunt people," Alex Brown said.

In many families, children often choose—or are guided toward—the same profession as their parents, whether that be in medicine, law, education, or a multitude of other jobs. But the stunt business in Hollywood was different. It was a very small industry, there were very few of these highly sought-after and lucrative jobs, and the people who controlled the business had no interest in sharing the work. So the BSA was not only fighting a system that excluded them because they were Black, but because they were trying to take work away from people who thought it was rightfully theirs, in perpetuity.

BSA members started getting work in the early 1970s, here and there. Even though some were working, they still had to battle discrimination and work hard to secure every job.

"I used to see a paint-down of a white dude that looks like a Black guy, or a Black woman, and all this other stuff. We had qualified stunt people to do the job. The excuse all the time was 'We was looking for a Black stunt man or a Black stunt girl, and we couldn't find nobody.' They never wanted to look for us," Upton said.

In addition to all the roadblocks put in their way when they were trying to get hired, the inequities continued on the set. Just because they may have had a job doing stunts on a production, that didn't mean they were going to get paid the same amount as a white stuntman for doing the same job. The standard daily rate in SAG in the late 1960s was $178 a day for doing stunts, but the good money came in adjustments, which were the premiums handed out for doing more difficult stunts.

"When you did stunts, and you did something over and above what it required, they had adjustments. I could go in at $178 and do a job and get no adjustment. A lot of white guys would go in and they could get like $100 over, $200 over for the same job. Somebody could come out with $378 by getting a $200 adjustment, plus overtime. Now back then it was a lot of money," Alex Brown said.

The entire process of handing out work revolved around nepotism and cronyism, according to Lawrence.

"The stunt coordinator picks the stunt people because he knows them, he likes them, or he is related to them, and those are the guys that get the stunts that pay the most money," Lawrence said.

Stunt coordinators were also motivated to pay the BSA members less because it helped the production's bottom line.

"It makes the stunt coordinator look really, really good because they operate on a budget, so if they've got a $2 million budget, and he comes in with new stunt guys, and they don't pay them what they should be paid, which is what they did with us all the time. Example: a white guy would get for a car chase, $500, we would get $300, and that's the way it always went. Matter of fact, when I retired, it was still that way to a certain degree," Lawrence said.

In an atmosphere where they were often the only Black person on the set, and generally made to feel unwanted, the BSA members survived by sticking together and supporting each other. Willie and the other guys especially looked out for Upton, as he was just a 14-year-old kid when he joined the group.

"I was adopted by the guys, and the guys taught me know not to get killed, or get hurt, in this business," Upton said.

Willie explained to the teenage Upton that his gymnastic ability was a gift, but he needed to be careful in order to be successful.

"Willie told me that means your body is agile, that means your bones are flexible. What we are going to do is teach you how to use that expertise you have to put it to good use where you can make some money off of it and also show you how it will look good in front of a camera, and so I wouldn't get hurt," Upton said.

Most importantly, Willie told Upton to stand up for himself and if he ever felt unsafe, just say no to doing a stunt.

"Upton, don't be afraid to tell a director, a unit production manager, or even a stunt coordinator, if you see something that might get you hurt or killed, say no. Say no, because all they care about is the shot," Willie said.

"Really? Why would they ask me to do it if it wasn't safe?" Upton said.

"You gotta remember," Willie said, "Some of these people don't like us anyway, so they always want to see us fail, or see us get hurt."

"But if I say no, won't that look bad?" Upton asked.

"Don't believe that crap: if you don't do it, you'll never work in this business ever again. They say that to everybody," Willie said.

However, when you did your job, you had better do it well, or you were sent home. Hollywood sets were not places where compassion was abundant, and the veteran stuntman had ways of trying to intimidate the newcomers.

"They called us the BSA, but the BSA also stands for Boy Scouts of America, and Bullshit Association. When you call us the Bullshit Association, or you call us Boy Scouts of America, that's not respectful. I was called a nigger when I came on the set sometimes, and I didn't even know what a nigger was at 13," Upton said.

Many of them were told that perhaps they didn't have the mental capacity to handle complicated stunts. Maybe they were great athletes, but it took more than that.

"A Black person is not supposed to know anything. A Black person is not supposed to be able to do stunts. A Black person doesn't have the mentality to do those things. I used to get that thrown in my face," Upton said.

As much as the members of the BSA stood up and fought to get jobs as stuntmen in Hollywood, once they were on the set, they needed to be calm and just go about their business. If they were getting harassed or abused, they couldn't fight back, as that was a sure way to get kicked off the set.

"Back then you didn't cause any trouble on the set, because a producer would get you kicked off. Someone might say, 'Hey, the nigger is over there giving me a hard time,' and the producer would say, 'Well, fire his ass.' You didn't do that. You had to sit there and smile," Upton said.

Eddie Smith instilled in Upton the notion that they could not afford to be seen as a disruption—even if the disruption was totally justified—if they wanted to continue to make progress.

"He said, 'I don't care how mad you get, I don't care what you do, don't hit back.' And I didn't. I took it, just like all the rest of the guys took it," Upton said.

One area where they did hit back was during fight scenes. When they first started working, instead of fake punches being thrown their way, they were getting clocked by actors and other stuntmen who thought it was fun to actually hit the new Black stuntmen.

"When we worked with actors, the actors would actually use us as punching bags. So we wised up and we let everybody know, we weren't taking it anymore. If we got hit, we were hittin' back. Once we started doing that, we stopped a lot of that," Doug Lawrence said.

When a few BSA members started working regularly in the early 1970s, it was due to their activism and to help from people inside the business, such as certain Black actors who stood up for them, including Bill Cosby, Sidney Poitier, and Harry Belafonte.

"They were there in the beginning. They knew what we were fighting against, and a couple of them would be the ones to say I don't do this unless you put a Black stuntman there, not painting a white guy down," Lawrence said.

In addition, a few studio executives were sympathetic to their cause and made sure they got work. Lew Wasserman, the legendary head of Universal Studios, was one of their biggest supporters. Eddie Smith, Alex Brown, and a few other BSA members were often welcomed in Wasserman's office on the 14th floor of Universal's iconic Black Tower, and they would chat with Lew and explain what they saw as unfair hiring practices down on the lots. Wasserman would call downstairs and tell the producers they needed to hire some Black stuntmen, but even that could often be a struggle, as they would find that when they got down to the lot, the jobs wouldn't be there, so Lew would have to call again. Eventually, the group could count on getting work in productions at Universal, though the same could not be said for most of the other studios, including Warner Brothers and Paramount.

"After things got started, it was more or less an understood thing that any show that came to Universal, you would have Black stunt people, and then you would have people behind the camera," Alex Brown said.

The largest and most powerful stunt group in Hollywood was the Stuntmen's Association of Motion Pictures, and it was all white until they admitted African American Bob Minor in 1973. Minor had grown up in Birmingham, Alabama and was a former bodybuilder. He was a highly skilled stuntman and would go on to have a decades-long career with hundreds of credits in stunts, acting, and as a second unit director coordinating stunts. He was not a member of the BSA, and when the Stuntmen's Association of Motion Pictures admitted him, it was not well-received by the BSA. They saw it as tokenism: the group that dominates stunts in Hollywood now has one Black member, and they feel like they've done their part. They are now "integrated."

"So the group decides to hire one Black guy, take one member into the organization, so he acts like it was all because of his efforts that he was accepted into the group, but we had already fought, so naturally they would go get somebody and put them in, so he claims the fact that he was the first Black guy in the Stuntmen's Association, and it kind of rubbed the (BSA) guys the wrong way. Because the only reason they took him in was because of our efforts, and the fighting we had been doing in Hollywood," Alex Brown said.

Throughout the 1970s a few more Blacks were admitted to the Stuntmen's Association and other white stunt groups, and by being in those groups, they had plenty of opportunities to work, since the vast majority of stunt coordinators who hired stuntmen were in those groups.

"They were getting a lot more work than we were. We made the noise and they got the jobs. A lot of them made out pretty well from us raisin' hell," Alex Brown said.

It was ironic that some of the Black stuntmen who benefited the most from the BSA's efforts were not members of the BSA. The traditionally white stunt groups would admit a very small handful of Black stuntmen, but they let them know they couldn't be associated at all with the BSA.

"(The Black stuntmen admitted to the white groups), they didn't want to get involved with us because they were afraid that they would get blackballed, 'cause the white stunt guys were saying that we were too militant. And a lot of them white guys would tell them don't fool with us. And if they wanted to work, don't be messin' with the BSA. They would tell them do not correspond, or mess with us, and they didn't," Willie said.

The BSA's mission was to stop the practice of putting blackface on white stuntmen so they could double Black actors, to open up opportunities for Blacks to work in Hollywood productions, and to move the industry to a place where its artistic output more accurately represented the diversity of American society. Those are all noble and reasonable goals and characterizing them as "too militant" was just a way of stereotyping Blacks as violent in order to discredit them. The first excuse for not using Black stuntmen was they didn't exist. The second excuse was they weren't qualified. The third excuse was they're too militant. It was one massive roadblock after another that was erected to stop them, but they kept going, kept pushing, and kept chipping away at the discrimination and hypocrisy that poisoned the industry.

However, not every original BSA member was able to keep the fight going. They had rent or mortgages to pay, and families to feed. There were about 40 members who trained in Athens Park in 1967-68, but with the dearth of stunt jobs available before the early 1970s, about half of them just could not continue, and by the early 1970s, about 15 to 20 members were active.

"People thought it was a great idea, but you know, along the way, things were so hard, people had regular jobs during then, they thought, it was all exciting, but it was a hard fight. So people began to drop out along the way... It was very few of us that could make a real true living as a stuntman during that time, and that could survive, you know, all the indiscretions and insults in the motion picture business. 'Cause some of us were doing extra work, and some were doing other things. The motion picture business is a hard thing to get jobs in. You had to give up everything if you were really dedicated to it. A lot of guys quit and went on back to their regular jobs," Alex Brown said.

For those that remained, there were brighter days ahead, as the 1970s saw an explosion of movies and TV shows with action-packed plots, as well as a new genre of films, Blaxploitation, and the industry would need many Black actors, stunt performers, and other professionals to help churn out the new material.

**13**

—— • ——

# HIT ME WITH YOUR BEST SHOT

In early 1970 a 37-year-old Black actor, director, screenwriter, play-wright, painter, composer and renaissance man named Melvin Van Peebles was tapped by Columbia Pictures to direct a comedy called *Watermelon Man.* Up to that point, very few feature films produced by Hollywood studios had been directed by Blacks, and this was Van Peebles first shot at directing a feature produced by a major studio.

The plot centers on the experience of a bigoted, suburban white man, Jeff Gerber, who wakes up one morning to find he has been transformed into a Black man, and he completely flips out. Herman Raucher wrote the script, which was inspired by Franz Kafka's *Metamorphosis* and John Howard Griffin's *Black Like Me,* the true story of a white journalist who darkened his skin in 1959 and set out on an illuminating six-week journey through the Deep South to try to experience life as a Black man during Jim Crow. The movie has several themes, but the viewer is left with at least one inescapable conclusion: if a white man were to become Black, it would be just about the worst thing that could ever happen to him. The tagline on the movie poster was "A very funny thing happened to Jeff Gerber. It won't happen to you, so you can laugh."

Gerber is depicted as white in the opening scenes, and then as Black for the majority of the film. During casting, the studio suggested to Van Peebles that they hire a white comic actor such as Jack Lemmon or Alan Arkin to play Gerber and paint him down in blackface after his transformation. Van Peebles said I have a better idea: let's hire a Black actor and put whiteface on him for the opening scenes, and that's what he did, casting Godfrey Cambridge in the lead role.

Van Peebles had gotten to know Willie the year before when he directed an episode of *The Bill Cosby Show* in which Willie had portrayed a boxer. Van Peebles called Willie up and told him he had a small part for him as the elevator operator in Gerber's office building. It would be the second time Willie worked on a movie in a role larger than an extra, with the first occurring when he was in a gang fight the previous year in *They Call Me Mister Tibbs!* In one scene in *Watermelon Man,* the elevator is full of people heading to work in the morning, and Gerber (the whiteface version) pretends to make a pistol out of his index finger and thumb and sticks it in the back of Willie's head. The passengers on the elevator look very uncomfortable, but Willie's character is seemingly oblivious, and he continues to do his job.

In what was perhaps an attempt to make the film's white audience feel better as they walked out of the theater, the final scene Raucher wrote was the clichéd "it was all a bad dream" ending, with Gerber waking up white and realizing his metamorphosis had never happened. He was still white. Thank God. However, Van Peebles wanted to send a distinctly different message, and he prevailed. He filmed the final scene with Gerber, still Black, practicing martial arts with other Blacks—an apparent indication of his conversion to Black militancy. He was embracing his Blackness, not shunning it.

The film was commercially successful, and Columbia Pictures offered Van Peebles a three-picture contract, but the young director said no thank you. *Watermelon Man* was not only the first studio film he directed; it would also be his last. In order to have complete creative control, Van Peebles produced all his films independently for the rest of his career.

In the spring of 1971 the film *Skin Game* was produced at Warner Brothers Studio. It was a comedy western set in the 1850s and starred James Garner as the slick conman Quincy Drew, and Louis Gossett Jr. as Jason O'Rourke, a well-educated free Black man who was born in New Jersey and finds himself hooked up with Drew on a romp through the American West. The plot involves the pair going from town to town with Drew pretending to sell O'Rourke as a slave, but after they get the money they hightail it out of town and run the con again somewhere down the road. Garner, a civil rights activist and self-proclaimed "bleeding-heart liberal" who participated in the 1963 March on Washington where he was seated not far from Dr. Martin Luther King Jr. while he delivered his "I Have a Dream" speech, called the film "a funny movie if you don't mind jokes about slavery."

One thing the BSA didn't think was funny was when a white stuntman was painted down to portray Gossett Jr.'s character as he drove a covered wagon in the film. This was the number one issue for the BSA and the primary reason the organization was formed: to stop the paintdown of white stuntmen. The BSA was now in its fourth year, and it had trained at least two dozen Black stunt men and women, some of whom were working frequently around Hollywood. Directors and studios could no longer use the crutch that they had to paint down white stuntmen because "there weren't any Black stuntmen." But old habits die hard, and some white directors and stunt coordinators were still dining on the malignant stew of racism, cronyism, and economics, giving work to their white stuntmen friends that should have gone to Blacks, and hoping that no one would notice (or just not caring if anyone did notice).

The swiftest way to stop a paint-down is for the Black actor to say no, I won't let you use a white stuntman to double me. The more prominent Black actors in the 1960s, such as Sidney Poitier, Harry Belafonte, and Bill Cosby, could make this demand and it would be heeded. But for an actor who was not yet as powerful in Hollywood, it was more difficult. When Gossett Jr. was cast in *Skin Game*, it was just his fourth film, and he was not yet the Oscar winner and Hollywood legend he would become.

"Lou wasn't a big-time actor at that time. I think the *Skin Game* started really making a name for him. He didn't like it. He didn't like it at all, and he didn't want to go along with it, but you know, if you wasn't Cosby or somebody really, really big then, there wasn't too much you could say if you were Black. But as Lou got bigger in the business he spoke out against it," Willie said.

Gossett Jr. was actually working through other race-related issues on the set of *Skin Game*. Since it was a western movie, there were many cowboys on the set who managed the horses and worked with the actors. Gossett Jr. said many were Southerners who had come to California in search of better work, and they were not happy working with a Black man, particularly one who was starring in a movie. Many of them did their best to sabotage Gossett Jr. on the set, but he handled it with the same dignity and class he showed throughout the rest of his career.

> There were so many ways they could trip me up: put me on a poorly trained or wild horse; place feces in my dressing room; give me a particularly uncomfortable or broken saddle. The first time I found feces in my dressing room, I became physically sick, but I refused to let anyone see my reaction. Calmly, without any emotion, I called for some help from housekeeping, and together we removed the disgusting mess. This type of harassment continued, yet I never allowed myself to express my anger over such repulsive behavior.

Many people in Gossett Jr.'s position would have reacted to these provocations by either starting a fight with the cowboys or raising an issue with the producers over the outrageous treatment, but he did the opposite: he worked to befriend these men. He knew that their actions were not caused by any personal hatred of him, but were done out of ignorance and the intolerance that their culture had fostered in them since they were little boys. And it worked: he ended up forming treasured friendships with many of the cowboys.

When Eddie Smith heard about the paint-down of Gossett Jr.'s stunt double, he immediately went to the studio to complain.

"Eddie Smith went to Warner Brothers about it, and he told Warner Brothers if they didn't do something about it, he was going to go to the NAACP and all of that to create a nightmare for them," Willie said.

At that time Warner Brothers was producing a movie that would be shot right after *Skin Game* in the late spring and summer of 1971. The film was *Dirty Harry* starring Clint Eastwood in the title role, and it would go on to be the fourth highest-grossing movie of the year, as well as spawn a new genre of movies that featured urban cops who bent or broke the law in pursuit of justice. As a movie that featured plenty of action, violence, and chase scenes, there was a need for several dozen stunt performers. In an apparent attempt to make up for the *Skin Game* paint-down, Warner Brothers told Eddie they would hire as many BSA members as possible. They ended up hiring about half a dozen, including Eddie, Willie, Ernie Robinson, Alex Brown, and Richard Washington. It was Willie's first break doing a stunt in a feature film. He was chosen to double Albert Popwell, whose character robs a bank and then fires a shot at Harry, who is calmly shooting at anyone who comes running out of the bank. The fact that everyone running out of the bank was Black may have just been a coincidence, but probably not.

Coincidentally, Willie had gotten to know Popwell the prior year when they spent a few weeks in Las Vegas working with Sammy Davis Jr. filming an episode of the TV drama *The Name of the Game*. Willie was playing Sammy Davis's Jr.'s bodyguard in the episode, and

Sammy could have used an actual bodyguard, especially since his life had been threatened years before for dating white actress Kim Novak, and then repeatedly threatened during his eight-year marriage to white actress May Britt.

As often happens with stunt doubles, Willie got the job in part because he and Popwell resembled each other, as both were very tall with similar features. Willie's stunt in *Dirty Harry* comes right after Popwell's character shoots at Harry, and misses. Harry shoots back and the bullet hits Popwell's character in the right arm. Willie, as Popwell's character, is thrown into the air by the force of Harry's .44 magnum and collapses on the sidewalk. Harry saunters up to Popwell's character, and after some unpleasantries utters the iconic line:

"You've got to ask yourself one question: 'Do I feel lucky?' Well, do ya, punk?"

Willie and some of the other Black stunt performers kept busy by doing extra work when there were not a lot of opportunities to do stunts. Extra work only paid a small fraction of what they could earn doing stunts, but it was better than not getting paid at all. Willie worked as an extra on the TV shows *The Partridge Family, The Fugitive,* and the film *Lady Sings the Blues,* as well as many others.

Several months after *Dirty Harry* was shot, Willie went out partying all night and got home at four or five o'clock in the morning. He went to bed, only to be awakened by the shrill ring of the telephone.

"Hello," Willie mumbled in his baritone.

It was Alan Oliney calling. Alan was a Black stuntman who was working as the stunt coordinator on the set of *Top of the Heap,* a film being shot at MGM. Oliney had gotten his start in the business in 1968 in *Mod Squad,* doubling Clarence Williams III, the actor who portrayed Linc, one of the three members of TV's first—and possibly only—groovy police trio.

"Hey, Willie, this is Alan. Listen, we're on set and we need a big dude to do a fight scene. You want a job today?"

Willie's head felt like someone was banging a gong next to his ear.

"No," he said, and hung up.

Alan was with Harold Jones, Willie's friend and fellow BSA member.

"Let me try," Harold said, and he dialed Willie's number again.

"What?" Willie asked, getting annoyed.

"Willie, this is Harold. Listen to me. This is a really good fight scene. You want to do this."

"Well, when do you need me there?" Willie asked, rubbing his eyes.

"It's nine o'clock now. Can you get here by noon?"

"I'll be there as soon as I can," Willie said, and he got up, showered, and drove to MGM, where a pass was waiting for him at the gate.

Until he got to the set, Willie didn't know anything about *Top of the Heap*, and the only thing he knew about Christopher St. John—the film's writer, director, and lead actor—was that he had a supporting role in the wildly popular film *Shaft*, which had been released the previous year.

*Top of the Heap* is a long strange trip through the mind of St. John's character George Lattimer, a Black man in his 30s who grew up in a small town in Alabama and went on to become a cop in Washington, D.C. The film is set during the week after Lattimer's mother dies, and the scenes weave back and forth between the struggles of his daily life and dream sequences. Lattimer has a complicated and painful life: most Blacks he encounters don't respect him because he represents the establishment that has been abusing them for centuries; whites don't respect him because he is Black; his wife doesn't respect him because he is always angry and not a good father to their daughter; and his girlfriend he keeps on the side lacks self-respect and is always looking to George for money. About the only person George gets along with on a regular basis is his white partner, who also happens to be a crook who shakes down criminals every chance he gets.

Throughout the film, George tries to pretend his mother's recent death doesn't bother him, but it actually is eating away at him. The thing he wanted most in the world was to make his mother proud of him. And he wonders, is she proud of me? What have I done with my life? I became a police officer, but no one really respects me or loves me. Am I just a complete failure? The dream sequences transport George to his alter ego as an astronaut. George wants to be special. He wants to do something great, and what would be greater than being the first Black man to walk on the moon? The viewer sees clean-shaven Black Cop George morph into Astronaut George. The fantasy astronaut wears an orange jumpsuit with the NASA logo emblazoned on the back, sports trapezoidal mutton chops and a finely trimmed goatee, and looks like the most badass fake astronaut who ever pretended to walk on the moon.

The film is melodramatic and absurd at times, but the simple message it conveys is that being a Black man in 1970s America is difficult—extremely difficult. No matter what path you take, you are going to be instinctively disliked and marginalized by at least some segments of society, and as a Black cop seething with rage, George had found a way to alienate just about everyone in his life. The film ends with Black Cop George getting shot in the head in a dark, deserted alley, just as Astronaut George is assassinated in JFK-esque fashion during a victory parade in his hometown following his triumphant moon landing. Despair and despondence. Nothing else is left. The credits roll over the film's title song that begins with the lyrics: "Why do we try to make it better? Tell me what this will get you."

As was *Shaft* and dozens of other films released in the 1970s, *Top of the Heap* was soon labeled a Blaxploitation film. What most of these films had in common is that they featured Black urban characters who were often drug dealers, gangsters, and prostitutes. There was usually a lot of action, fighting, and gunplay, and the heroes and antiheroes were frequently trying to evade or outwit the law. But like all labels, calling something a Blaxploitation movie reduces it, and ignores its intent, nuances, and artistic achievement. When you dig deeper, you see how the themes in these films often address very important issues facing people, both psychologically and physically, even if they do it in a comical or farcical way. It is entertainment, after all.

Willie didn't know any of this when he showed up on the set. All he knew was he had a wicked hangover and Harold had promised him it was going to be a great fight scene.

Oliney told Willie the fight scene takes place in a bar, and they were going to do it together. Oliney would double St. John's character George, and Willie would play the bouncer in the bar. The setup for the fight scene was that George had come to the bar to tell his girlfriend, who was wearing a shimmering gold jumpsuit, sporting a huge afro, and singing that night in the bar, that he was taking her with him. The bar owner intervenes and tells George she has to work and can't leave. George responds with the signature line that he menacingly spews repeatedly in the film:

"I'll do any goddam thing I want," and punches the bar owner in the stomach, knocking him to the floor. Then Willie enters the room as the bouncer and all hell breaks loose.

Oliney and Willie rehearsed the scene a few times and were ready to shoot when St. John changed everything.

"When they got ready to shoot it, Christopher St. John, who was the actor, he decided that he wanted to do it with me, not Alan. That was the worst decision I ever made," Willie said.

Oliney and Willie were very leery. St. John was not a trained stunt-man, and this was an intense fight scene. It may have been that St. John thought doing the scene himself would make the scene look more realistic in the final cut, or it may have been that as the writer, director, and film's star, he felt he could do—as his character would say—any goddam thing he wanted.

Whatever his motivation, Oliney and Willie reluctantly agreed. St. John was the man in charge, and there wasn't really anything else they could do, other than quit.

Oliney and Harold Jones were right about one thing: it was an awesome fight scene. Epic. Pure cinematic gold.

Here is how it looks in the film: Willie the bouncer is planning to toss George out of the bar for punching the owner, but not before he beats the crap out of him. Willie walks through an arch with a flourish, taunting him with "C'mon, you nigger pig." The camera zooms in on George's face and you can see the rage that consumes him when he hears those words. He rears back and punches the much larger Willie in the face, sending him crashing through a thin glass wall. Game on. Willie tosses him into a jukebox, smashing its glass. They wrestle on the bar's bright red carpet. George punches Willie in the stomach, elbows him in the kidney, and sends him sprawling into a table which splinters from the impact. Willie recovers and hurls George across the room, sending him through another thin glass wall. Willie gets George in a headlock and appears poised to finish him off, when George does something that seems to defy the laws of physics. Willie is no longer a wiry rebound machine, but has become a 6'8", 270-pound behemoth, yet George somehow flips the big man over his shoulder and Willie lands on his back. George pummels him viciously in the head. As Willie lies on the ground, seemingly unconscious, St. John holds Willie's right hand and lifts his right side up off the ground, to give him a clear shot at his back.

"Nigger!" George yells, and he kicks Willie in the back.

"Nigger!" He kicks him in the back again.

"Nigger!" He kicks him a third time, and then two guys from the bar jump on George, but the bar owner says, "Let him go." George grabs his girlfriend's hand and, breathless, triumphantly exits the bar with her.

While moviegoers were treated to a scintillating fight scene, it had far more serious and long-lasting implications for Willie.

"Even before he kicked me, we were wrasslin' and hasslin' on the floor, and some way he fell across my right knee," Willie said.

It got worse.

"He knocked me down, and he got me by the right arm, and kicked me in the back, three or four times. That's when he busted my fourth and fifth vertebrae in my back. 'Cause he kicked me wrong, he kicked me straight in with the toe of his shoe, which you're not supposed to do. If Alan had done it—Alan was a stuntman—Alan would have known better, how to kick me."

Willie was hurting when he left the set and he went home to rest, hoping he would feel better in a few days.

"The next day, I had a bad pain in my knee. My back wasn't hurtin' me that bad, but it was hurtin' me. So as the week went on, three or four days later, it just got worse and worse. So I called the Screen Actors Guild, and they told me to go to the doctor. I knew this lawyer, named Harold Gamer. When I wasn't working, I delivered subpoenas and stuff for him, and I called him."

Gamer connected Willie with an orthopedist, and he set up an appointment so they could assess the damage. First, they examined his right knee and told him his kneecap was cracked. Next, they put dye in his spinal cord and conducted a myelogram to see what was wrong.

"They told me the fourth and fifth vertebrae was crushed. One of them, it was cracked and was pressing down on the nerve that went to my right leg. 'Cause today my right leg is slower than my left," Willie said.

The orthopedist explained that he needed knee surgery. He had torn cartilage in his knee, and they were also going to go in and shave the kneecap down. The back surgery would come later, and they would likely need to remove at least one vertebra. Simply put, Willie was a physical wreck. He went home to recuperate, and they set up a date to operate on his right knee at St. Francis Medical Center in Lynwood, just south of LA. With many months of healing ahead of him, his stunt career was on hold.

Willie was lying in a recovery room after the knee operation when the surgeon walked in. His name was Dr. Walter Woods.

"How are you feeling, Willie?" the doctor asked.

"I'm okay. I'm tired, and sore, but other than that, I'll make it."

"Well, the operation went pretty well. We went in there and shaved the kneecap down, and it was soft, real soft. We put a small plate in there to try to stabilize it," the doctor said.

"Okay," Willie said.

"Willie, when did you get steroids?" Dr. Woods asked.

That's an odd question, Willie thought. "I ain't never had steroids," he said.

"Have you ever had injections in that knee?"

"Yes, both knees, when I was in the Air Force," Willie replied.

"How many injections?" Dr. Woods asked.

"Oh, jeez, I don't know, Doc. Too many to count, to be honest with you. I hurt my knees when I got flipped around dunking a basketball, and they shot me up every Thursday, because we had games on Friday and Saturday. That went on for a couple of years. They told me it was just to kill the pain."

"What did they inject into your knees?" Dr. Woods asked.

"Cortisone."

"Willie, cortisone is a steroid. It should be used sparingly. If you get too much of it, then it damages your cartilage, bones, and tissue. Apparently, you received far too much of it. The tissue behind your right knee is like a banana," Dr. Woods said.

"Well, what do we do now?" Willie asked.

"We'll monitor how your body reacts to the plate we put in there, and we'll assess you every couple of months. I'm sorry to have to give you this news, Willie. For now, you should get some rest," Dr. Woods said, and he walked out.

Willie lay there, stunned. If he wasn't so angry, he might have cried. Now it all made sense. The aches, the recurring pain that got a little worse each year. All those shots in my knees. For what? So the Kirtland Air Force Base team could win basketball games? They destroyed my knees to win basketball games? They told me they couldn't win without me, so they did whatever the hell they had to do to get me on the court. I could have been a pro basketball player, or at least I had a shot, and they took that shot away from me. And now they are taking my career away from me. Major Cosner. The doctors. Those sons of bitches.

Willie spent the next year going through operations, recuperating, and doing painful physical therapy. By the fall of 1972 he could get around fairly well again, so he looked for work, and landed a small role as the Watusi chief in the African adventure film *Trader Horn*. They were filming in Bronson Canyon, which was located just north of Hollywood, and included a tunnel that was used to depict the entrance to the Batcave in the *Batman* TV series. The role required him to run down a hill, and then run back up the hill. His knees wouldn't let him. He told the producer he couldn't do all that running. It's okay, the producer said, we'll shoot around you, so they did. But it wasn't okay. One of the things Willie always prided himself on was being a superior athlete, and now he couldn't run, and he could barely jog. He could see his career coming to an end.

A year later, he was offered a small part as a basketball player in a skit on *The Carol Burnett Show*. He didn't know it before he got there, but they needed him to do some jogging in the skit, and he limped through the episode. That's it, he said. I'm done. I can't do this and I'm starting to embarrass myself. But what should he do next? He was receiving a small VA disability pension and with Maureen working, they would be okay. He could sit on the front porch, feel sorry for himself, read the newspaper and listen to the birds sing, but what kind of life is that when you are in your thirties? What would his mother think? No, he didn't go through all that hell in Mississippi to fade away. He always said that whenever he got out of Mississippi, wherever he went, he was gonna be dynamite. So he hatched a plan.

He went to a BSA meeting in 1974 to pitch his plan. All the guys were there, and Eddie Smith was presiding.

"Eddie, listen, I have an idea," Willie said.

"What's up, Willie? The floor is yours."

"Well, you know  how I can't do any more stunts since I broke my back and cracked my kneecap," Willie said.

"Yes," Eddie said.

"Well, the directors and the stunt coordinators keep doing the paint-down, taking work from us. I can't work anymore doing stunts, but I got a little VA pension from the Air Force, and with the wife working, it's enough to get by. Let me be the guy to speak out when shit goes down. Since I can't do stunts anymore, they can't blackball me. I've been dealing with this crap practically my whole life, and I won' take any shit. Let me help you guys," Willie said.

Eddie thought about it. Since he started the BSA seven years earlier, he had always been the front man, the one to mix it up with studios and directors when they didn't do the right thing.

"Well, what do you guys think about Willie's modest proposal?" Eddie asked the group.

"I think it's a great idea," one said.

"Me, too," another hollered from the back.

"Me three," one said as he chuckled.

"Well, Willie Darnell Harris, I hereby name you the new public relations mouthpiece of the Black Stuntmen's Association," Eddie said with a flourish.

"Thank you," Willie said, smiling.

# 14

## An End Leads to a Beginning

Admitting that his stunt career was over was bittersweet for Willie. He had always been a proud and dominant athlete, and knowing that his body couldn't do the things it used to was very painful, both physically and psychologically. However, saying out loud that he was done doing stunts meant he didn't have to pretend to do things his knees and back simply would no longer allow. Thankfully, he had a new mission. Serving as the spokesman for the BSA freed him to broaden his gaze and instead of worrying about his next job doing stunts, he could seek to correct injustice wherever he saw it, or at least give it one hell of a shot.

One of his first crusades involved the Kemper Insurance corporation. From the 1970s through the end of the millennium, the insurance giant marketed itself as the "Kemper Cavalry" in its advertising campaigns. They ran television commercials that showed two dozen men on horseback clad in nineteenth-century U.S. Cavalry uniforms charging across the western plains, their horses kicking up dust and the Kemper flag waving gloriously in the breeze under a pristine blue sky. The concept was that when you needed your insurance company to come in and save the day after an accident or a natural disaster, you could count on the heroic men of Kemper to be there to take care of you. It was a very powerful, persuasive, and patriotic message.

However, when Willie and the other BSA members saw these commercials and ads, they saw something else. They saw all white faces on the cavalrymen. Since the majority of BSA members were also honoring the Buffalo Soldiers through their work riding in parades and educating the community, this was a very big deal to them. They saw the lack of Black cavalry representation in the advertising campaign as another sign of their marginalization. You held us in complete bondage for three hundred years. Then you set us free, only to keep your boot on our throats through the creation of discriminatory laws, economic and educational deprivation, and systemic racism. And even in a case like this, where Black people were given the opportunity to do something great, something worthy of everyone's acknowledgment and respect, you dismiss it. Like it never happened. But it did happen. The all-Black Buffalo Soldiers of six regiments, including the 9th and 10th Cavalry Regiments, served honorably from their formation in 1866 until they were finally disbanded during the Korean War. They were stationed mostly west of the Mississippi because whites in the South and East were not comfortable seeing Black U.S. Army soldiers protecting their communities. Of course, the only reason all-Black regiments even existed in the U.S. military was due to the racism that was prevalent in the armed forces and society overall.

So Willie decided to do something about it. He called Kemper Insurance's headquarters in Chicago and spoke to their public relations officer.

"Hello, my name is Willie Harris, and I am calling from the Black Stuntmen's Association in Hollywood."

"Good morning, Mr. Harris. What can I do for you?" the officer said.

"I would like to talk to you about your TV commercials with the Kemper Cavalry, and all of that," Willie said.

"Yes, we are very proud of them, and we have gotten great feedback on them from a lot of people."

"Well, I don't like them as much as those people you are talking about," Willie said.

"I'm sorry to hear that. Why is that?" the officer asked.

"When I watch them, what I don't see are any Blacks. There are no Blacks in your commercials. Did you know there were Blacks in the U.S. cavalry back in the old west days?" Willie asked.

"I have to be honest and tell you I don't know if there were or not," the officer said.

"Well maybe you should do some research. You will find that there were two cavalry regiments, the 9th and 10th, and they were formed right after the Civil War. They were all Black, and they escorted white settlers across Arizona and New Mexico on their way to California in the 1870s. They protected wagon trains as they moved west, they fought the Indians and captured cattle rustlers, and a whole bunch of other things. They were true American heroes of the wild west, but most folks ain't never heard of them," Willie said.

"Wow, that's really interesting, Mr. Harris, and they were all Black, you said?" the officer asked.

"All Black," Willie said. "You see, the problem with having all white cavalry in your commercials is you are not fully representing United States history."

"Well, it certainly sounds like something we should look into," the officer said.

"Let me tell you something else. Some of the guys in our stunt group are members of the Buffalo Soldiers here in Southern California. They were in the movie *Hello Dolly,* and they rode in the Rose Bowl Parade, and all of that. They would be honored to represent the Buffalo Soldiers in your commercials," Willie said.

"Thank you very much, Mr. Harris. I am definitely going to look into this, and I will get back to you," the officer said.

"Thank you for your time, and I appreciate you looking into it," Willie said, and he hung up.

Willie wasn't sure if he would ever get a call back, or if he would have to call Kemper back to let them know he wasn't going away. But to Kemper's credit, they did call him back, and they asked to be put in touch with the Buffalo Soldiers to discuss putting some Black men in their cavalry commercials. Alex Brown, Henry Kingi, and a few other BSA members were hired to ride in the commercials.

After the problem was presented to them, Kemper did the right thing. The issue is that corporations and advertising firms would consistently need to be reminded that their marketing is lily white and not representative of all Americans.

This type of omission—ignoring the seminal contributions of Blacks in various areas of society—is linked to the cultural appropriation of Black skill, art and influence that has a long and entrenched history in the land of opportunity. For example, the most common perception of an American barbecue pitmaster is that of a jolly and obese white guy who sports a robust beard, sauce-stained apron, and charming Southern drawl. He can be seen on TV food shows explaining the nuances of patiently smoking meats over smoldering hickory sticks and making obtuse references to the secret ingredients in his signature marinades. The truth, however, is that the original American barbecue pitmasters were enslaved Black men in the seventeenth and eighteenth centuries who honed their skills to serve their white masters, and then passed that knowledge on to them. Similarly, Jack Daniel, born in 1849 in Tennessee, has always been considered an archetype of the American craft pioneer. He grew up poor in the tiny city of Lynchburg and created what has become the world's best-selling brand of whiskey. However, young Jack did not create his legendary whiskey by himself, though you would certainly think he came up with the recipe and had the skill to make the smooth libation all on his own, especially since his name is synonymous with Tennessee whiskey. In fact, it was a Black man who taught young Jack how to make whiskey. What some people have known for 150 years was admitted by Jack Daniel Distillery in the mid-2010s—Jack learned the craft of whiskey making as a boy by a former slave named Nathan "Nearest" Green in the mid 1860s. Green is now rightly recognized by the company as one of the most important people in the company's history and his story is told in their marketing materials.

Perhaps the most widespread white appropriation of creative Black innovation and energy occurred in the entertainment industry. In music, for example, the explosive popularity of rock-n-roll in the 1950s and 1960s amongst young white Americans was largely the result of white musicians and record company executives using Black rhythm and blues as the basis for the new genre dubbed rock-n-roll, and creating white stars that achieved far greater popularity than their Black forerunners, a process that scholars have termed "Black roots, white fruits."

Willie and his family lived in Compton for most of the 1970s, and he took Route 110 to get home every day, getting off at exit 10 in Gardena, 10 minutes from his house. As soon as he got off the exit, he could not help but see the sprawling headquarters of the American Honda Motor Company. It was massive. Three blocks long. And every time he saw it, anger swelled in his breast. Willie had been seeing advertisements for Honda motorcycles for years, and they had always bothered him, because he never saw any Black faces.

While Honda became one of the top automobile manufacturers and retailers in the United States in the 1980s—and has remained so ever since—the 1970s was a different story. Before entering the U.S. auto market, Honda was the dominant motorcycle retailer in the country. In fact, the company was founded in 1948 as a motorcycle manufacturer, using leftover engines from World War II generators to power their first models. While Honda made slow inroads into the American auto market in the 1970s, its motorcycle business exploded following the introduction of the CB750 in 1969. It was dubbed the first affordable "superbike," a term for a high-performance motorcycle, and its sales skyrocketed. It became very popular with many demographics, including Blacks. But you wouldn't know that judging from the campaign orchestrated by Grey Advertising. The many magazine ads and TV commercials depicted the freedom and glory of riding a CB750, but they might lead you to believe only white men rode them. Occasionally a woman would be featured, and she was certain to be white, pretty, and usually blonde. For Hondas more economical models, Grey ran a campaign from 1963-1975 focused on the concept that "You meet the nicest people on a Honda." The campaign was designed to change the perception many Americans had that motorcycle riders were rough and unpleasant outlaws. Instead, they showed clean-cut white men riding their Honda bike to work or to an acceptable all-American activity like playing baseball or tennis. When women were included in the ads, usually as a passenger hugging their man, they would be sensibly dressed maidens ready for an innocent frolic on the beach. The campaign was a huge success, but again, no Black faces to be seen.

*Willie Harris, circa 1980*

Willie thought about all of this every time he got off exit 10 and drove past the headquarters. He and his fellow BSA members had been complaining about it for years and they got no satisfaction. They complained to Honda and the company said the ads were created by Grey Advertising. They complained to Grey and the agency told them they couldn't include any Blacks without Honda's approval. One day Willie decided that he was sick of all this crap and figured he would do something about it. He pulled his car into the parking lot of the headquarters, walked in the front door, and asked to see the director. A secretary called upstairs, and a manager came down to speak to Willie.

"Can I help you?" he said.

"Yes, I want to talk to you about your hiring," Willie said.

"Well, you see that sign on the wall? That says we are an equal opportunity employer. If you fill out an application, we will be happy to take a look at it," the manager said.

"I'm not interested in a job here. I want to talk to you about your hiring for Honda commercials."

"What about it?" the manager asked.

"You know the Honda 750?" Willie asked.

"Of course, it is our best seller. What about it?"

"Well," Willie said, "did you know that a lot of Black guys ride the 750? Maybe even more Black guys than white guys?"

"Maybe they do, maybe they don't. I really don't know. I don't understand your point.".

"Well, when I see a TV commercial or an ad in a magazine for the 750 or any other Honda bike, it's always showing white guys, never any Black guys. Why is that?" Willie asked.

"I've never noticed one way or the other, but I really can't help you with this, because I don't have anything to do with it," the manager said.

"I can tell you why it is," Willie retorted, "it is because Honda is racist, and they don't want to show any Blacks in their commercials.

They just want to show white-bread folks because they think show-ing Blacks will give a bad impression, even though Blacks are the ones buying the bikes."

"Listen, I've heard about enough of this," the manager blurted. "I can't help you, and you are going to have to leave."

"What would you say if I told you we are going to picket Honda for being racist?" Willie asked.

"I would say you need to leave before I call security."

"No need for that," Willie said, walking toward the door, "I'm leav-ing, but did you get my name?"

"No."

"Well let me give it to you. My name is Willie Harris. I'm the public relations guy for the Black Stuntmen's Association. If I were you, I would write it upside the wall in red, 'cause you are going to hear from me again," Willie said, and then paused, letting that sink in.

"One more thing: what did MacArthur say after he left the Philip-pines?" Willie asked.

The manager stood silent, apparently unable to retrieve that nugget from his ninth grade Civics class.

"He said 'I shall return.' And believe me, sir, I will return," Willie said, and he walked out.

Now that Willie had put Honda on notice that he was serious, he had to put things in motion. He decided that picketing the headquar-ters was the best way to draw attention to the issue, and he also knew that if he wanted to make an impression on Honda, he needed more than a handful of bikers from the BSA, and the rest of them on foot holding signs. He called a BSA meeting and told the guys they needed reinforcements. Kingi said his cousin ran a motorcycle repair shop and he knew a lot of the bikers, so maybe he could help. Willie went to see Kingi's cousin and was directed to the Chosen Few Motorcycle Club. It was appropriate that he sought help from the Chosen Few, as the club had started as a Black club in the 1950s, but a few years later it became the first integrated motorcycle club in the country. Their white members would get called "nigger lovers" by other bikers, but they would just give them the finger and ride on.

When Willie went down to the club's hangout, he was actually a little scared. He may have been 6'8" and a badass, but an outlaw motorcycle club was a completely different level of toughness. It turned out he had nothing to worry about. Willie explained the situation to the club's leader, and he was very happy to help out. He would spread the word and could certainly get a few dozen bikers down there to support the cause.

Next, he went to downtown LA to the office of a Japanese newspaper. He paid them $100 to run an ad in the edition of their paper that was distributed in Osaka, Japan, the home of one of Honda's founders. The ad accused Honda of being racist for not using any Blacks in their commercials, despite the popularity of Honda bikes among Black men and women.

Then he called the *Los Angeles Times* and was directed to one of their freelance writers, Jack Slater. He explained that they had been fighting with Honda for years about not hiring Blacks in their commercials and they had filed a suit against Honda with the Equal Employment Opportunity Commission, but Honda had generally ignored their pleas. He asked Slater to be at the Honda headquarters the day they picketed and report the story.

Finally, he went to the county sheriff's office—something he could not imagine himself doing voluntarily in Mississippi—and told them they planned to hold a peaceful picket and protest outside Honda's headquarters in Gardena, and he told them the date: Friday, October 31, 1980.

The BSA members and their supporters showed up on Halloween morning and started picketing, walking up and down the sidewalk in front of the headquarters, chanting and displaying signs such as "Over the hill, over the track, Honda won't let me ride because I'm Black." The excitement grew with the glorious roar of several dozen Chosen Few bikers as they came off the highway exit ramp.

Willie and other BSA members were interviewed by the media.

"It seems we're good enough to buy Honda motorcycles, but we're not good enough to sell them," Willie said at the time.

William Upton was at the protest and the cause was personal to him.

"Back in the days, Black people rode Honda motorcycles. Lots of them did, they bought 'em like crazy. But on the commercials you saw on television back then, it was all people who didn't look like me, and Willie went after them," Upton said.

After a few hours of picketing and people driving by honking their horns, the Honda executives looked out the window and decided this needed to end.  They were seeing guys riding Honda motorcycles protesting outside the company's U.S. headquarters. If there is anything corporations detest, it is a hit to their image, so they sent a messenger outside who told Willie they wanted to negotiate. Willie said he didn't want to talk to them, but Ernie Robinson went in on behalf of the BSA. The Honda executives told Ernie they would hire Blacks to ride in their commercials as long as they stopped picketing. When Ernie came out and told everyone, they all agreed to take them at their word, and they ended the protest. High fives all around.

A couple of weeks later, Willie was in Centinela Valley Hospital for another knee operation. The doctors had put a piece of steel in his knee to try to support it, but his body had rejected it, so they were taking it out. While lying in the hospital bed recuperating, he received a call from Honda executive Bill Post Kemp. Honda was ready to deliver on its promise.

"Mr. Harris, we want to get this commercial together, and we would like to offer you the job riding in it," Kemp said.

"Thank you, Mr., Kemp, but I can't ride a motorcycle. I am lying in a hospital after another of many knee operations I have had," Willie said.

"Oh, I'm sorry to hear that, is there someone else you can suggest?" Kemp asked.

Willie thought about it and said "Sure, you can hire James A. Watson Jr. He is an actor doing some part-time work riding on *CHiPs* now, so he would be perfect."

Honda hired Watson Jr. for the commercial and they also hired Black stuntwoman and friend of the BSA Jadie David for the print advertisement.

The battle with Honda was another example of Willies' grit and resolve. He had a way of spotting things that were wrong, assessing the options for making them right, and not giving up until things were changed for the better, or at least until he has tried to right the wrong in every conceivable way. The way Honda had marketed their motorcycles had bothered him for a long time, and he would not let it go.

"Some people think they can keep steppin' on you, keep steppin' on you, and you ain't gonna do nothing, just like if the dude across the street come in here and slap you upside the head and go back across the street, and you don't do nothing, he'll be back tomorrow, he's going to slap you again. So these are things that you have to let people know, wait a minute, I'm not stupid. I can stand up to you. And you stand up. If you believe you're right, you stand up for it. And if you get knocked down, you get up. If you get knocked down again, you get up again. And you let people know, you have pride. You're going to respect me, you don't have to like me, but if you're around me, and I'm dealing with you, you're going to respect me. I don't give a damn what you think about me, but respect me," Willie said.

Alex Brown believes it is Willie's singular tenacity and determination that helped him when he was fighting for justice on behalf of the BSA.

"Willie is very instrumental, and he's got the kind of attitude that he doesn't give up. So a lot of our success is really, truly due to Willie's efforts because he said, 'They can't hurt me 'cause I'm getting a government check anyway.' You know, the more you talk, the less they would work you. But Willie said, 'I'll just keep pushing 'cause they can't stop my check, I'm gonna get paid anyway.' So Willie just kept the fight going with a lot of advertising agencies for one thing. So Willie made a lot of noise. Willie is the kind of guy who don't care about who he asks for things that he thinks are right. So he continues to fight. He really doesn't get a lot of benefit out of what he is doing, he just loves doing what he thinks is right," Alex Brown said.

In the late 1970s Willie went back to Mississippi for a week to visit his mom, who was now living in an apartment in Tchula. He was driving through town one day when he saw his old high school friend Shelly standing in front of the Western Auto store smoking a cigarette, so he pulled into the lot, got out of his car, and started chatting with him. A minute later Bill Turner, the store manager, walked up and spoke to Shelly. Willie stared him down. This was the son of a bitch who had stuck a gun in his face 20 years ago in the Howard Store and threatened to blow his brains out.

Turner looked up at Willie.

"Who are you?" he asked.

"You don't remember me, do you?" Willie asked.

"No," Turner said.

"I was the kid who supposedly stole your cigarettes and called you a liar, and you threatened to shoot me," Willie said. "Do you remember me now?"

"Yeah, goddammit, I do," Turner said.

Willie started walking toward him.

"I hope you don't have your gun on you, but you'll never get into the damn store to get it if that's where it is," Willie said.

"You go to hell, you bastard," Turner said.

Willie got closer and was ready to clock him when Shelly stepped between them. "Willie, don't do it. This isn't smart. Just get in your car and leave."

"Not as long as he's standing here. I'm not going to give him a chance to run in the store and get his gun and shoot me. You promise me that he'll stand here until I get my car and I'll be more than happy to leave,"

"I promise, Willie, he won't move," Shelly said.

Willie looked at Turner.

"You're a lucky son of a bitch that I don't wring your neck off," Willie said.

Willie never could have spoken like that to a white man in Mississippi when he was growing up in the 1950s. It was still dangerous to do it in the 1970s, but it wouldn't result in him getting lynched and the fact that Willie lived in California made it less precarious.

After he had cooled down a bit, he got in his car and drove off, and he never saw Bill Turner again.

"I never forgot about him puttin' a gun in my face. You don't never forget that. It ain't no good feeling," Willie said.

Things didn't get any better for Willie when he tried to obtain part of his dad's estate from his widow Ruby. He had called her several times since his father died to ask about it, and she always said it was still going through the courts. Willie was no fool, and he knew when he was being played. It doesn't take 15 years to settle an estate. Ruby had sent him $500 and he was hoping that was a down payment on what he would receive down the road. He was skeptical, however, that she would do the right thing. He called the courthouse and asked about the estate and was told it had been settled years ago. He wasn't surprised. Ruby had never liked him, though that certainly wasn't his fault. He decided he wanted to go after her to get a piece of his father's estate. He called Mr. Shure from the N. Shure department store, as well as the man who ran the shoe store. He asked both of them if they would stand up for him in court and they said yes, they would be happy to verify that Andrew Davenport had taken responsibility for Willie and Robert when they were boys and always bought their clothes.

Then he called Ruby.

"I'm calling about my dad's estate, again," Willie said.

"What about it?" Ruby said.

"Well, you been tellin' me that it is still going through the courts, but I called the courthouse and they told me it had been settled years ago. Why did you lie to me?" Willie asked.

"Listen, you don't deserve nothing from Andrew. I was his wife. You were lucky you got the $500 I sent you. You ain't nothing but a bum," Ruby said.

"I don't care how you feel about me, but what is right is right. I'll see you in court," Willie said.

"You go ahead and do that. Bring me to court. But tell me something, big man, what do you think the people of Lexington will do to you when I tell everybody you got a white wife? Do you think the Klan will like that?" Ruby asked.

Willie froze. He knew that she had him. Some things had changed since Willie left Mississippi, but many things remained the same. A Black man being with a white woman was still the ultimate taboo, and if everyone knew about it, he wouldn't be safe, so he gave up on his effort to attain part of his father's estate.

The CBS television network has a sports program that has been running under various names since 1960, and it is most commonly known as *CBS Sports Spectacular*. In the late 1970s, in addition to showing a wide variety of sporting events including boxing, tennis, and auto racing, it often featured stuntmen engaging in various contests, such as motorcycle racing and horseback riding. They would set up a decathlon of sorts, with the stuntmen going from one activity to the next to see who was the fastest or the most skilled. Along with millions of other Americans, Willie watched the show on Saturday afternoons, and he noticed one thing that wasn't surprising, but it was maddening: no Black stuntmen were ever featured. So he decided to do something about it.

Barry Frank was a legendary television sports executive, agent, and producer. He created hit shows such as *The Skins Game, Battle of the Network Stars,* and *American Gladiator.* From 1976 to 78 he was also the president of CBS Sports. Willie decided to try to persuade him to hire Black stuntmen for *CBS Sports Spectacular.*

Willie called CBS Sports headquarters in New York City and asked to speak to Mr. Frank.

"Hello, my name is Willie Harris. I am calling from the Black Stuntmen's Association in Hollywood, and I would like to speak to Mr. Frank," Willie said.

"I'm sorry, Mr. Harris, but Mr. Frank is not available. Can I take a message?" the secretary said.

"Yes, thank you. Please tell Mr. Frank that we do not appreciate him doing a stunt show with all white stuntmen and no Blacks. And if we have to, we know where y'all shoot it at, up at Indian Dunes, I'll get some Blacks together and we'll go out when you are shootin' and we'll picket it because we will not stand by and watch us suffer, while y'all pay the white guys," Willie said.

Willie waited about a week and when he did not hear back from Barry Frank, he made his next move. The CBS affiliate in LA at the time was KNXT, and Willie called the station and asked for the sports department. He spoke to Ted Dawson, a gregarious sports reporter, and told him that CBS was being racist by not using Black stuntmen in the sports spectacular program. Dawson offered to come out and interview Willie, so they met at BSA member Len Glascow's house. Willie told them that he had spoken to the CBS sports headquarters in New York and requested that they hire Black stuntmen but had received no response. He asked Dawson if the KNXT wanted to get caught up in this, or if they wanted to report on it. Dawson said he would have the station manager call the New York headquarters and see what he could find out.

A couple of days later, Willie's phone rang.

 Is this Willie Harris?"the caller asked.

"Yes, who is this?" Willie asked.

"The name is Corbett, from Unlimited."

"Yeah, what do you want?" Willie asked.

"Well, I hear you been asking around about getting some of your Black stunt friends on the CBS show," Corbett said.

Hmmnn. Willie didn't like the sound of this.

"Maybe I have. What business is that of yours?" Willie said.

"Well, I'm just telling you, you don't need to be doin' that," Corbett said.

"I'll do whatever the hell I want to do. It's a free country," Willie said, his blood pressure starting to rise.

"I'm just tellin' you, for your own good. If you want to stay healthy, leave it alone," Corbett said.

"Listen, you little punk," Willie started.

Click. Dial tone. Corbett had hung up.

"Son of a bitch!" Willie said as he slammed the phone down.

He could feel the old anger growing inside him. Calling my house. Threatening me. Trying to intimidate me. That's bullshit. I've dealt with a whole lot worse than you. So bring it.

Willie had always spoken to people with respect. His mother taught him that. But it had to go both ways. If someone disrespected him, they did not earn his respect, and calling someone's house and threatening him is very disrespectful indeed.

About a week after Corbett called Willie's house, the phone rang again.

"Hello, is this Mr. Harris?" a woman on the other end asked.

"Yes, ma'am," Willie replied.

"Mr. Harris, I am calling from Barry Frank's office, and Mr. Frank would like to speak to you. May I connect you to Mr. Frank?" the woman asked.

Willie was shocked.

"Yes, please do. Thank you," Willie replied, and she connected the call.

"Mr. Harris?"

"Yes," Willie said.

"Hi, Mr. Harris, this is Barry Frank from CBS Sports. How are you doing today?" Frank asked.

"I'm doing fine, thanks," Willie said.

"Mr. Harris, I've been thinking about your proposal regarding hiring some Black stuntmen for our sports show, and I want to take you up on it. We have decided to use several Black stuntmen in our next show," Frank said.

"Thank you, Mr. Frank, I appreciate that very much," Willie said.

"You're welcome. You know, I had never heard of the Black Stuntmen's Association until I received your message, but we are happy to work with you. Can you give me the names of some stuntmen we can contact?" Frank said.

"Sure, you can call Len Glascow, John Sherrod, Henry Kingi, and Alex Brown," Willie said.

"Great. How about you? Would you like to perform?" Frank asked.

"Unfortunately, I had to retire from doing stunts a few years ago due to injury. I actually just had my seventh knee surgery a couple of months ago," Willie said.

"I'm sorry to hear that. We are going to be shooting up at Indian Dunes. Will you come out and watch us shoot?" Frank asked.

"I would love to, but my knees won't let me drive all that way," Willie said.

"Okay, this is my last pitch," Frank said, "and tell me how this sounds. I will send a car to take you to Indian Dunes and you can serve as one of the judges on the show. Can you do that?"

"I would love to," Willie said.

A black limo pulled up to Willie's house on the day of the shoot, and he got in. They arrived at Indian Dunes after an hour's drive and when Willie got out of the car, he saw Henry Kingi standing with his wife Lindsay Wagner, star of *The Bionic Woman,* and several guys. Kingi introduce Willie to everyone and when he got to the last guy he said, "This is Corbett."

Willie looked at him. He was a little short guy, not much taller than Eddie Smith.

"Corbett," Willie said, and started walking toward him. "You're the little son of a bitch who called my house and threatened me!"

Willie moved closer to Corbett and was about to whoop his ass when Kingi stepped between them, putting his two arms up on Willie's chest to hold him back.

"Willie. Willie. Don't do it. Calm down," Kingi said.

"Listen, Corbett. Don't you ever call my house and threaten me! You don't know me. You don't know anything about me," Willie shouted.

Corbett said nothing and Kingi was able to move Willie away from the group and calm him down. After he shook off his anger, Willie was able to enjoy the rest of the day, watching his guys compete.

The incident with the CBS sports show exemplifies the two things Willie fought so hard for after leaving the Air Force: fairness and respect. It always went back to his mom and the lessons she taught him about always trying to do the right thing, and respecting others, but only if they have earned your respect.

**15**

—·—

## Help on the Way

Marge Ryan was an idealistic yet savvy 26-year-old white woman with a freshly minted law degree from the University of San Francisco when she began her career as a trial attorney in the LA office of the Equal Employment Opportunity Commission (EEOC) in 1979. Spending three years in San Francisco in the late 1970s gave her a chance to see the epicenter of America's counterculture firsthand: the city had become a haven and center of political activity for gays and lesbians who were demanding equal rights; in the early 1970s a group of Native Americans occupied the former federal penitentiary on Alcatraz island for 19 months, claiming the island should be returned to indigenous peoples, as it had been declared surplus federal property in 1964; and the music of the Grateful Dead and aroma of marijuana wafted through the air. It was a groovy place to be, where people with many different backgrounds and interests spouted revolutionary ideas in a setting where they felt free to express themselves.

While many of Ryan's classmates had designs on landing a job at a prestigious law firm, making a boatload of money, and eventually becoming partner, she aimed to use her talent and energy to help improve people's lives.

"It was the 70s, I wanted to change the world. And it wasn't unusual, I was a normal kid. We all wanted to change the world," Ryan said.

Ryan was drawn to the EEOC through an internship.

"My third year in law school I had an internship with the state department of Fair Employment and Housing, which is the state agency that is the same as the federal EEOC. When I got out of school there were tons and tons and tons of jobs that were looking for new law students to take. And the only one that seemed interesting to me was this one with the EEOC, and I thought, that is the kind of work I want to do," she said.

The EEOC was founded in 1965, and its purpose was to enforce the federal Civil Rights Act that had been enacted the previous year. For much of its history, the commission has been criticized for being ineffective. It has historically had a mountainous backlog of cases, coupled with a very low percentage of cases that resulted in a positive outcome for people who have made claims of discrimination against their employers.

However, when Ryan joined the EEOC in 1978, there was a buzz of excitement due to the dynamic leadership of its chair, Eleanor Holmes Norton. When President Jimmy Carter appointed her in 1977, she became the EEOC's first female chair, and she planned to change how the commission operated. She sent Ryan and other newly hired lawyers to Maryland for a six-month boot camp of sorts, and then dispersed them around the country so they could spread what they had learned to the field offices. Norton's idea was for the EEOC's lawyers to learn how to use the law effectively and actually bring lawsuits that changed society, and not just changed the working lives of a few people who actually brought the charges. The goal was to do something grander and more far-reaching, something that could have a positive impact on American culture.

"It was a real exciting time to be at the commission. Everybody was real enthusiastic about what they could do to make a difference in the world," Ryan said.

Being sent to work in the LA office fit perfectly with Ryan's goals. When she got there, the plucky new lawyer saw that the office was operating inefficiently and was overwhelmed with cases. She decided she was going to shake things up—she was young and didn't know any better. She talked to the office's director Jesus Estrada Melendez and said help me, Jesus.

"I said what I want to do is do something for the entertainment industry. And the reason I wanted to do something for the entertainment industry is because I thought what better way to make a difference in culture than to change what we see up on the TV screen or on the movie screen. If we saw Blacks and Hispanics and women being judges or doctors or in everyday jobs that we normally didn't see them in on television, then we would find it more acceptable to have them do those kinds of things in society," Ryan said.

Melendez was on board with her idea, and when cases related to the entertainment industry came in, they were all sent to Ryan, and they also gave her all the backlogged entertainment cases.

"Find one in here that interests you, that you think we can take to trial, and we'll do it," Melendez told her.

She started poring through the cases, looking for the special ones that could have the most impact on society.

"The charges were coming in. We had people bringing in charges on a daily basis. Our offices were always full with people. But when the entertainment cases came in, they would go through an intake process and then be given to me. And I would look at them to see if they were just regular rank and file cases that were like every other case that came in, or if there was something about it that we could take to the next stage. And that's what the Black Stuntmen's Association, that charge was about, that was the first charge that come in that was one of the charges that could make a difference," Ryan said.

The charge that Hollywood studios had discriminated against Black stuntmen was first brought in the mid-1970s. In fact, multiple charges were brought that claimed a system was in place in which jobs were handed out through nepotism and cronyism, thereby excluding just about anyone who wasn't in the inner circle from getting work. In the late 1970s lawsuits were filed against more than 20 studios, claiming that stunt work was not being fairly distributed. In particular, the complaint was that non-descript stunts, which are stunts done by someone who is not doubling a specific character, were not being posted publicly and were all being given to the same people over and over, thereby excluding people who wanted to break into the business, as well as some established stunt performers who wanted to further their careers.

Soon, Ryan got to know many of the Black stunt performers, including Willie, Alex Brown, Richard Washington, Tony Brubaker, John Sherrod, and Jadie David.

When they first met Ryan, Alex Brown and many of the other guys were skeptical that "this little white girl" was going to be able to help them. She was just a kid in her 20s, after all, and she was taking on major Hollywood studios.

Willie remembers how surprised the guys were when they realized they had such a powerful advocate in this young, white female lawyer.

"The EEOC gave us a lawyer and about six months later he got sick and they gave us Marge Ryan, a female, she was just fresh out of law school, and she's the one stuck it to the studios, and things started to change at that time, and then we were beginning to get better jobs, also, because we weren't even gettin' the same pay that the white guys were gettin', and we didn't have the proper equipment needed either, until Marge Ryan started filing charges with the EEOC against the studios and all of that, so they had to come up with a plan to do better by minorities. 'Cause when we started, there were no Black producers, directors, wardrobe, makeup, sound, you name it. We the one opened the door for all of that," Willie said.

"They came in saying, look, we filed 20 lawsuits against all these studios three or four years ago, and they promised us all they were going to put more Blacks in non-descript stunts and they were going to post all stunts at the Screen Actors Guild every day so that we could go in and find the jobs. 'Cause one of the complaints had been, look, we're skilled stuntmen, but we have no way of knowing when the jobs are going to be available because it's only word of mouth, and if you don't have a place where it's posted, then there's no way we're ever going to know. So they agreed to post it at the Screen Actors Guild and then they didn't do it. And they had entered into what is called a consent decree, under a federal court case, and that consent decree gave us the power of a decision that a judge could enforce. So I took the consent decrees, went back to the federal court judge, and said, your honor, these people have promised to do these 15 things. They have done none of them. I think it is time to hold their feet to the fire, and actually make them hire these people now. It's not just a question of did they or didn't they, they absolutely didn't, and they went out of their way not to," Ryan said.

It was a painstaking process to calculate how many potential jobs had been lost. They sat around a table and figured out how many non-descript stunt jobs that had been awarded, but that they hadn't known about, and therefore could not apply for.

"I met Willie and all the other guys came in, and they came in with the stories that they had been to the Screen Actors Guild and not been able to see any jobs posted, that they hadn't been hired for anything, and we were able to go through call sheets for each of those three studios to show exactly how many jobs had been lost for that period of three years. There were probably 25 of these guys that were involved in the litigation, but there really were only 7 or 8 of them that were actively involved. That came to every meeting, helped with providing evidence, and really worked hard on making the case happen," Ryan said.

One of the stipulations in the case that Ryan explained to the BSA guys was that they could not file on behalf of Black stuntmen alone—it had to be on behalf of all minority stunt performers, including women. She requested that the studios be required to pay the amount of lost wages for these stunts to anyone who was of color and who had done two or more stunts in the past three years.

"They said, we can't sue for one group of people, we have to sue for everybody, so we said okay, but nobody else is out there fighting but the Blacks, they said, well, we can do it, but we've got to do it equally for everybody. So we sued, we won. Then everybody out there became a minority," Alex Brown said.

Willie was also frustrated that some others took advantage of the opportunity to cash in on their hard work.

"It was for minorities. We didn't file for Blacks. It was for minorities and women. That's how everything got changed around. And at that time also, when the EEOC commissioner stated that they must hire more minorities, and start an apprentice program for minorities, and don't discriminate against minorities, well some of the white boys went out and got them notarized letters that they were part Indian. Now ain't that something?" Willie said.

While charges had initially been brought against more than 20 studios, Ryan decided to pursue just three, including Warner Brothers and Paramount, as some other studios had made some efforts to comply with the consent decree, but those three had not.

Ryan asked a judge to force the studios to pay the minority stunt performers for all the non-descript jobs, rather than just paying them for the amount that may have gone to minorities, based on the percentage of minorities in the U.S. population.

"I said it was their problem that they didn't post the jobs, so they had to pay for them all. We said they would have had them all if they had the opportunity. You prevented them from having that opportunity." And the judge agreed.

The case was similar to a class action lawsuit, but technically it was the enforcement of a consent decree. Ryan was working with the BSA members to build a case to take to trial, but then the studios conceded.

"We got really close to the trial, but at the last minute, the studios all decided to settle. They decided they would give a certain amount of money, to be divided among the stunt actors, and that they would again post the jobs, and again guarantee non-descript stunts. And this time the (BSA) guys were going to monitor it. Each person got $1,700. So it wasn't a lot of money, but there were people who came out of the woodwork that had done two days of stunts in the past three years, so we had lots of people in this group of all colors that got some of the money," Ryan said.

After the settlement, things did start to improve in Hollywood in terms of diversity, at least to some degree. It did not immediately become an equally represented melting pot reflective of all American citizens, but it was better than it was in the 1960s.

"A number of different things happened at the same time. They started hiring EEO experts. Each studio got an EEO officer who was responsible for making that sure that both in front of the camera and behind the camera, was reflective of society, and so they took the percentage of people of color and tried to get that many people hired on each project. That was their job as EEO director, to try to encourage that kind of hiring," Ryan said.

The experience of fighting the studios together helped create a 40-year bond between Ryan and the BSA members. Whenever they have had a legal question, Marge has always been their first call.

"It was like going to war. It was so hostile with the studios. And nobody had stuck with them for very long, and I stuck with them through the end, until they actually got something, some money, and some work. And I think that is what it was. Nobody had done that before. And I genuinely liked them all. It was always fun to be around them. They would joke with me, and they were just very kind to me. So it was easy to have that relationship grow," Ryan said.

Doug Lawrence is one of many BSA members who is thankful that Ryan took an interest in their case.

"She took it upon herself to go arm in arm with us, into the studios and into corporate America. Every fight that we had legally, she was there with us and for us," Lawrence said.

Ryan was also working on other somewhat similar projects while at the EEOC, including a report on discrimination in the entertainment industry, and issues surrounding the lack of female directors in Hollywood. When future Supreme Court Justice Clarence Thomas was appointed Chair of the EEOC by President Ronald Reagan in 1981, her role at the commission changed, and she eventually served as special assistant to Thomas. As far as the other projects she was working on, the report on discrimination in the entertainment industry was buried, and when she stopped working on the issues related to a lack of female directors, no further progress was made on that front. As an example of how long it can take for any meaningful change to come to some of the more entrenched institutions in Hollywood, the EEOC started investigating why there are so few female directors running major studio projects in 2015—more than 30 years after Marge Ryan was working on the same issue.

# 16

## CRASHING THROUGH THE GLASS CEILING

Evelyn Cuffee grew up as the only Black girl in the small, corn-loving city of Mitchell, South Dakota in the 1940s. Back then, 12,000 souls abided within the city limits, which is located 80 miles west of Sioux Falls. It's claim to fame was—and has been for over a century—that Mitchell is home to the "World's Only Corn Palace." It seems one is enough.

With Mitchell being surrounded by endless farmland and vast open spaces, Evelyn had the chance to ride horses and motorcycles as a kid. She also had six brothers, five of them older than her, and all of that made her a tomboy. She was slightly more than five feet tall, but though she was little, she was fierce.

It may have been because Evelyn's was the only Black family in Mitchell, but the city was not fractured by segregation, like every square inch of the South at the time, as well as places like Sioux Falls. At Mitchell High School she became the first Black cheerleader in South Dakota, a feat that was trumpeted in newspaper headlines as far as Minneapolis, though she couldn't understand why anyone thought it was a big deal. The only thing close to segregation that afflicted her early life was imposed by her daddy: while all six of her brothers regularly dated white girls, she was forbidden to go out with any white boys. He told her that she could date when she graduated from high school and either went to college or left to go live in another city. This, of course, prevented her from dating anyone before she was 18, as the only Black boys in Mitchell were her brothers.

Everyone in Mitchell knew Evelyn and her family, and the only time she felt the sting of racism was when kids from the outlying farms would come into town on Saturday nights, as there really wasn't anything to do on the farm after the sun went down. She was 17 years old in 1950 and was having a good time with her friends downtown until a car rolled up.

"This one little farm girl came into town, riding up and down the street. They would all come on Saturday night to ride up and down our Main Street. So she was in the car with her boyfriend, and she leaned across him and hollered 'Nigger, nigger, nigger, nigger!'" Evelyn said.

Okay, Evelyn thought, I know they are going to go down the street, turn around and come back. So she picked up a rock. Then they did exactly as she predicted, and when they got close, the girl leaned out the window, was about to holler at her again and pow! Evelyn hurled the rock at her and hit her in the eye.  Flabbergasted, the girl and her boyfriend took the rock directly to the police station and filed a complaint against the Black girl who had assaulted them. When Evelyn got home that night, Officer Kellogg was sitting on the front porch with her daddy. There were only two police officers in town, and Kellogg was the one who worked evenings.

"Hi Evelyn," Kellogg said.

"Good evening, Officer Kellogg," Evelyn said.

"Evelyn, what happened tonight?" Kellogg asked.

"What did the girl tell you?" Evelyn replied.

"She said you brought a rock down there and you threw it and hit her in the eye," Kellogg said.

"I did that, but she called me nigger, nigger, nigger, nigger. My name is Evelyn. Everybody in town knows my name is Evelyn," she said.

"That's true, but you can't throw a rock."

"She can't call me that name either."

Evelyn had to go to court with her father the following Monday to answer for her crime. The judge fined her $5 and let her go.

Evelyn left Mitchell after high school, got married, had four kids, split with her husband, and then became something of a globetrotter, working as a singer and dancer in shows across Europe and Asia. By the late 1960s she had settled in Los Angeles and was working as a physical therapist when she met some of the BSA members who were starting to train to be stuntmen at Athens Park. They asked her to come and work out with them, and her spirit of adventure wouldn't let her say no.

Soon she was jumping off the bleachers doing high falls, learning how to throw and receive punches without getting hurt, and learning all the same things the guys were learning.

"I did everything they did. We had to do everything they did—and do it better. Because of how guys think: 'Girls, they can't do this,'" Evelyn said.

Evelyn became an original BSA member because she joined the group shortly after they started training, along with the second woman who joined, Marie Louise Johnson.

In 1971 Evelyn got a call from Calvin Brown and he asked her if she wanted to come out and do a stunt in a movie he was working on, *The New Centurions*, starring George C. Scott and Stacy Keach. Calvin had a bit part as a bank robber, and they needed a young Black woman who he could take as a hostage when the police came to break up the bank robbery.

Evelyn said absolutely, as it sounded like her chance to get back into show business, and maybe this could lead to other work.

It was not surprising that Calvin was playing a bank robber. Thieves, prostitutes, pimps. They were some of the standard roles available to Black actors in the 1970s.

"Back then, that's what they wanted to just portray us as: low-class people," Evelyn said.

So Evelyn went down to the shooting location at an actual bank on Wilshire Boulevard in Los Angeles.

"Calvin and I were in the bank. I was in front of Calvin. When I got up to the teller, he grabbed me and pulled out a gun and said I'm going to shoot her if you don't give me the money. So she gave him some money. He was supposed to drag me out the front door, but he missed the door and hit the window. And the window broke, but the window wasn't the breakaway window, the door was. And we were so lucky, because we didn't get cut by none of the glass or nothing," Evelyn said.

It would appear that they had just filmed a scene similar to dozens of others you would see in a 1970s movie about city cops. However, this was historic. Evelyn had just become the first Black woman to do a stunt in a Hollywood movie, and she did it with Calvin Brown, a man who almost a decade earlier had been the first Black man to do a stunt in a Hollywood movie. Evelyn did not see herself as a pioneer at that moment.

"I was just a stuntwoman. We were just out there. It wasn't that we were trying to put our name up in lights. We wanted to make money, just like the white stunt people did. That's all we wanted," she said.

Evelyn didn't find out until after the filming that the production did not have a permit to shoot, so the local police didn't know that the robbery was staged. Things could have gotten ugly.

"You know, we were Black. And we were coming out of a bank. And a policeman, a real policeman, was going up and down on Wilshire Boulevard. And we could have got shot by the police for real. I was so mad. And they didn't even have any police over there, but the regular police were running up and down the street and looking at us, and we were just lucky."

Evelyn was right that this job would lead to others through word of mouth. In her favor was the fact that she was a Black stuntwoman, which practically made her a unicorn at that time. If a stunt coordinator didn't want to paint down a white stuntwoman—or white stuntman—to double a Black actress, he had very few other options besides Evelyn. Her next job was the following year in *Buck and the Preacher*, a western film starring Sidney Poitier, Harry Belafonte, and Ruby Dee that was shot in Durango, Mexico.  She went on to work in more than 30 more productions, including the epic thriller *Earthquake*, *Hooper*, *Top of the Heap*, and *Airport '77*. She was a stunt double for Pam Grier, Ruby Dee, Diahann Carroll, Teresa Graves from the *Get Christie Love* television series, and others.

Though she did high falls, jumped out of a moving train, climbed a rope hanging from a helicopter and other dangerous stunts, she never suffered any serious injuries, and that was very unusual for anyone who did stunts, man or woman. Compared to her male friends in the BSA, it was also unusual that she never felt discriminated against or made to feel less worthy than anyone else on the set. It may have been because she was so small, her cheerful personality, or she was always needed in productions because as a Black stuntwoman she was such a rare commodity. Whatever it was, she didn't suffer the same abuse as her male friends in the BSA.  She was treated well by the other white stuntwomen she worked with, and she thinks she received equal pay, but she had no way of knowing for sure.

One of the other Black stuntwomen to get her start in the early 1970s was Jadie David. One day she was riding her horse in Griffith Park when Bob Minor rode up next to her and said what she thought was a pickup line: "I'm going to put you in the movies." Jadie was a 21-year-old nursing student at the time, and she planned to get her degree and become an RN, just like her mom. She was a little surprised a few weeks later when Minor called her up and said he was going to help her start her training. She went to Paul Stader's gym and worked out. Stader had been the stunt double for Johnny Weissmuller in the Tarzan movies. She was trained by Bob Yerkes, a stuntman who had run away from home at age 15 to become an acrobat in the circus and did his first stunt in a Hollywood production in 1948. They were some of the mentors who helped her develop her skills. Jadie was well equipped to attempt the daunting world of the Hollywood stunt business, as in addition to riding horses, she rode motorcycles and could swim and dive.

Her first stunt job was in the 1972 blaxploitation western film titled *The Legend of Nigger Charley,* which starred Fred Williamson. She was hooked. She realized she had the chance to make a lot more money as a stuntwoman than a nurse, and it would be much more exciting. She gave up nursing school to pursue a full-time career as a stuntwoman, and she became the fourth Black stuntwoman in Hollywood, after Evelyn Cuffee, Marie Louise Johnson, and Peaches Jones.

The early 1970s turned out to be a good time for someone like Jadie to get into the sunt business.

"I was fortunate because of the other stuntwomen, African American women, where probably the tallest one was 5'6", I was 5'9". And during the period of the Black exploitation films, a lot of the actresses were tall, and one of the actresses that I regularly doubled was Pam Grier. So I fit into a niche," Jadie said.

Jadie knew that situations occurred in the early 1970s where white stuntwomen—and even white stuntmen—were painted down to double Black actresses.

"The (Screen Actors) Guild had sort of lax rules, and it was kind of grey, in terms of paint-downs and men doubling women," she said.

She believes that her status as a tall, Black female stunt performer had its pros and cons, in terms of her getting work.

"Sometimes I wasn't hired because I was a woman and I was Black, but other times I was hired because I fit a niche," she said.

Jadie knew all the guys in the BSA and was friendly with them, but she never officially became a member of the group. She did join the United Stuntwomen's Association, which was multiracial. It was not important to Jadie at the time that she officially join the BSA—what was more important to her was they were all working toward the same goal.

One incident where she was treated unfairly was when they were filming a scene with her driving a car that was to end up in a lake. The stunt coordinator told her to drive the car up to the edge of the lake. Then he told her to get out of the car and they replaced her with a white stuntman, who proceeded to drive it into the lake. The stunt coordinator told her that they didn't want her driving it into the lake because she wasn't scuba certified. However, after the scene she learned that the stuntman they used to drive into the lake was not scuba certified either. One reason the stunt coordinator would give the job of dumping the car in the lake to someone else is because that part of the scene is what earns the big money.

"That is kind of common in this business, in that stunt coordinators, not all the time, but often, will hire their friends, other legitimate stunt people. They want to give the work to their friends. It's like, if I give you a job, you'll give me a job," she said.

So Jadie may have been denied the lucrative money for that stunt due to racism, sexism, the fact that she was not part of the old boys' network of stuntmen, or a combination of all the above.

In 1977 the television series *Logan's Run* was being produced at MGM Studios. The series was based on the 1967 science fiction novel by William F. Nolan and George Clayton Johnson which depicts a dystopian future in the twenty-third century where all humans are required to submit to voluntary execution when they turn 21 years old. A casting call went out for stuntmen which specifically stated they were not looking for any African Americans. Jadie and her fellow Black stunt performers saw the posting and joked to themselves: "What, are there no Black people in the future?" But they were annoyed, so they complained to the studio and as a result, both she and Tony Brubaker got hired to work on the show. It was this constant vigilance, this relentless pursuit of equity that characterized the fight of the Black stuntmen and women. In their totality, all of these moments that drew attention to an unfair situation were responsible for Hollywood eventually opening its doors to people of color.

"Sometimes these weren't major things, but they were small things that marked steps along the way," Jadie said.

Unlike Evelyn Cuffee, Jadie was not as fortunate when it came to injuries. One of her worst occurred during the filming of the 1977 thriller *Rollercoaster*, which starred George Segal and Timothy Bottoms. They were filming a scene at the now defunct Ocean View Amusement Park in Norfolk, Virginia, which was located directly on the Atlantic Ocean. Jadie was amongst a group of six stunt men and women—Black and white—who were there to do a stunt in which they would be thrown from The Rocket, a big, rickety old rollercoaster that was built in 1927. The group of stunt performers surveyed the planned stunt and decided it was too dangerous. They told the stunt coordinator they wanted more money. There was a back and forth between the stunt coordinator and the producers and the stunt coordinator came back to the group with a simple message: you're fired. Jadie thought that was the end of it, but as they were getting ready to leave town the next morning, the producers came back to them and told them we really need you to do this stunt.  There were three stuntmen and three stuntwomen in the group, and the other two stuntwomen said no, we're leaving. Jadie thought about it and said, well, if the guys are doing it, then I'm going to do it. The four remaining stunt performers made a deal, and the stunt was back on.

The plan was to have two stunt performers get thrown to the left, and two to get thrown to the right. Jadie was to be thrown to the right along with the big, brawny, blonde stuntman Diamond Farnsworth, whose father Richard Farnsworth was a stuntman and actor who had done his first stunt in the Marx Bros. film *A Day at the Races* back in 1937.

The crew had prepared the landing spot for the stunt performers by digging up the sand the night before, softening it up. The problem was that being on the Atlantic Ocean, the morning dew rolled in and packed it down hard, really hard.

"When we went off the rollercoaster, we just hit hard sand. And it felt like when the rollercoaster went off of the tracks it pitched us a little bit, so instead of going down, we kind of went up and down. It was like a disaster. Diamond broke his pelvis, and I broke my back," Jadie said.

While those injuries forced Jadie and Diamond to take a few months off to recuperate, both were back at it shortly thereafter, and each did stunts for the following two decades. Such are the lives of stunt performers.

As painful as the broken back was on the set of *Rollercoaster*, that was not even Jadie's worst injury doing stunts. A few years later she was asked to do a stunt in the television game show *Truth or Consequences*. The premise of the show was that contestants would be asked a question that they generally were unable to answer, and if they didn't come up with the "truth," (and the producers made sure that getting the answer correct was almost impossible), then they would have to face the "consequences," which usually meant performing some outlandish stunt. Sometimes the contestants would perform the stunt, and sometimes they would be done by a stunt double. In one episode, Jadie was doubling a woman and had to jump off a building. The idea was that the woman's husband would be watching from the ground and be stunned and terrified that his wife had just jumped off a building. That's Hollywood.

Jadie flew off the building onto an airbag set up several stories below, but rather than landing on her back, she landed on her buttocks, and she blames herself for that, calling it "pilot error."

"I hit the air bag, and I hit kind of like rear end first, and my vertebrae jammed into each other, and decimated one of my vertebrae. There was nothing left there, nothing to protect my spinal cord. Luckily, I'm walking today, because for all intents and purposes, I should be paralyzed. And it resulted in like nine hours of surgery. I lived in sort of a body casing, which was like a new kind of cast, that was riveted shut, so for a year I had to wear this thing."

Other than breaking her back and crushing her vertebrae, Jadie suffered from the usual ailments that afflict stunt performers: bad knees, bad hips, and the general bodily abuse that is part of the profession.

Jadie's work in the stunt business, however, did not start and end with her risking her health and life. In the 1970s in particular, she worked very hard to expand opportunities for minorities to work in greater numbers in many different jobs on Hollywood productions. She was one of the people who documented cases where minority stunt performers were missing out on job opportunities due to the entrenched old boys' network of the Hollywood stunt industry, and she brought those cases to Marge Ryan of the EEOC so she could tell a judge: Look, this is what is happening out there.

Jadie is proud of the work Black stunt men and women did to move things forward in Hollywood.

"I often like to think that the work we did back then opened up the door for more African-American people of color and women, and there were some amazing people that walked through that door. I am so proud of the talent that is there now. I have nothing but praise about them, because some amazing people walked through that door."

Jadie fought side by side with the BSA in their struggle, and she understands and appreciates everything Willie and the other guys in the Black Stuntmen's Association did to help open up Hollywood: every insult they suffered, every dangerous stunt they attempted with little support from their peers, and every time they didn't give up when it seemed no one wanted them around.

"It was absolutely essential that the BSA be there to pave the road."

While very proud of all the changes they were able to effect in Hollywood, Jadie realizes the work is never done. No one is holding up a sign that says Mission Accomplished.

"There was a huge change, and it had a lot to do with the work that we did in terms of diversity. We were pretty vocal and were responsible for a lot of change. Unfortunately, even though the business now isn't as bad as it was back then, there are still some huge problems and things that need to be mended because we should be further than we are right now," Jadie said.

The mindset is similar to that voiced by John Lewis, the eloquent civil rights icon from Alabama who served 33 years as a member of Congress representing Georgia's 5th District.

"Our struggle is not a struggle that lasts for one day, one week, one month, or one year, or one lifetime. It is an ongoing struggle," Lewis said in 2013.

# 17

— · —

## WATCH YOUR BACK

Working as a professional stunt performer is intrinsically one of the most dangerous jobs there is, but if you are a newcomer, and someone who is not welcomed by the more experienced colleagues you are working with who—if they displayed a baseline of concern for their fellow human beings—should be helping you to be successful and stay safe, that increases the danger exponentially.

The BSA members endured insults, inequities, and abuse that others who felt entitled would never tolerate. Those who were born into white families of stunt performers felt that the work was their birthright, and that they could and should do whatever was in their power to stop others, especially upstart Black stuntmen, from taking *their* work away from them. The paint-downs, the doubling of women, and the old boy network had worked just fine for them for decades, so they saw no reason for it to change.

When someone is new at a job they are normally guided by the existing staff and shown how to get the work done so they can be successful and contribute to the organization. On the contrary, a Hollywood set in the 1960s and 1970s was often littered with selfish independent contractors, each primarily concerned with their own fortunes, not interested in helping anyone else—and sometimes actively working to sabotage their co-workers—especially if they believed the new person threatened their ability to earn money, or if they were just straight-up racist.

William Upton is very clear about the lack of support the new Black stuntmen received from most of the white stuntmen when they started working.

"Back then, we had a lot of racist sons of bitches. They were Caucasian, yes they were, they would try to get us killed in this business," said Upton, who performed stunts that involved scuba diving, high falls, fire, motorcycles, horse falls, car stunts, air ramps and explosions.

"That's how so many Black guys got hurt." Willie said. "We didn't have proper safety equipment. And if you got busted up, they'd say 'I told you them darkies didn't know what the hell they was doing'. It wasn't that we didn't know what we was doing, we didn't have the type of equipment to protect us as they did. And if you didn't do it in one or two takes, you got fired. But the good old boys, they take as long as they wanted to do their stuff. But we didn't have that luxury. They'd tell you to meet them somewhere. They didn't tell you what to bring, or nothing. Say they wanted you at Universal at 9:30 in the morning to do a stunt on one of them shows. They don't tell you what you need or nothing. And you'd show up, you might be falling off a truck or whatsoever. You have no pads or nothing, and they wasn't going to loan you any."

Eddie Smith injured his leg doing a stunt in which a helicopter crashed on the set of the film *M*A*S*H* in 1969. The injury gave him a limp for the rest of his life, but at the time he didn't mention it to anyone on the set.

"I couldn't mess it up for the rest of the group, man. We fought too hard. We had to show ourselves," Smith said.

Henry Kingi is one of the BSA's original members and is of Native American and African American descent. After breaking through with the BSA, he went on to compile more than 200 credits for his stunt work, and more than 80 acting credits in Hollywood productions. Some of his films where his work appears include *Live and Let*

*Die, Close Encounters of the Third Kind, Scarface, Predator, Bad Boys,* and *The Lost World: Jurassic Park.*

"Our thought was that you'd have to be better than good to get the job. All they needed was to have one of us mess up so they could say, 'See, they don't know what they're doing,'" Kingi said.

Henry Graddy was one of the original members of the BSA who had been recruited by Eddie Smith at its inception. Like Willie, Henry had grown up in Mississippi during the 1940s and 1950s. He was born in Meridian, which was also the birthplace of James Chaney, one of the three civil rights workers murdered in 1964 in nearby Philadelphia, Mississippi. Chaney, Andrew Goodman, and Michael Schwermer were murdered by a gang of Ku Klux Klan members after having been handed over to them in a deserted area outside of town by the local deputy sheriff, a fellow Klansman. Their murders and the aftermath inspired the 1988 film *Mississippi Burning,* which was nominated for seven Academy Awards. Graddy knew what discrimination felt like. He had felt the sting of racism during the first 18 years of his life in Mississippi. He felt it when he moved to Detroit and Chicago as a young man, and he felt it all his time in California, where he moved in 1957. He had been discriminated against so much that when he started working on Hollywood sets in the late 1960s that sometimes he didn't even notice the discrimination. He was so used to it—it was such a regular part of his daily life.

"After you've been discriminated against so much, you kind of forget about that, not forget about it, you just do something and keep going," Graddy said.

Doug Lawrence agrees that when the BSA members first started working, they were mostly out on their own and had to navigate what was usually a treacherous work environment.

"The white guys wanted us hurt, and then they didn't have to hire us if we were out hurt where we could not work. So they put us in situations where we were more prone to be hurt, as opposed to getting our little money, and going home every night. On a show up in San Francisco, as an example, the guy that taught me how to use an air ramp, he was a stunt coordinator, very well known. I'm not giving his name. But he was the coordinator on this show in San Francisco. I was being chased by a car, and we simulated me being hit by the car, where I flew through the air and landed on the hood of another car. Well, he didn't turn the air ramp on, and I did not know that the final responsibility was mine, so I did not check. I'm guilty as charged. But I got hurt. My knee hit the bumper and that blew up, and my face and mouth hit the hood, and of course, that blew up. But we turned around and said, let's do it again," Lawrence said.

As hard as it was, what they endured in the early days of their careers helped forge a lifelong bond amongst the BSA members, and the fact that they succeeded is something they can look back on and be proud about.

"My biggest pride was the fact that, all the way back in the 70s, once our six guys started working pretty regularly, we realized what the white guys were doing to us. They put us out on the jobs, sure, but we didn't get any rehearsal times, practice, or any of that, where those guys, the white guys, always did, so we were being subjected to a lot of danger, and working in the blind, so to speak. We had a car stunt to do, we hadn't driven the car, where those guys had the opportunity to do the actual stunt in rehearsal, we never did," Lawrence said.

Alex Brown remembers that when they first started working on movie and television sets the BSA members would routinely get insulted and called nigger by the white stuntmen.

"You were always a little apprehensive about who you were working with, because you could get some of them that didn't buy into the fact that we wasn't going away, so you were subject to get hurt," Brown said.

Black people were rarely found on the sets back in the late 1960s and early 1970s, before the Blaxploitation films started being made. The BSA members were usually one of the only Black people on the set, and importantly, there was almost never any Black person working in the production who was in a position of authority. The BSA members were usually out there on an island, and they had to have guts and determination to keep going, because there was rarely anyone there who was inclined to help them.

"You are only as good as the people you work around. So any job you were working around that involved explosions you were susceptible to getting hurt. So you would never know where it would come from. You know, it could come from the special effects man, it could come from the stunt guys. So you would always have to watch your back," Brown said.

Once the BSA members started working as stuntmen, they realized that in order to continue to get work on a regular basis, they would need to have some of their members advance into roles as stunt coordinators, because the stunt coordinators hire the stuntmen and women. This has been a decades long struggle.

"There are still not a lot of Black stunt coordinators," Brown said. "That's the key to success in this business: being a coordinator. Now you have a lot of responsibility because we did have a couple of guys coming along, like Alan Oliney used to run a lot of stuff, but then somebody got killed on his show. Once somebody gets hurt on your show, it kinda stays with you. A lot of deaths happen on jobs, because the director is going to look at that coordinator and say 'what do you think. Is this possible?' Directors, all they have is an idea, and they want to see it come to fruition. So the coordinator has got to be very imaginative."

# 18

## TAKE IT TO THE HILL

When Willie was fighting for the rights of his brothers and sisters in the Black Stuntmen's Association and the Hollywood community at large, he was finally able to exercise some of the privileges supposedly granted to all Americans in the Bill of Rights—the freedom of speech, freedom of assembly, and freedom to petition. Up to that time, he had spent most of his life being told what to do, when to do it, and how to do it. Back on the plantation it was Peyton Abbott Jones and his teenage son controlling his family's life. In the Air Force it was his superior officers telling him he had to play basketball, despite his injuries. Willie had an innate and ferocious pride and iron will. He wanted to be great. He knew he could be great. But like every other person born into a poor Black family in America in mid-twentieth century America, it was a constant uphill struggle. Straight uphill, with roadblocks forever being placed in their way.

Working for the BSA to help open up Hollywood was fulfilling yet exasperating. For every victory, there were just as many setbacks, usually more. People don't release their power willingly; it must be taken through a struggle. As hard as it was, it made Willie part of a community of people working for a goal much bigger than themselves. The bulk of their work occurred during the late 1960s and the decade of the 1970s. America was changing, incrementally, and they were helping change it. By 1980 the America that Willie saw was different than the one he had grown up in. There was more opportunity for Blacks, but it was relative. They had been down for so very damn long that any improvement felt like a step forward.

After more than a decade of fighting, the BSA could be rightly proud of the fact that where there once was only one Black stunt performer—Calvin Brown—now there were about two dozen, and many of them had carved out long and lucrative careers. More Blacks were also seen on movies sets in roles more substantial than janitorial or food service. It was not a flood of dark faces, but some were there. While Willie could feel good about what they had accomplished together, he was simultaneously fighting his own private battle. His knees kept deteriorating. The words Dr. Walter Woods said to him after his first knee surgery echoed in his head: "Cortisone is a steroid. It should be used sparingly. If you get too much of it, then it damages your cartilage, bones, and tissue. Apparently, you received far too much of it. The tissue behind your right knee is like a banana."

As his knees got worse, his nightmare began. The number of surgeries piled up. Between 1972 and 1990 he had 15 knee surgeries, and long, thick scars from the surgeon's scalpel kept getting etched into his skin, zigzagging across his flesh like a horribly ill-conceived piece of modern art. At the same time, his regularly occurring pain increased, and his mobility decreased. By the mid-1980s, this once graceful and dominant athlete was in pain every time he stood for more than a few minutes, and his limp had now become a regular part of his gait. The surgeries were done to try to reinforce his failing knees and hopefully keep him from being stuck in a wheelchair someday. But every time they operated, the recovery period meant even more pain, and more anger. He was consumed with rage at what they had done to him, all so he could slam dunk a basketball for his base's team.

He needed to make the Air Force pay. They had ruined his health, and when you don't have your health, a slew of other terrible things can conspire to bring you down, and if you can't stop things from continuing to disintegrate, you may never get back up.

Willie's quest to obtain reparations from the Air Force began shortly after his first knee surgery in 1972. The pain and lack of mobility were relatively mild back then, as long as he didn't stay on his feet for long stretches at a time. However, the doctors had told him it would get progressively worse, and he dreaded the future. He had a friend named Ruth Sparkman who was a law student at California Western School of Law in San Diego. Willie had heard about something called a Correction of Military Records. It involved petitioning the Air Force to change his discharge documentation to indicate that the excessive amount of cortisone injections had caused his knee problems, and therefore, the Air Force would be liable for starting the process that would eventually destroy his knees. When he left the Air Force, he was only given a small severance payment and the right to free health care at the VA hospital, but nothing else. So Ruth and Willie headed off to the Orange County Public Law Library in Santa Ana, just south of LA. They researched the procedure and requirements for filing a request for a Correction of Military Records. Willie filled out the paperwork and filed the request. The Air Force rejected it. They disagreed with his contention that the military doctors had caused his injuries. For most people, that would have been the end of it, but Willie was not most people—he was just getting started. In hindsight, he knew he had rushed into it. If you are going to attempt to obtain justice from something as massive and powerful as the U.S. military, you had better be prepared with experts and influential allies to help plead your case.

In March of 1973 Willie was examined by orthopedic surgeon Dr. Robert B. Salisbury, and after the exam the doctor wrote a letter to the VA Regional Office in LA with his opinion regarding Willie's knee injuries:

"As regards the patient's prior history, it is my feeling that his onset of chondromalacia [inflammation under the kneecap and softening of the cartilage] symptoms in the service coupled with multiple hydrocortisone injections would make the service liable for his disability. I believe it has been well established that multiple cortisone injections, while stopping the pain for the moment, do hasten the degenerative phenomenon in arthritic knees.

The patient's present status is that he is incapacitated for any work requiring prolonged standing or walking or any active use of his lower extremities. He has had acute bouts of depression secondary to this situation, having been an extremely active individual in the past. As a former military orthopedic surgeon and an attending orthopedic surgeon for the Veterans Administration Hospital in Long Beach, I believe it would be in the best interest of the patient and the Veterans Administration to have his disability status reviewed in light of these findings."

Now Willie had documentation that he had been wronged, and it was from a respected orthopedist who also worked for the VA. The doctor believed the Air Force was liable for Willie's diseased and deteriorating knees and he thinks they should review his disability status. Shortly after receiving this letter Willie ran into a lieutenant he knew from the Air Force who told him about a lawyer named Richard P. Fox. "Go see him, Willie. I think he can help you," he said.

The lieutenant had told him that Fox was a former military man who had served in the Judge Advocate General's Corp (JAG) in the Army. So Willie went to Fox's office and sat down in a cushy leather chair.

"Willie, I think you have a pretty good case to have your disability reviewed and increased," Fox said.

"I sure hope so," Willie said. "When they rejected my request for a Correction of Military Records, they told me the statute of limitations, which was two years, had run out."

"Well, there is a statute of limitations, but the clock starts ticking on that when you find out that your disability was service related. You just found out about the steroids last year, so we are in good shape there," Fox said.

Willie just sat there and smiled. It felt great to finally talk to someone who might be able to help him fight the Air Force.

"Don't worry, Willie. I know how the military lawyers think. I used to be one of them. We'll take care of this," Fox said.

"I like what I am hearing, but how much is this going to cost?" Willie asked.

"I'll charge you $700," Fox said.

"I don't have $700."

"Don't worry, Willie, you can pay me in installments," Fox said.

"That sounds great," Willie smiled. He pushed himself up out of the chair, reached across the desk and shook Fox's hand, which disappeared inside Willie's massive paw.

"Thanks for coming in Willie. Just make sure you duck when you go through the doorway. We don't need any more injuries," Fox said.

"I'll be careful," Willie chuckled.

Fox was able to help Willie convince the Air Force to increase his disability rating from 20% to 30%. This was significant, because if your rating is at least 30% you qualify for a military retirement. It took a couple of years to finalize, but in 1976 Willie started receiving a small monthly pension check from the Air Force, as well as a $17,000 lump sum payment for his pension from 1967-1976.

Willie wasn't done, however. Far from it. The pension gave them a little base of funds and with Maureen working they could get by. But the slim pension didn't address the medical malpractice the Air Force doctors committed with all those steroid injections. He began fighting battles on two fronts. As his knees continued to deteriorate, he petitioned the VA to increase his disability percentage, which they slowly did over the next two decades.

His main foe became the Air Force, as he wanted to sue them for crippling him. Willie built up more evidence to bolster his case. In 1981 he asked Dr. David Casey, Chief of Internal Medicine at Kaiser Permanente Medical Center in Bellflower, California to write a letter to the Air Force on his behalf. Dr. Casey had been treating Willie for several years for osteoarthritis and he stated in the letter:

"His condition was undoubtedly exacerbated by repeated injections of corticosteroids intra-articularly, a treatment that is now known to precipitate early changes in the cartilage of knees which in turn progresses to osteoarthritis at an early age. It is my opinion that because of these circumstances, every consideration should be shown to Mr. Harris regarding his application for disability."

He obtained his medical records and found a handwritten note in his chart from his examination by Dr. Pamela Prete, the Chief of Rheumatology at the Long Beach VA Medical Center. Prete, a 21-year Air Force veteran who had attained the rank of colonel, wrote "Mr. Harris, a former basketball athlete received numerous steroid injections into his knees. This was not standard medical practice for the medical community," and she underlined the last sentence.

In 1982 Willie filed a claim for damages with the Air Force, stating that his knees had completely deteriorated from the steroid injections he received from the military doctors. He quickly received a letter from the USAF Office of the Judge Advocate General denying his claim. The denial letter stated:

"Your claim, alleging medical malpractice in February 1963 at Patrick AFB, FL, has been considered under the Federal Tort Claims Act. 28 U.S.C. 2671-2680, and is denied. The reason for this decision is that the available medical evidence fails to establish a connection between any Cortisone injections you received in 1963 and your present condition. Additionally, as your claim is barred by the statute of limitations, as well as by the holding in the United Sates Supreme Court case of Feres vs. United States, 340 U.S. 135 (1950), which excludes claims arising out of active-duty service."

In other words: you can't prove that the military doctors crippled you. Even if you could prove they crippled you, you're too late to seek compensation. And even if you weren't too late to seek compensation, a Supreme Court case from 1950 set a precedent that prevents you from suing the military for damages anyway. One. Two. Three strikes. You're out.

Feres vs. United States. Willie had never heard of that, and he needed to learn more about it, so he looked it up. Lt. Rudolph J. Feres had served in World War II as a member of the 501st Parachute Infantry Regiment. He jumped into Normandy on D-Day and fought in Europe for three and a half years. He earned three Bronze Stars, the Croiz de Guerre of the French Government, as well as awards from the Dutch and Belgian governments. Rudolph had enlisted in the U.S. Army in 1935, and in 1940 he married his sweetheart, Bernice Bunnell. When he returned from the war, they had a son in 1946 named Ward, but less than a year after the birth of their son, Rudolph was burned to death on December 10, 1947, in a barracks fire at a U.S. Army base in Pine Camp, New York, just a few miles from the Canadian border. He had been training with 1,600 other soldiers in Exercise Snowdrop, a U.S. Army experiment designed to test human endurance and the effectiveness of equipment if they were to fight a war in sub-zero conditions. The fire started in the middle of the night and quickly engulfed the barracks. At least eight officers escaped the inferno by jumping to safety out of the two-story building's windows, but Feres and four other officers—all WWII veterans—were killed in the blaze.

There were indications that the fire was caused by a faulty boiler in the barracks, and that the Army knew it was dangerous. In addition, the staff assigned to fire watch was insufficient, and it took 45 minutes for the fire department to respond, even though it was located on the base, not far from the barracks. Bernice filed a $100,000 lawsuit against the Army for negligence under the Federal Tort Claims Act. The act permits private parties to sue the federal government for injuries or deaths caused by the intentional actions or negligence of anyone acting on behalf of the federal government. The suit was dismissed in court, but she appealed it all the way to the U.S. Supreme Court. When it got to the Supreme Court the Feres case was considered in combination with two other suits brought by soldiers or their families. In one, an Army doctor left a 30" long towel marked "Medical Department U.S. Army," inside a soldier during surgery, and the other involved an alleged botched surgery by Army doctors that led to a soldier's death.

The Supreme Court ruled that the federal government is not liable for injuries or deaths of service members that occur while they are on active duty and that are caused by the actions of others in the military. This means that if an active service member is subjected to medical malpractice by military doctors that—if it happened to a civilian—would result in liability for the doctor, the injured party cannot sue. Even if a service member is raped by another service member, they can't sue. This ruling—which became known as the Feres Doctrine—has had lasting implications for military members and their families for decades, including Willie.

Willie was up against another brick wall with the Feres Doctrine. In early 1985 he reached out to his district's member of Congress, the larger-than-life former actor and talk show host Bob Dornan. A hard-right Republican on the surface—he earned the nickname "B-1 Bob" for his support of the B-1 Bomber—Dornan was a complex character. His personal credo was Faith, Family, and Freedom. He was an Air Force fighter pilot in the 1950s before acting in several television series and hosting his own radio show in the 1960s. He also participated in the March on Washington for Jobs and Freedom in 1963 and helped get Blacks registered to vote in Mississippi the following year. He participated in the civil rights movement because the U.S. Constitution was sacred to him, and he believed in fighting for equal opportunity for all Americans. Like Willie, Bob had enlisted in the Air Force at a young age, and like Willie, he always stood up for the underdog. Though they came from different worlds, they felt a bond when they met.

Bob listened carefully as Willie sat in his office and told him the story of what the military doctors had done to him 20 years earlier. Bob loved and respected the U.S. military. It was the shield that protected the greatest country on earth. He had proudly served five years active duty and another seven years in the reserves. However, he believed in the rights of the individual, and it galled him to see someone get squashed by such a behemoth with no way to fight back.

"So Bob, is there anything you can do to help me?" Willie asked.

"Actually, I think there is," Dornan said. "Have you ever heard of a private bill?"

"No."

"Well, Willie, a private bill is a bill that if made into a law, would apply to only one person. It is different from the vast majority of bills, which are essentially public bills, and they apply to everyone," Dornan said.

"Well what would this private bill do for me?" Willie asked.

"Well, if we can get it passed, it would allow you to sue the military for medical malpractice. That's the only way to get around the Feres Doctrine."

"Yessir! That would be great," Willie said as he clapped his hands.

"Well, don't get too excited just yet, Willie. These bills are hard to get passed, but I am going to try like hell to push it through for you," Dornan said.

"I appreciate that very, very much. Thank you," Willie said.

And that is what Dornan did. On August 1, 1985, he introduced House Resolution 3223. The bill started with the following text:

"The United States shall be liable to Willie D. Harris for any injuries he suffered in connection with steroid injections administered to him by armed forces medical personnel during his service in the United States Air Force."

Dornan issued a press release the following day which explained his support for the bill.

"At age 19 Mr. Harris could slam-dunk a basketball. But at 43, he can barely stand long enough to make a pot of coffee... Mr. Harris played basketball in the early '60s for Kirtland AFB, New Mexico. For two of those years he played on injured knees with the help of steroid injections. He did so upon the recommendation and concurrence of military physicians assigned to the base at that time. His doctors now claim that the steroid treatments made him a cripple for life... My bill, plain and simple, will give Mr. Harris a well-deserved 'day in court.'" Dornan said.

Before the bill could be considered by the full House of Representatives it had to be approved by a committee, and it was assigned to the Judiciary Committee, and then to the Subcommittee on Administrative Law and Governmental Relations. With the backlog of bills being considered by Congress, it would be a while before Willie's bill was considered. He embarked on a prolific letter writing campaign to try to garner support for his bill. He wrote to just about every member on the committee. He repeatedly wrote to the subcommittee chairman Dan Glickman of Kansas, sending him more and more supporting documentation. He wrote to his California senators Alan Cranston and Pete Wilson. He wrote to President Ronald Reagan. The responses he received were a mixture of "I'll take a good look at the bill when it gets to me," and "I'm not in a position to help you." He also wrote several letters to the top brass at the Air Force, asking them to reconsider his case. The answer was always the same: No.

With the support of Bob Dornan and other members of Congress, Willie was hopeful that he would prevail, but like thousands of other bills introduced each year, his withered and died, like an untended grape scorched by a drought. Dornan didn't abandon him, and in March 1987 he reintroduced the same bill for Willie, but once again, it didn't gain any traction and died.

The 1980s was a very difficult time for Willie. Many of the men and women he had fought with in the BSA had become well established in Hollywood and he was rarely needed to act as their bulldog. Every time he thought he was going to be able to make the Air Force pay for its negligence, his quest hit a dead end. The pain in his knees kept getting worse, his mobility kept decreasing, and his mood got progressively darker.

His sons Darnell and Andrew were teenagers and they wanted to play ball with their dad. All the other kids' dads played with them, so why couldn't he? They didn't understand, and they resented him. Here he was: a mountain of a man, a formerly great athlete, completely handicapped by his knees.

His relationship with his wife Maureen was even worse. They argued frequently, and they both sensed a divorce was inevitable.

"I wasn't sleeping. Your kids are mad at you. You're going through a divorce. You're living in pain, and everybody done kick you in the ass for something you didn't do," Willie said.

Willie's knees caused him constant pain. He slowly became an emotional and psychological wreck because he couldn't be the father and husband he wanted to be. When he was hunched over in the cotton fields as a boy, picking for hours in the sweltering heat, his white t-shirt plastered to his back and stinking to high heaven, he kept thinking: "I don't know what I'm gonna do whenever I get the hell out of Mississippi, but whatever I do, I'm gonna be dynamite." What was he now? He felt like a broken man. His gregarious nature and ready smile were gone. He was just angry. Angry that he couldn't do any of the things he wanted to do. Angry that he was a cripple. Angry at the Air Force. So he started self-medicating. He smoked three packs of Winston cigarettes a day. He started drinking more—a lot more. Bacardi and Coke was his go-to beverage. He would just sit in his room and drink one after the other, and it slowly masked the pain in his knees, heart, and mind. Though he was a man who loved the game of basketball, he found he couldn't even bear to watch it on TV.

His friend and fellow stuntman Clifford Strong would come over and spend time with him as he drank.

"Willie, look at you," Clifford said.

Willie glanced over at a mirror, ran his hand over the three-day stubble on his cheek, and smiled.

"I look good, don't I?"

"You look like a piece of shit," Clifford said.

"What are you talkin' about?"

"Willie, you're goin' down the wrong road, my friend," Clifford said. "You're so full of anger and you drink to try to feel better. It doesn't work. Your aunt drank herself to death. Your sister drank herself to death. Do you want to be next?"

"Listen, I can't work. I can barely walk. Everybody is givin' me shit about something or other. What the hell else am I supposed to do? And by the way, I would like to see you walk a mile in my shoes. Actually, I would like to see you walk a hundred yards," Willie bellowed.

"I know, I know. You got a shitty deal. I get it. But this anger, you need to let it go. I've seen it before, it is eating you up inside and it will consume you sooner or later, partner, and probably sooner," Clifford said.

Willie just waved him off. Cliff didn't know what he was talking about. But the pain, frustration, and anger all took their toll. His kids couldn't relate to him. Maureen no longer saw the happy, energetic guy she met in an Albuquerque bar two decades earlier. They divorced in 1986.

Willie got a call from his cousin in Mississippi the same year. It was about his mom. She had suffered an aneurism and was in a coma. Willie talked to the doctor treating her and asked if he should come home. "She wouldn't know you," the doctor said, so he stayed in California. A few days later his cousin called back and told him his mom had died. She was 86 years old. Willie and Robert flew to Mississippi to attend the funeral. This was almost too much to take.

His personal life was a mess, and now he had lost the one anchor he had in the world. He sat in the church and listened to the preacher and Curtiss Ross say nice things about his mom. He felt like a lost sailor.

"It was really weird. 'Cause I got up and walked out halfway through the funeral. It was just, you know me and my mom, you know she had went through thick and thin for me. You know she had went hungry, abused, and all kinds of shit for me, you know. I been to quite a bit of funerals, and ain't nothin' like going to your mom's funeral, 'cause you know that's the end of the line, and she ain't comin' back. And it sticks with you for quite a while. You might forget, but you'll never get over it, 'cause that was my mom."

With both of Bob Dornan's bills in support of him dying in committee, Willie felt like he was at another dead end. He was getting nowhere by petitioning the Air Force, and if Congress wouldn't help him, what else could he do?  It was in his nature to keep trying, keep fighting, but he was at a low point in so many ways, maybe giving up would just be easier. He was tired. But then, in the spring of 1988 he heard about a private bill that was passed into law to help a young Canadian become an American citizen so she could compete for the U.S. Olympic team in Seoul, South Korea. Wait. What? Did he hear that right? Now Congress is making special deals to alter the requirements for citizenship in the United States of America to help someone get on the Olympic team? With all he had been through, that was hard for Willie to fathom.

Tracey McFarlane was an exceptionally talented swimmer who was born in Canada in 1966 and moved to Palm Springs, California when she was a teenager. She competed for the University of Texas Longhorns swim team from 1984-1988 and wanted to compete on the U.S. Olympic team in 1988, but she was not a U.S. citizen, as she had not lived in the U.S. long enough to meet the requirements for naturalized citizenship. She needed help. She needed Congress to pass a law circumventing the normal requirements for obtaining U.S. citizenship, one of the most deeply cherished and highly sought-after designations in the world. That help came in the form of a bill introduced in the House of Representatives titled House Resolution 2819: For the relief of Tracey McFarlane. It was introduced by Rep. Jerry Lewis, a Republican who represented California's 35th District and who, coincidentally, was also the captain of his high school swim team in nearby San Bernardino back in the 1950s. By unanimous consent, the bill was approved by the House Committee on the Judiciary and sent to the full House for consideration on March 22, 1988. It was quickly passed by the House on the same day, then passed by the Senate on March 31, presented to the President on April 1, and Ronald Reagan signed it into law on April 12, 1988. Bing. Bang. Boom. Done. Three weeks from committee discussion to a newly enacted law. It is amazing how efficient Congress can be when it involves something really important, like a shot at Olympic glory.

That summer McFarlane went to Seoul as a member of the U.S. Olympic team and won a silver medal swimming the breaststroke as part of the 4 x 100 medley relay.

Willie was pissed, but he had also found what he needed to reenergize his quest.

"Those were some tough times. I went to bed thinking and sleeping it, and got up fighting," Willie said.

He restarted his letter writing campaign to senators and members of the House to draw attention to his plight.

"The tragedy in the United States today is that the Congress and Senate are more interested in winning medals in the Olympics than helping a military malpractice vet who has been butchered by military doctors. Why does someone who has not served one day or contributed anything to protect this country get preferential treatment over people whose blood has been spilled all over this world to protect this country? But, I guess one day Tracey McFarlane can tell her kids how great America is. But what will I tell my kids who have lost a father because of this country? When will Congress or the Senate stand up and fight for military malpractice vets who have suffered for years? What has Tracey McFarlane suffered from? My private bill has been in Congress since 1985. Only one Congressman came to my defense. How many got on the bandwagon for Tracey McFarlane? I am 49 years old today. This government made me a cripple at the age of 24. I have had 15 knee surgeries. I will have to have more surgeries until I reach the age of 65, when I will have to have plastic knees," Willie wrote in August 1988.

Willie found an ally for his cause in Barney Frank of Massachusetts. As a Jew and the first openly gay member of Congress, Frank knew what it felt like to be treated unfairly. He thought the Feres Doctrine was unjust, and he wanted to pass a law that would essentially overturn it and allow active-duty service members to sue the government when they were harmed by negligence. Any law he may have been able to get passed, however, would not be retroactive, so it would not apply in Willie's case. However, he was willing to do whatever he could to help Willie's cause.

In the fall of 1988 Willie heard about another private bill that had just become law and it made him even angrier than he already was. Michael Wilding was born in California in 1953 and his parents were the legendary actress Elizabeth Taylor and the English actor Michael Wilding, which made him a dual citizen of the U.S. and England. In 1971 the 18-year-old Wilding renounced his U.S. citizenship to avoid getting drafted and possibly sent to fight in the Vietnam War. The young Wilding had better things to do than serve his country, like live on a farm in Wales and grow pot. In 1974 he was arrested in England for cultivation and possession of marijuana—twice. He returned to the United States as an English citizen and worked as an actor on the soap opera *The Guiding Light* beginning in 1986. He ran into a problem in 1987 because he was going to be deported, since you are not allowed to legally live in the United States indefinitely if you are not a citizen. Wilding could have applied for status as a permanent U.S. resident, but U.S. law barred him from obtaining that status due to his drug convictions in England. Luckily for Wilding, his mother was Elizabeth Taylor, and his former stepfather was John Warner, the U.S. Senator from Virginia and former Secretary of the Navy who held that post, ironically, during the Vietnam War. Warner was Taylor's sixth husband, and they were married from 1976 to 1982. Warner got to know Wilding during this time and said he developed respect for him. "He should not be excluded from the United States for the rest of his life because of a youthful mistake," Warner said. So Warner, a veteran of World War II and the Korean War, and former Secretary of the Navy, thought the man who renounced his U.S. citizenship to avoid getting drafted was worthy of a private law just for him.

So on December 4, 1987, Warner introduced Senate bill 1919 which stated that the law which bars those with drug convictions from gaining permanent residence would not apply to Wilding. The Senate Judiciary Committee approved the bill on September 14, 1988, and it then sailed through Congress before being signed into law by President Reagan two months later. For Wilding, he was certainly fortunate to be born into such a rich, famous, and powerful family. For him, America truly was the land of opportunity.

Willie had seen a lot of Hollywood scripts, but if someone pitched this plot they would have been laughed out of the producer's office. It was too ludicrous. If Willie was not in so much pain, he would have found it comical.

Willie also heard about the case of Jack Kent Cooke, the millionaire broadcasting mogul and famously arrogant owner of numerous professional sports teams. Cooke, a Canadian citizen, wanted to become a U.S. citizen, so in 1960 he reached out to his friends in the Senate and a bill was passed that allowed him to bypass the 5-year residency requirement. "It was done entirely by friends of mine in the United

States who wanted me, desperately apparently, to come down here," Cooke said.

Money. Power. Connections. You can get a lot done in America if you have these advantages. The more Willie heard about these cases, the more he needed to speak up. He noticed that many of the people benefitting from special laws made just for them were wealthy, and he also could not find one that was passed to help a Black person, certainly not one to help a Black person who grew up picking cotton on a plantation in Mississippi.

The letter writing campaign to senators and representatives continued.

"I served my country from 1962 to 1967 in the U.S. Air Force. Because of my stature of 6 feet, 8 inches, the military wanted me to play on their basketball team. When I became injured and not able to play the game, the military doctors injected me with steroids (a "quick fix"). I had no idea of the long-term side effects this drug would have on my body.

I am not a white man, and my mother is not Elizabeth Taylor and I do not have a stepfather named John Warner. I have never been convicted of any crime.

In 1988 I had a bill that would allow me to get justice for what the military did to me. Yet Congress refused to help me to pass my bill.

However, Michael Wilding is a white man and is the son of Elizabeth Taylor and did have a stepfather named John Warner who just so happens to be Senator John Warner. In 1971 Michael renounced his citizenship in the U.S. to avoid the draft. He went to live in England where in 1974 he was cultivating marijuana and was convicted. U.S. immigration laws say that no one who has been convicted on drug charges can become a permanent resident in the U.S. Yet, Congress still passed his bill with the help of James Sensenbrenner and Senator John Warner. A quote from a newspaper article in Virginia says, 'Would Warner write new laws for someone else's son?'," Willie wrote.

Like Socrates did in Athens in fifth century B.C., Willie was holding up a mirror to American society and saying "Look at this. What do you see? Is this fair? Is this just? Does this look like a place where all men and women are created equal, where they all have the same opportunity to achieve their goals, or where they are treated fairly, or is their treatment actually based on their background, the size of their bank account, and the color of their skin?"

In 1990 Willie moved to Highland, California, an hour east of Los Angeles. This meant Bob Dornan was no longer his representative in Congress, and he had moved into the district represented by George Brown Jr., a Democrat who had been in Congress for more than three decades. A longtime champion of science and human rights, Brown had a history of standing up for others, as way back in 1938, as a college freshman at UCLA, he started a student housing cooperative that enabled Black students to live off-campus in the Westwood section of Los Angeles, as Blacks were forbidden from living in that neighborhood at the time.

Just like Dornan, Brown saw the merit in Willie's case and vowed to try to help him. In 1990, he assigned his legislative assistant Bill Grady to research Willie's case and help craft the legislation for a new private bill. Both Brown and Grady were convinced that Willie's case had a lot of merit and that he should be allowed to sue the Air Force.

"We looked at the Willie Harris case and Congressman Frank had sort of the same view, too, of here was a military service member, he was not harmed by a medical decision made in a military field hospital. It wasn't something, a rushed decision that had to be made to save his life in the heat of battle. He was at a military base, and he was on the base basketball team, he was the star of this basketball team, and the commander so liked having a winning team that when Willie hurt his knees, he told the doctor do whatever you have to to get him back out on the court. So there was no pressing military need for that to happen. The doctor wasn't being told, get him back in that plane, only he has the skills to fly that plane and we need him to protect the country. It was to get him back out on the basketball court, so he was given repeated injections over I think a several year period of steroids in his knees and other joints and it enabled him to play, but doctors later said that was what went to your crippling," Grady said.

Grady and his colleagues researched whether the Air Force could be forgiven for crippling Willie based on the available medical information in the early to mid-1960s. They found that they could not.

"We did some research on what was known about steroid injections in the early 1960s. Because we felt like our case might not be very strong if steroids started out as a miracle drug. If you go back in the 40s and 50s you read all about the miracle of steroids and nothing, no warnings are given about them at all. And it could be a little hard to blame these military doctors and the military for malpractice if 20 years later it's discovered that steroid have problems, but at the time, nobody knew that. But what we found is starting in the late 50s and into the early 60s that's when medical journals started to publish articles about the risks of long-term steroid injections and cautions about it. So when Willie had these injections in the early to mid-60s we felt that there had been enough period of time in there where warnings had come out about steroids that doctors should have been careful and cautious about those injections," Grady said.

George Brown introduced the private bill House Resolution 760 on January 30, 1991, in support of Willie's case. The bill included especially harsh words about the Air Force's negligence in treating Willie's injuries: "Such exploitation of athletes is sad when performed by colleges or professional sports teams, but colleges and professional sports teams and their doctors are subject to legal action concerning their activities. The United States Armed Forces and its medical personnel normally are not, making their exploitation of an athlete like Mr. Harris even more shameful."

The letter writing campaign began again in earnest. Willie wrote letters to members of the House and senators to make them aware the bill was coming up for debate. Brown wrote letters to his colleagues in the House, explaining his position and asking for their support, and Dornan also contacted his colleagues to let them know he supported Willie's cause.

Barney Frank, chair of the Administrative Law and Governmental Relations Subcommittee of the Judiciary Committee, set a hearing on Willie's bill for March 7, 1991. Frank invited Willie to come testify. The kid from the cotton fields was traveling to Capitol Hill to state his case against the U.S. government. Oh mama, mama, many worlds I've come since I first left home.

Willie flew into D.C. by himself and went to the National Mall. On the way his taxi drove by the Jefferson Memorial and the red brick towers of the Smithsonian Institution's Castle. He stood at the base of the Capitol on the east side of the mall, admiring the image of the Ulysses S. Grant memorial in the reflecting pool. A mile and a half away stood the Washington Monument, an Egyptian-style obelisk piercing a crisp, blue early spring sky. Then he turned around and looked up at the soaring dome of the Capitol building—and all those damn stairs it would take to get up there. Shit. He hadn't thought about that. He would just have to soldier through it, like he had done his whole life.

"It was terrible. I had my knee braces on, and I just made up my mind that I've got to do it," Willie said.

When Willie got into the hearing room, he sat down in front of the committee and thanked Barney Frank for inviting him to testify. He had on his best suit, and he felt like he was back in the movies. Unfortunately, this movie was a tragedy. He would turn 50 years old a few months later, and his knees had been failing for more than half his life. He spoke passionately, eloquently, and forcefully for 15 minutes to a rapt audience. He spoke of the repeated steroid injections and poor medical care he received from the Air Force. He spoke of the aftermath and how it had altered his life. Mostly, though, he spoke about pain—the physical and emotional pain wrought by his crippling.

"These past 24 years I have suffered physically, emotionally, mentally, financially, maritally, and paternally. I wish I could relate to you the anguish and torment I have experienced to this day. Do you know what it feels like to be cheated? To miss out? To suffer and feel like there is no one out there to care enough to help relieve any of the torment? How can you undo the years of physical pain, loss of use, and repeated surgeries to knees that can barely support oneself to even cook a meal? Knees, once strong and able, one minus a kneecap and both still degenerating so that surgeries are required to clean them out. Surgeries that will need to continue until I am age 65. When I reach age 65 plastic knees will be inserted. There is also the probability that I may be confined to a wheelchair.

And then there is the family life that I missed out on—and not of my own choosing. I could not be the active father my sons needed. I had sons who were interested in the same thing as their dad, but because of the disability and pain, we could not enjoy the bonding or the sharing. I could not pass on or teach to them the skills, or practice with them as they were growing up. I couldn't take them to Disneyland, the park, or play any sports with them. This created or added to problems I had with them or relating with them. They could not understand why their friends' dads could do these things with them and theirs could not. As they grew older, they were able to understand, but that did not make up for them having to miss out. That hurt!

There is not a day that I do not live in constant pain. Each and every day and night I am constantly reminded and tormented by the physical results of what happened at the hands of Air Force doctors so I could continue to play basketball for the Air Force. I ask you to put yourself in my place. Remember your most excruciating pain. Each second seemed like an eternity. What if you were told you would have to suffer that pain every minute of every day for the rest of your life?

And that it would get worse and worse! Have you been through that yet?

I am not a statistic. I am real. What my life has suffered is real. My plight is real. It is so real I had to come to you so you would see me as a real person who is so determined about seeking justice that he strived to come this distance of years and miles to be heard by members of Congress. I put myself and my plight before you. I am worth the effort. I am deserving of your assistance."

When he was finished, he got up slowly, leaned on his cane, and walked out.

George Brown also spoke at the hearing in support of the bill he had introduced.

"Currently, military personnel are the only individuals I know of in America who can suffer medical malpractice but are then prevented from seeking full compensation for their damages. H.R. 760 should be seen and used as a way not only to bring justice to Mr. Harris individually, but to help reform the military legal service system as a whole so that military personnel have the same legal protections as the rest of our nation."

They had made a strong case for Willie. His quest to get a private bill passed was written up in many newspapers, including the *Los Angeles Times* and *Stars and Stripes*. In June his bill was approved by the Judiciary Committee and sent to the full House of Representatives for consideration. The Judiciary Committee's report stated the following:

"The Committee believes there is a direct causal relationship between the actions of the Armed Forces medical personnel, motivated by a desire for a winning basketball team, and the present condition of Mr. Harris' knees. Mr. Harris now has problems walking, let along running, and his possibility of a career playing professional basketball has been destroyed."

Willie had been working with Bob Dornan and George Brown for six years to try to get a bill passed, and this time he was feeling like it might actually happen. But nothing in his life had ever been easy, so why should this? It turned out that there was an immovable object standing in the way of Willie finally getting his day in court against the Air Force. It came in the form of Frank James Sensenbrenner, Jr., or Jim, as he likes to be called. Sensenbrenner was a Republican congressman from Wisconsin who served on the Judiciary Committee. He was also an heir to the Kimberly-Clark personal hygiene products fortune. Sensenbrenner had never known what it was like to be misused and abused by the system. He attended a fancy private school as a child and didn't have to worry about serving his country during the Vietnam War, as he was an undergraduate at Stanford University and a law student at the University of Wisconsin in the 1960s, before going directly into politics after graduation. He wasn't misused or abused by the system—he was the system.

Sensenbrenner was named Frank after his father and great-grandfather. His great-grandfather was the vice president of Kimberly-Clark in 1920 when he invented the Kotex sanitary napkin. More than eight decades later Jim Sensenbrenner was one of the fiercest champions of the Partial Birth Abortion Act of 2003 that was signed into law by President George W. Bush. The Sensenbrenner men had a surprisingly long history of getting in the middle of women's business.

One of Sensenbrenner's duties on the Judiciary Committee was to serve as the Republican Party's official objector. The more than 400 members of the House did not have the time to look closely at all the private bills that came through, so each party appointed an official objector in their committees, and it was their job to report to the rest of their party if they thought the party should not back a bill. If either objector didn't back a bill, that bill would not go to a vote in the full House. It would be dead. And Sensenbrenner didn't like Willie's bill.

"Sensenbrenner was the roadblock," George Brown's aide Bill Grady said. "He took the position that the Department of Defense did, and he supported the Feres Doctrine. He wasn't using an unusual argument, but it was disappointing to hear that, and the bill didn't go anywhere. We worked on Sensenbrenner. Willie definitely worked on Sensenbrenner over the next year or two, both writing, and I think getting some letter writing campaigns going, having different people call him, but he didn't change his position."

Willie never got anywhere with Sensenbrenner. He wouldn't return Willie's calls and he refused to meet with him to discuss the bill. Willie thought it was racially motivated. Sensenbrenner has received poor grades from the NAACP and the American Civil Liberties Union related to his voting record and whether it furthered or impeded their agendas. However, those poor grades are not unusual, as most Republican members of Congress of his era received similar ratings.

The news media was happy to report on Willie's story in the early 1990s and he kept corresponding with members of Congress and trying to shine light on his plight. However, he started to realize that as hard as he tried, he wasn't going to be able to get the bill through. He had taken it as far as he could.

"I knew in '92 that I was fighting against a brick wall. And I said to myself: 'I gave it my best shot. Just me, the lowly guy, the guy from the plantation had enough brains and backbone to stand up to society and fight back.' And that's what I did," Willie said.

Along the way, he made an impression on a lot of people and raised awareness about an important issue. Bill Grady felt especially glad to have had the chance to get to know Willie and work with him.

"Willie is a very personable guy. I like Willie personally and I always enjoyed interacting with him. This is something I've never told Willie, but my dad, he's from the South. And sometimes when I'd hear Willie talk, it would sound like I was talking with my dad, like I was hearing my dad's voice. I mean, they were different people, different backgrounds, but I could hear my dad's cadence and the sound of my dad in Willie's voice," Grady said.

Letting go of his struggle with the Air Force made him less angry. His anger had been driving his drinking, and in the early 1990s he realized he needed to stop drinking so much. Maybe his friend Clifford Strong was right after all. The anger had been destroying him. He started listening to Cliff and stopped his heavy drinking.

"One thing about me, I've got a strong mind. I ain't goin' out the back door as a drunk—which I was on my way—and once you get turned around, you look for something else. You do things different. You change your lifestyle. You change your friends. And because of this, there are better things out there for you. But it's not gonna come to you. You gotta go get it. So that's what I felt like I had to do, and that's what Cliff would tell me," Willie said.

Fortunately for Willie, his steely will helped him avoid getting addicted to painkillers. He occasionally needed painkillers when the agony in his knees was unbearable, but he was cautious with the Hydrocodone his doctors prescribed.

"I don't take it all the damn time because if you do, you're gonna pay for it. I only take it when I am in excruciating pain. My first surgery was in '72, and I'm in the room next to this old lady. I guess she had been there for a little while. She would be screamin' every night for her pain medication. I asked the nurse, what the hell is wrong with her? She said, man, she's hooked on that stuff. And I said then, I'll take one here and there, but I ain't gonna get hooked on it. I've seen too many people get hooked on that stuff, especially going to the VA. I've seen people going to pharmacy and they're ready to fight saying they need their medication, but the pharmacy is saying you're taking your other medication too quick. My doctor said you must have a high tolerance for pain, because you aren't asking for pan meds. I learned to live with pain. Because if you get hooked on the pain pills, now you got two problems. You've still got the pain and you're hooked on them damn pills. So what I try to do is deal with the pain as much as I can and not get hooked on that other damn stuff. So that is what my life has been like for the last 40 or 50 years."

After he had stopped drinking and gained some peace of mind by letting go of the anger that was consuming him, Willie met a fellow veteran at the VA, and they started talking about Willie's life. The vet was intrigued. He worked with kids in the Crenshaw District of LA, trying to keep them on a path to success, and away from all the crime and gang activity that can afflict impressionable teenagers. Willie said he would be happy to talk to them, and he ended up going four or five times. Willie would walk slowly into the gymnasium of a beat-up community center, with a few dozen teens sitting on the bleachers watching him lumber along.

He stood in front of them, and every eye was fixed on him, waiting to hear what this giant of a man had to say.

"Listen to me. It doesn't matter where you're from, it's where you're goin'. Sometimes you may think you have it rough here, and I'm sure you do. I grew up on a plantation in Mississippi picking cotton. We worked from can to can't, which means you start working when you can see, and you stop working when you can't see. Black people were at the bottom of society, and most had no hope of a better life off the plantation. But I got out, and I made something of my life, and so did a lot of my friends. Remember this:  Never give up. Never take no for an answer. And when you speak, you make sure you know what you're talking about. You have the same rights as anybody else. Only thing about being Black, your rights come a little harder, but don't back up. Don't quit. If you get knocked down, get up."

**19**

**WHAT A LONG STRANGE TRIP IT'S BEEN**

When you are struggling through something difficult and painful you often don't have the time or possess the necessary perspective to appreciate how monumental it might be. When you are in the heat of a battle you don't have time to think about how history will record the unfolding events. When Martin Luther King Jr. was working to secure the rights of African Americans in the late 1950s and 1960s, he was feared and reviled by those who felt he threatened the status quo that was built on white supremacy. However, he was also seen by many others as an eloquent and righteous leader who was fighting for the equal treatment that had been denied to African Americans for more than three centuries. It was only after his murder that the magnitude of his life and work was fully realized, and he became an American icon.

When the Black Stuntmen's Association was formed and they began fighting through the prejudice and roadblocks put in front of them by the white stunt groups and the Hollywood establishment in the 1960s, they weren't thinking about how history might look upon them. Their mission was to stop the insidious practice of painting down white stuntmen, and to secure jobs, both for themselves and other minorities and women seeking to break into the very tough and unforgiving world of Hollywood film and television productions. They weren't thinking that they were breaking down a door that others would pass through much more easily than they did. They weren't thinking that they were making history, but that is exactly what they were doing.

Some BSA members, including Henry Kingi, William Upton, Tony Brubaker, Richard Washington, and Alex Brown, began working regularly in the 1970s and kept on doing stunts in hundreds of Hollywood's biggest productions well into the twenty-first century, including *Glory, Pirates of the Caribbean, Scarface, Batman Returns, Apocalypse Now, Armageddon, Fast & Furious*, and many, many more. Their work has also included acting roles and advancing to become stunt coordinators and assistant directors. In addition, Kingi has three sons who have built careers as some of the top stuntmen in Hollywood.

As more and more Black stuntmen and stuntwomen began working regularly and encountering less discrimination, the practice of the paint-down became exceedingly rare. As the spokesman for the BSA, Willie had fewer battles to fight as the 1980s rolled into the 1990s. His stunt buddies had established themselves and many others had followed and were now enjoying lucrative—albeit very dangerous—careers. The fact that the studios no longer had to brace themselves for a protest or a challenge from the BSA when discrimination had been exposed was a good thing. It meant that the old boys' network of white stuntmen that kept jobs from going to anyone outside the cabal of white males was broken, and the opportunity to work in Hollywood productions had been opened up to men and women of many different backgrounds. This didn't mean that Willie and his mates were not still vigilant. They would occasionally hear about a situation where Blacks were being denied the chance to work, where a production may have a few dozen stuntmen working and all of them would be white, and Willie would make a call to protest. However, this happened much less frequently as the twentieth century drew to a close. The BSA became much less active and became a legacy organization, representing something special that had happened in the past, and it had served its purpose extremely well.

In the early 2000s Willie started thinking about all they had accomplished, and he didn't want their work to be forgotten. Their legacy needed to be inscribed in the history of the American civil rights movement. He started talking to his fellow BSA members about his plan to resurrect the organization and help it receive proper recognition, and the BSA members named him President of the Black Stuntmen's Association in 2004. Willie organized the first BSA reunion and it was held in Las Vegas in 2008. Most of the original members, many of whom were now in their 60s and retired from stunt work, attended the event, but Eddie Smith, the man who started it all, had died in 2005 at the age of 81. The first big award the group received was the NAACP Image Award - President's Award, an honor that is given to one recipient each year, and other honorees have included Muhammad Ali, Colin Powell, Spike Lee, Rihanna, Venus and Serena Williams, and LeBron James. It is given in recognition of special achievement and distinguished public service and was bestowed upon the BSA at the 43rd NAACP Image Awards ceremony in February 2012. Fittingly, the original BSA members were presented the award by Sidney Poitier and Harry Belafonte, two of the prominent actors who helped them gain their footing in Hollywood when they were first starting out. "Harry (Belafonte) and Sidney (Poitier) bent over backwards to do everything that they could to make sure that we were there in the first place," Brubaker said.

Growing up in the cotton fields of Mississippi in the 1950s, Willie could not wait to get out of there and go somewhere—anywhere but Mississippi. He had seen too much and felt the sting of racism and segregation too intensely. He had watched his mom work too hard for too long and have nothing to show for it. He never liked working in the fields or the life of a country boy. Many people enjoy being out in the sun, smelling the sweet scent of everything growing anew each spring, and watching the birds soar through the sky. Willie liked all that, too; he just wasn't interested in doing it from sunup to sundown, bent over picking cotton with his aching fingers and a sack filled with 50-100 pounds of the cash crop on his back. What he really didn't like was what being a Black sharecropper in Mississippi represented—a second-class, or perhaps third- or fourth-class, citizen. Considered a lesser being. Going to a rundown and underfunded school while the white kids enjoyed the best the town could afford. Don't even think about going into that nice restaurant. Don't use the clean public bathroom—you can go in the meadow like a feral dog. He couldn't take it, so he left, and he returned only occasionally to visit his mom, his childhood friends, and attend reunions of his high school class and the Howard Bottom community. It was still home, however. This place had formed him and put the gravel in his gut and the fire in his eye. If he had grown up in a comfortable middle-class suburb, he couldn't have fought as hard and as long as he had for the Black Stuntmen's Association. The fields of Mississippi created the kid who was boiling with rage at the injustice all around him.

So when Bryant Clark, an attorney and member of the Mississippi House of Representatives from the town of Pickens in Holmes County, told Willie in 2015 that he had arranged for the Black Stuntmen's Association to be honored for their heroic contributions at the Mississippi state capitol in Jackson, he was moved beyond words. Willie had never been to the state capitol. Now he was going to be honored there.  Oh, if only his mama could see him now. All the memories of the fields and segregation and the family history he was told came flooding back.

"Black people pass down things. And I found this out from my mom. My mom didn't have a birth certificate. The old people back in those days would write your birthdate in the Bible. It was the midwife who delivered us, 'cause we didn't go to no hospital. I was born at home, and my mom was telling me about her grandmother.

Her grandmother came over from Africa on a ship. My mom was born in 1900. My mom's mom was born in 1875, and I think that her grandmother was born in the 1830s or 1840s, but she came on a ship. I remember my mom tellin' me about her granny, and great-grandmama was tellin' them about the people dying, how they slept, and how they was chained together on these ships and when they died, they would throw them overboard, and how the women got raped on these ships and stuff. And you know, I got slave records of my great-great grandfather I researched. And that when he was brought to America, he was brought to Anderson County in South Carolina. And that was on my mom's mother's side. On my mom's dad's side he was brought to Virginia," Willie said.

Willie headed home to Mississippi in early March for the ceremony at the state capitol, and he was not alone. He was accompanied by BSA members Alex Brown, Henry Kingi, Joe Tilque, William Upton, and Henry Graddy, who was also a Mississippi native. More than 40 years after they started fighting together, the BSA members always supported each other. These are people you can count on. Dewitt Fondren, another BSA member from Mississippi, had planned to attend, but he became ill and couldn't make it.

Willie leaned on his cane as he walked up the long granite promenade to the massive state capitol, an impressive building which is more than 400 feet wide. The capitol bears some resemblance to the U.S. Capitol in Washington, D.C. It is elongated and constructed of grey stone with spacious chambers on the left and right sides, and it is also topped by an iconic dome in the center. A 15-foot wide and 2,800-pound solid brass eagle—the symbol of American freedom—sits perched atop the dome, soaring 180 feet above the soil. The building and the eagle face south. Always south. Built in 1903, the capitol features lush artwork depicting scenes from Mississippi's history. Those responsible for the building seem not to grasp the irony of displaying a replica of The Liberty Bell alongside a statue honoring the women of the Confederacy.

When Willie and the others walked into the capitol, they were brought to a small conference room where they would wait to be called into the chamber to receive their honor. When he stepped through the door, he stopped for a moment when he saw who was sitting in the room waiting for him. It was Robert G. Clark, Jr., the father of Bryant Clark. The elder Clark was a legend in Mississippi, especially to Black folks, and especially to those from Holmes County. He was born in 1928 in his family's home in Pickens, a tiny town out in the country, 25 miles south of Lexington. The home was built by his father in the early twentieth century, and it sits on a former plantation where Clark's great grandparents had toiled as slaves. Upon emancipation, the plantation owner sold the land to Clark's great grandfather. As was the case for Blacks all over the South for the first two-thirds of the twentieth century, being a landowner—as opposed to a sharecropper or tenant farmer—gave the Clarks something of an advantage over most of their Black brothers and sisters. It gave them a certain independence. Landowning Blacks could do things, and sometimes say things, without fear of being thrown out of their homes. One of Robert's grandfathers who helped raise him was born in the early 1850s and had been a slave for the first 11 years of his life. He told Robert that things were going to get better in America for Blacks, but they were only going to get better if young people like him grew up and did something to make it better. He carried that mission with him for the rest of his life. Robert worked his way through Jackson State University, earning a bachelor's degree, and then he received a master's degree in Administration and Educational Services from Michigan State University before coming back home to Pickens in the 1950s to manage the family homestead, as his father has asked him to. He became a teacher and basketball coach at Louise High School. He knew Willie from his coaching days, as he had coached against him.

Clark became involved in the civil rights movement in the early 1960s, working to register Blacks to vote, the kind of activity that was often too risky for Blacks who did not own their own land. His involvement in politics progressed, and in 1967 he ran for office, hoping to represent Holmes County in the Mississippi legislature. He ran on the ticket of the Freedom Democratic Party, a party that had been formed in 1964 to combat the Mississippi wing of the national Democratic Party, the party that had been responsible for disenfranchising Blacks in the state for so many decades. The Mississippi legislature is composed of 177 elected officials, and between 1894 and 1967 not one Black person served in the legislature. Clark sought to change that. Three-quarters of the people who lived in Holmes County were Black, and that had been the case throughout the twentieth century. Yet, due to their disenfranchisement, neither they nor any other Black person in Mississippi had an elected representative who looked like them for more than 70 years. Bolstered by the federal Voting Rights Act of 1965, as well as the work done by countless activists in Mississippi and across the country, Clark won the seat to represent Holmes County. He would remain the only Black representative in the legislature for almost a decade, and in 1977 he became the first Black committee chairman in Mississippi's history, when he was named to head the Education Committee. He would go on to serve in the legislature for 35 years until his retirement in 2003, and the following year he became the first Black person in the history of Mississippi to have a state office building named after him.

Willie knew all this, and it is why he was so moved that Robert Clark was there. He was 86 years old, yet he still radiated the same dignity and determination that made him so beloved and successful.

"Mr. Clark, I didn't know you were coming," Willie said.

"Oh, I wasn't going to miss this, Willie. It is not every day that the state of Mississippi honors Black people for being civil rights heroes—especially those who gave me nightmares when I was coaching against them 60 years ago," Clark said.

Willie laughed and sat down next to Clark.

"Willie, when I was elected representative for Holmes County and came here in 1968, I had no idea what it would be like, but I knew it wouldn't be easy. I won the election, and my opponent challenged the results in court. I didn't know until 15 minutes before I was sworn in if I would even be seated in the legislature. They would do anything to keep me out of here. You look around this building, you see all the beautiful statues and the ornate woodwork and the grand chambers and domes. You know, when I started serving as a representative, Black people weren't even allowed in this building. The only ones allowed in were those that were cleaning the toilets and polishing the brass," Clark said.

"This is the first time I have ever been in here," Willie said.

"Exactly," Clark continued, "they didn't build this place for people like us. When I became a representative, no one would sit next to me for the first eight years. No one would talk to me. When I wanted to address the chamber, I would stand up and raise my hand, and the gentleman who was presiding would call on someone who had stood up after me—every time. I thought about quitting a few times because it was so hard to get anything done, but I couldn't do it. I had to keep going. Being one Black among 121 whites did not intimidate me at all. Because I knew what I knew, and the one thing I knew I was going to zero in on was what I was an expert in, and that was education. I knew no one there knew as much about education as I did. And eventually, it paid off. When you want to change things, it is a marathon, and not a sprint, unfortunately."

"Oh, I know that," Willie said.

After they were ushered into the chamber for the reading of the proclamation honoring the Black Stuntmen's Association, Willie and the other BSA members received a standing ovation. Willie spoke on behalf of the group to thank the state of Mississippi for this honor, and as he walked up to the podium, his mind started to wander into the darkness that is Mississippi's history.

"When I was up there speaking, I was thinking about all the trees I saw on the capitol grounds. I know Blacks been hung in Jackson, but I just didn't see it because we lived out in the country. But this plays on your mind. Now I'm standing in this podium speaking, looking out where all the senators and the congress people sit, and thinking: what have some of them done?"

He kept those incendiary musings in his head and was gracious when he spoke.

"On behalf of the Black Stuntmen's Association and the Coalition of Black Stuntmen and Stuntwomen, I would like to thank the legislature for this tremendous honor. I want to especially thank Representative Bryant Clark for putting this all together. Your dad was a pretty good basketball coach, but he was a great statesman, and he is someone I always looked up to."

Willie paused and took a deep breath before continuing.

"Ladies and gentlemen, I stand here before you amazed that this is even happening, that we are receiving this honor from you. I ain't never been to the state capitol, and none of my friends have neither. It was just not a place where we felt welcome. So thank you for making me feel welcome. I spent the first twenty years of my life up in Holmes County, picking cotton on Clifton Plantation, living in a segregated society, and getting chased around by Sheriff Dick Byrd. It was a hard life, and to be honest, I couldn't wait to get out of Mississippi because there were no good prospects for a young Black man in Mississippi at that time. On top of that, my mom, my dear sweet mom who has since passed, she was worried about me. I wasn't the kind of person who took very well to bein' pushed around, and she figured that sooner or later I would do something or be in a situation where I would get myself thrown in jail for no good reason, or maybe even killed. So I left. I went to serve my country in the Air Force for four and a half years, and my last assignment was the Los Angeles Air Force Base, and right after I got out of the service I met Cal Brown, the first Black stuntman in Hollywood. I knew when I started working with these guys that we were doing something important. The old boys' network of Hollywood stuntmen was painting down white stuntmen with makeup to double Black actors. We said no, no, no. That ain't right. We're here. We've been trained. We're qualified. Hire us. We faced all kinds of racism: you ain't good enough, you ain't smart enough, you ain't tough enough."

Willie stopped to take a drink of water.

"It was very dangerous work, and at first, almost none of the white stunt guys would help us. Just the opposite. They worked against us. Back in the late 60s, early 70s, when a Black stuntman went to work, one of three things could happen: he could come home, he could go to the hospital, or go to the graveyard. We would get paid sometimes half the money for the same stunt on the same day that a white guy did. But we kept pushing, and we never gave up. And eventually, we made it. Some of our members became some of the top stuntmen in the business, but nothing came easy, and nothing was handed to us. We had to work twice as hard and be twice as good to be accepted, but then things started to get better in the late 70s and 80s. What's more, our fight not only opened doors for Black stuntmen and stuntwomen, but for Black people and other minorities all over Hollywood."

Just before Willie spoke, the Mississippi House Concurrent Resolution 83 was proclaimed in the state capitol. An excerpt from the resolution states that "Whereas, it is the policy of this Legislature to applaud organizations that seek to tear down barriers and build bridges for all citizens of this country. Now, therefore, be it resolved by the House of Representatives of the State of Mississippi, the Senate concurring therein, that we do honor the many contributions of the historic founding and existence of the Black Stuntmen's Association and the Coalition of Black Stuntmen and Stuntwomen."

Willie never missed an opportunity to educate people about what the BSA had accomplished. He had become friendly with Beau Biden after meeting him at an event, and in 2012 the Democratic Party in Las Vegas called him to tell him that Biden requested he be invited to an upcoming event in Las Vegas where First Lady Michelle Obama would be in attendance. He happily accepted and when he met the First Lady he told her all about the Black Stuntmen's Association, as she had never heard of the organization.

*Michelle Obama and Willie Harris, 2012*

The BSA had also been honored in 2010 by the state of California and the United States Congress. On February 25, 2010, Senator Harry Reid of Nevada introduced a concurrent resolution of both houses of Congress, stating "I rise today to acknowledge a group that has created opportunities for countless African American men and women in the film and television industry. I rise to submit this Senate Concurrent Resolution honoring the Black Stuntmen's Association and the Coalition of Black Stuntmen and Women for their efforts to not only integrate but enhance the television and film industry.

Later that year Willie attended a speaking event at a library near his home in Las Vegas. The speaker was Antonio Vargas, best known for playing Huggy Bear, the slick-talking and flashily dressed police informant in the 1970s television series *Starsky and Hutch*. Fargas and Willie were friendly, so at the end of his talk, Fargas called Willie up to speak to the group about the Black Stuntmen's Association. As the audience was filing out, a man came up to Willie and started chatting with him about what Willie had just told them about the BSA. It was Merald "Bubba" Knight, a singer, songwriter, record producer, and the older brother of Gladys Knight. Bubba was one of the Pips. Willie and Bubba exchanged phone numbers and vowed to stay in touch.

Willie's phone rang about six months later.

"Hello," Willie said.

"Hey, Willie, do you remember me?" the caller asked.

"Who is this?" Willie asked.

"It's Bubba Knight. We met at the library."

"Hey, Bubba. How you doin', man?"

"Good. Good. Listen, Willie, I've been talking to a woman who is working on building a museum at the Smithsonian in Washington about African Americans. Anyway, I was talking to her, and telling her about what you told me about the Black Stuntmen's Association, and she wants to talk to you."

"Why does she want to talk to me?"

"Because she thinks y'all are history makers and she wants to talk about maybe putting your group in the museum. Can I give her your phone number?" Bubba asked.

"Absolutely," Willie said.

This was interesting. A national museum to recognize and honor African Americans in Washington, D.C., part of the Smithsonian. Wow. Willie had not heard about this as of 2010, though the idea for a building to honor the achievements of African Americans had been kicked around in the nation's capital for almost a century. However, like so many other things related to the progression of African

Americans in the United States, it took a painfully long time to reach fruition, hampered and impeded every step of the way by those who sought to keep Blacks down. The first U.S. president to endorse the idea was Herbert Hoover in 1929. Throughout the twentieth century the notion had been raised and defeated many times for many different reasons, and in the late 1980s legislation was again introduced by members of Congress John Lewis of Georgia and Mickey Leland of Texas. That bill was killed, allegedly because members of Congress thought it was too expensive. The Smithsonian Institution drafted legislation which would establish the museum in the early 1990s and presented it to Congress. Senator Jesse Helms of North Carolina, a man widely considered to be racist and someone who had fought to keep Congress from creating a national holiday honoring Martin Luther King Jr., prevented the bill from being considered on the Senate floor, and the effort stalled again. It wasn't until 2003 when bipartisan support in Congress finally coalesced and the Senate, House of Representatives, and President George W. Bush all agreed that this is something that needed to be done, and they passed the National Museum of African American History and Culture Act. The new law established the museum and provided funds for planning and site selection. The planning committee recommended that the museum be placed on the national mall, just northeast of the Washington Monument. Again, there was controversy, as some thought this site was too prominent for the museum. Eventually, however, the site was approved and work on planning the architecture and collections that would be housed in the museum began.

One of the people charged with building the collections was Dr. Dwandalyn Reece, the museum's Curator of Music and Performing Arts. She is the person who Bubba Knight talked to about the BSA, and she knew Bubba because Gladys Knight and the Pips would be recognized in the museum. She called Willie and told him she was coming to Las Vegas and wanted to meet with as many BSA members as possible and hear their stories. Willie sprang into action. He contacted the pioneering Black stunt performers who lived in Las Vegas, including Doug Lawrence, Evelyn Cuffee, and Jophery Brown and told them he was setting up a meeting with someone from the Smithsonian to talk about the BSA. He rallied the guys from California to come, including Alex Brown and Henry Kingi. In all, about a dozen of them came together to meet with Dr. Reece. Willie knew Shelley Berkley, the member of Congress who represented Las Vegas, and she agreed to let them meet in her conference room.

Dr. Reece knew right away that this was something special, and she was struck by Willie, whom she found to be "kind, lovable, and fiercely committed. I mean he had a story to tell, and he had a certain openness and willingness to share and to build a sense of community."

She spoke to the group about the possibility of having them recognized in the museum, and she interviewed them individually, recording their recollections. After that first meeting, she was hooked.

"I instantly knew it had to be (included in the collection). I think as I talked to people, I said this is fascinating. What people did, what they knew, what they learned, the multiple roles that they played. I think particularly getting beyond the profession as just being a stuntman or stuntwoman, but for its social justice, its civil rights framing of what they were doing, that this was a group that was not just a professional association but was its own kind of civil rights association. They were professionals and proud of their work, but they were also intently trying to create space and value for African Americans in the industry. I think some of those issues that came up, I think it was Willie who told me, you know, we talk about the stuntmen, but opening up opportunities for the food service people, and other entities those doors were not cracked open for. So it was very much a political effort, as much as it was an industry story, and that's what really took me," Reece said.

Dr. Reece came back to Las Vegas to meet with the BSA members a second time, to hear more of their stories, and to collect items to be donated to the museum, including a cherished jacket that William Upton received for his work on the film *Glory*.

The journey of the Black Stuntmen's Association fit perfectly with Dr. Reece's charge to help tell the story of the African American experience in the entertainment industry—the entire story, which encompasses all kinds of people who made important contributions.

"They become part of the national collection and the national story of the African American experience, and to me that says a lot, whether I was a curator or not. And I think what I appreciate about our museum is, it is not merely a hall of fame. We are looking at stories of real people from all walks of life and experiences. That's the national story. So the Black Stuntmen's Association, and the women too, I always have to make sure they are included, they're part of that story, very much part of that story, and we also make a point of saying that we tell the stories and elevate the voices that have yet to be heard. And that's from a variety of levels from the everyday people who contribute their experiences, but for me through the field it's the stories that are not written about in the newspapers or publicly covered in television or media, or even in the history books. It's just as important for me to create a complete picture of what entertainment was all about, and what drove it, and what opened these doors for all these people who relish in the riches and the wealth and the fame, of where they came from, and Black Stuntmen's Association is part of that story, and part of that foundation," Reece said.

The inclusion of the BSA's story in the museum's collection was also the pinnacle of Willie's effort to get their story heard.

"In the late 1960s, there was one Black movie producer that we knew of—Gordon Parks. There were no Black people in wardrobe or makeup or operating cameras. I don't like for it to come off as bragging. Young people will just say, 'Aw, you're full of it.' But we changed Hollywood. We busted down the doors for a lot of Black people in the movie industry. You can go out here today and ask, 'Who is the BSA?' Ninety-nine percent of the population do not know.

We accomplished a hell of a lot because we fought back, and I don't think that the studios will ever forget what we did, and I think it's time for the public and the world to know who we are, and what we did," Willie said.

Dr. Reece was certainly glad that Bubba Knight had told her about the BSA and that she was able to get to know Willie.

"I enjoyed working with him, his commitment, his passion, his honesty. I felt like he had been carrying, not a weight, in a bad way, but this tremendous story that he wanted people to know and looking for outlets to get it told and to understand what people had to go through, and what some men and women learned through their experiences. Not only to set the record straight, but to inspire and educate other people, and I was proud to play some part in that. I think with their donations it will be part of the museum forever. So that story is recognized and included on a larger level, and I have been happy to do that and do what I can within my own human and staff and museum resources," Reece said.

So back in 2010 the members of the BSA knew they were going to be recognized in the Smithsonian's National Museum of African American History and Culture, but then came the wait. Construction began on the museum in 2012 and it was ready to open in the fall of 2016, shortly before President Barack Obama completed his second term. Most of the BSA members were now in their seventies and several died between 2010 and the museum's opening. Of the approximately 30 original BSA members, a little more than half were still alive in 2016, and most of them traveled to Washington, DC with their families to witness the historic opening weekend. Some could not afford to make the trip, so Willie secured corporate funding to ensure everyone who was physically able could be there. Marge Ryan Kreeger, the attorney from the Equal Employment Opportunity Commission who had helped the BSA fight the studios almost 40 years earlier, also joined them.

Willie was one of the fortunate ones who was able to get a ticket for the opening ceremony in front of the museum. He sat in a folding chair that was two sizes too small for him, while thousands more watched from across the street, standing and sitting on the matted turf of the National Mall at the base of the Washington Monument. Like the nearly two million people who attended President Barack Obama's inauguration in January 2009—when the temperature was in the twenties—these people had to be there. They could not miss this moment. Willie marveled as speaker after speaker spoke of the need for this museum, and how long it had taken to come to fruition. They included John Lewis, former President George W. Bush, and Oprah Winfrey. Stevie Wonder gave an impassioned speech about the need for all Americans to come together and put away their hate. Patti Labelle received a standing ovation after singing "A Change is Gonna Come," 52 years after Sam Cooke first sang the song. Everything was building up to the moment when President Barack Obama would address the crowd, and Willie was tingling as he watched Obama walk across the stage and stand at the podium. It was otherworldly when he started to speak in his deliberately halting style, as he is someone who knows that the empty spaces matter. At times, Willie felt like Obama was talking to him.

"Too often we ignored, or forgot, the stories of millions upon millions of others who built this nation just as surely, whose humble eloquence, whose calloused hands, whose steady drive helped to create cities, erect industries, build the arsenals of democracy. So this national museum helps to tell a richer and fuller story of who we are. It helps us better understand the lives, yes of the president, but also the slave, the industrialist, but also the porter, the keeper of the status quo, but also the activist seeking to overthrow that status quo," Obama said.

Willie thought about his mom, bent over in the field, already looking like an old woman when she was in her 40s, a lifetime of sweat and toil behind her, yet so much more still ahead of her. He thought about how she would be positively glowing if she could be here. He also thought about all the men who had held sway over him before he became a grown-ass man—Oscar Harris, Peyton Abbott Jones, Sheriff Dick Byrd, Major Carson. They had power, and they wielded it to suit their own interests, not the interests of every person they were responsible for. They weren't trying to make things better. Most of them thought things were just fine the way they were. Obama was clearly different. He understood history. He understood that people have suffered. And he understood that things would only get better if people's eyes were opened, and we all worked together to see the injustices of the past and build a better future.

"The best history helps us recognize the mistakes that we've made, and the dark corners of the human spirit that we need to guard against. And yes, a clear-eyed view of history can make us uncomfortable. It'll shake us out of familiar narratives. But it is precisely because of that discomfort that we learn, and grow, and harness our collective power to make this nation more perfect. That's the American story that this museum tells, one of suffering and delight, one of fear, but also of hope, of wandering in the wilderness, and then seeing, out on the horizon, a glimmer of the Promised Land," Obama said.

At the museum's opening, the BSA's memorabilia was included in the Black Hollywood display, and the BSA items included the saddle used by Ernie Robinson, the association's co-founder and first president, a United Stuntwomen's Association jacket worn by Jadie David, and a BSA hat worn by Willie Harris. The memorabilia are displayed next to items and information honoring pioneering director Gordon Parks, Sidney Poitier, Whoopi Goldberg, Denzel Washington, Halle Berry, and many more.

After working on building the museum's collection for six years, Dr. Reece was able to see the impact that the museum had on the people whose achievements are recognized inside its walls, as well as all those who entered as visitors.

"What struck me as I sat out there and listened to remarks was how significant and important this was to people. I don't want to say I underestimated, but when you're really involved in all the doing, you kind of forget how symbolic, how emotional, I think when people come to the museum it's a pilgrimage, and I'm humbled. I was humbled not only by the enthusiasm, but how people were moved, either to see themselves or to learn stories they never heard. That never ceases to amaze me. I'm even thinking about the members of the stuntmen's organization, how when you're inside, you may take something for granted, but their excitement and pride that what we're doing—what we're all doing collectively—really can change minds, change hearts, and provide a balm to the soul," Reece said.

As the 1990s came to an end, Willie's life gradually improved. He still had daily pain, his knees kept deteriorating, and he still had to undergo the occasional knee surgery. He was not improving physically, in fact it was just the opposite, as his knees continued to worsen. Mentally, however, things improved dramatically. He had stopped drinking heavily, which helped him let go of the anger about his physical state, what the Air Force had done to him, and the hatred for people who mistreated him in the past. His outlook turned more positive, and it was aided by the fact that he started spending time with Cheryl Pritchett. Willie had known Cheryl for years and they had been friends when he lived outside Los Angeles in the 1970s. In 1998 Cheryl relocated from Texas back to California, and they became a couple, eventually marrying in 2006.

Cheryl shared the burden of Willie's physical limitations. They never went out dancing and were not even been able to go for walks together, as Willie's knee injuries prevented him from even walking around the block since the 1990s. But Cheryl reveled in Willie's buoy-ant spirit and enthusiasm, and they were simpatico.

Willie knew he was in a much better place mentally after he got together with Cheryl, and he was thankful.

"Last eight, nine, 10 years has been a hell of a change on me and my thinking and my lifestyle of being what I want to be. And trying to, I think I learned how to deal with pain and hurt. It took many years to deal with that. Even after all of the surgery that I've had, I'm dealing with that now, and it's always good to have a good woman on your side," Willie said in 2016.

Just because he was more at peace with everything he dealt with his in his life, that does not mean that he stopped fighting against injustice and pointing out wrongs committed in the past. He wanted people who have conveniently short memories to wake up and ac-knowledge that the way Blacks have been treated in this country is outrageous and cannot be accepted.

"See that's the difference. You can have this, but you don't want me to have it. I heard this all the time; we are not intelligent enough. I remember when there weren't any Black quarterbacks in the NFL. Marlin Briscoe was the first one. They called him The Magician. As he was gettin' good enough to really do things, well, the word got out. You can't have no Black guy runnin' no football team. They changed him into a wide receiver, and they phased him out. 'Cause he ain't supposed to be good enough to do this. It goes back to basketball. The people in Boston would go see Bill Russell, but he couldn't go to some of the exclusive restaurants there. Like the Blacks fought in World War II, and came back here, and couldn't even sit down in a lunch counter and have a decent cup of coffee. Those are the things that made so many people angry. And these people that are runnin' the show, you take like some of your top senators and stuff, they don't pay attention or either that they don't give a damn. They say, 'Well I don't know what's wrong with you, this is America, everyone is free'.

But look how long we've been slapped down in America. Look how many times that we've worked all day for nothing," Willie said.

Willie often thought about his odyssey from picking cotton to his NBA dreams, to the Air Force, and his work with the Black Stuntmen's Association. It had been a wild ride with so many heartbreaking moments, but many other euphoric triumphs. How did he get there? What factors came together to shape his life?

"I've thought many times, and stayed at work many nights, tryin' to figure out how did I get there? What made me different from anyone else? What was my calling to do these things? Then I got to thinking about what my mom said, and my mom couldn't read or write, but she told me: always respect your elders, always try to do the right thing. Son, nobody is perfect, but it takes someone to rise up against certain things to change things. And after the military, and I got to thinking about how I was shot up and how I was used to play basketball to get the base that I was stationed at the publicity for the base commander and all of that stuff, and after that I got to thinkin' well maybe it's time for me to step up to the plate. And I started steppin' up to the plate before I got out of the military. Because I spent four months after my discharge fightin' for my rights because of what they did to me. They used me. They crippled me. And I wasn't going to accept just walking out like a dog with my tail tucked between my legs without fightin' back, and that's what started all of this, and I said from then on, whatever I get involved in, I wasn't goin' to be used and abused. I was gonna stand up for my rights, and I'm gonna stand up other people's rights who can't stand up for themselves. That's how I got there," Willie said.

# 20

## A WONDERFUL SURPRISE

Amanda White was 28 years old in 2016 when she found a phone number that could hold the key to her origin. She had never met her biological father, and when she had turned 18 her mom Toni told her his name, and that was really all she knew about him. Her mom and this man had a fling when they were going through a substance abuse rehabilitation program in Cerritos, California in 1987. They were in their early twenties, and both were struggling. A few months after getting released from the program her mom learned she was pregnant and that woke her up. She quit doing drugs, reconnected with her high school boyfriend, and decided to turn her life around. There was a baby on the way, and it was time to grow up. She was now in a stable relationship with a supportive partner who became her husband. Together they would raise her new baby—and four more after Amanda—so she decided to cut ties with Amanda's biological father, not wanting his lifestyle to potentially influence her daughter. Amanda's biological parents never spoke to each other after she was born.

Amanda grew up in a loving family in Moreno Valley, California, a diverse city an hour east of LA which had a mix of white, Asian, Hispanic, and Middle Eastern residents, but very few Blacks. While she felt loved, she carried a burden around with her—she looked different than everyone else in her family. She had out of control, frizzy blond hair, while all her siblings had straight, shiny, mahogany brown hair. She had green eyes, while almost all her siblings had brown eyes. She had tan skin but looked practically pale compared to her siblings' bronzed skin, which had been handed down from ancestors who had spent centuries basking in a Mediterranean climate. The distinction first struck her one day when she was nine years old. She was looking at a family portrait hanging on the wall in her home. One of these things is not like the other, one of these things just doesn't belong. When she was a child, her parents never told her anything to explain the obvious differences. She was their little girl and the oldest of their five children. That was it. But it always bothered her. Since so much of how people are treated is based on how they look, that made things difficult, especially for a young girl. Her dad's extended family compounded the problem. They were a close-knit clan and would always get together for birthdays, holidays, and various family gatherings. When it came time to take pictures of all the cousins together, they would snap a photo and then say, "Come over here, Amanda, sweetie." When she was away from her siblings and cousins, they would take another photo of them without her. She already felt weird around them; did they think she wouldn't be hurt by this? Or did they just not care?

Amanda began to learn the truth when she was 10 years old. She was at a sleepover with her cousins when one of them said to her "You know your dad is not your real dad, right?" Just like that, from the teasing mouth of a 12-year-old she started to understand, just a little. She didn't really know what that meant, though she knew it was related to why she looked so different. She held it in for a few years, but eventually asked her mom about it.

"I had always struggled with issues of feeling like I was different than everyone else, and I just wanted to be normal, and I didn't feel that way. Ever. And so I held it in a for a long time and I think a couple of years later I finally told me mom, you know, my cousin said this to me, and she was stunned, and her and my dad sat me down and they told me that I was not his biological child. She did not tell me anything else really at that time, though, she just didn't feel like maybe I was old enough to grasp the situation that she was in back at that time. They told me that he wasn't my biological father, and that one day when I was old enough, they would tell me more," Amanda said.

One day when she was 13 years old Amanda became upset because her best friend in middle school—a biracial girl named Cynthia—had such cute, tight curly black hair, and Amanda's mane was so incorrigible.

"I just want my hair to be like Cynthia's," she sobbed to her mom.

"Do you know why your hair is like that?" her mom asked.

"Why?"

"Because your biological father is half-Black."

When she was in her twenties she started to search for her biological father. She thought about the fact that half her genes came from a man she knew almost nothing about. A man who was essentially responsible for how awkward she had felt her whole life. And this man probably had an extended family of his own who she was related to. It was a little scary—and exciting—to think about all the ramifications.

She took the name her mom had given her and searched on Google, Facebook, Instagram, and LinkedIn. She looked at pictures of people who she thought might possibly, perhaps, conceivably, be her relatives. Did she look like any of them? Maybe. Maybe not. It was really hard to tell. Finally, her searching produced a phone number that she believed was her biological father's. It was a number for a house in Las Vegas.

She had written the number on the back of an envelope, and she had the number for two weeks, but was too scared to dial it. One day she looked at it and rubbed it with her fingers, trying to find the courage to dial it. Finally she did. It rang a few times and then someone picked up, and she heard a majestic baritone on the other end, a voice as deep as a well on Clifton Plantation.

"Hello," she heard the voice say.

She hung up immediately. Holy shit! That was scary. It took her another 10 minutes to summon the courage to dial the number again.

"Hello," the voice said again.

"Hi, I'm, um, I'm looking for Andrew Harris."

"Andrew doesn't live here, but I'm his dad. Who are you?" Willie asked.

"My name is Amanda White, and I am pretty certain that Andrew is my biological father."

He was shocked, but then a huge smile engulfed his face.

"That makes you my granddaughter!"

Amanda couldn't believe it. All the years of wondering. All the years of feeling like an outsider. It all melted away. She felt welcome, and that was not something she felt often.

"He didn't even hesitate. I still can't even believe just how gracious and kind he is. He could have said 'well no, you're not,' or 'who are you?' He didn't question me at all, and I think that has been the craziest thing with him in all of this. And so after talking with him I learned that we have a lot of similarities in our growing up, and that he has a similar situation with him finding out about his biological father. He didn't know, and we both found out at the same age," Amanda said.

Willie and Amanda talked for about 20 minutes, learning about each other's lives and families. Amanda was stupefied to learn everything Willie had been through, and his heart broke when he heard about her struggles, but he was excited and energized that Amanda found him. He called her back half an hour later and told her he had to meet her. When could she come see him? Labor Day was in two weeks. How about then?

"I wanted to say it last time before we got off the phone, and I don't know why I didn't, but I love you," he said.

Amanda's heart was full. It was so surreal and unbelievable to her. Willie immediately sensed her pain. They had a deep connection based on their similar childhood experiences, and he was there to comfort her. Come here, he was saying, I'll give you shelter from the storm.

Willie didn't know Amanda existed before she called his house, as Andrew had never told him about her. Now he had a new grand-daughter to love and care about.

Willie gave her Maureen's phone number and Amanda called and spoke with her. Maureen told her that Andrew would be coming over to her house the following day, and she could call and talk to him. So she did, and they spent a half hour on the phone together. Andrew told her that he tried to go see her right after she was born, but when he went to her mom's family's home, they turned him away. They were racist, and when they saw a Black man coming looking for his daughter, they told him he was mistaken.

"Toni had a beautiful white baby, and she is not your daughter. Now get your Black ass out of here," they said.

Andrew tried to see her numerous times, kept getting thwarted, so eventually he gave up.

Amanda happily agreed to visit Willie at his home in Las Ve-gas on Labor Day weekend. She and her husband Travis loaded their two-year-old daughter London into the car and set out on the four-hour drive.  When they got off the freeway and were getting close to Willie's house, she started freaking out a little bit.

"I started kind of hyperventilating, not out of fear, it kind of just felt like all this time I've looked for anybody for over 10 years at that point, and it just didn't really even feel real."

When they arrived in his driveway Amanda walked toward the front door with London on her hip. She wore a black dress with white polka dots and London had on a white dress with black polka dots. Willie opened the door as they got closer and then they just hugged for a long time, with Amanda shedding tears of joy and relief.

"I'm so happy I finally found out who I am. I have been looking for years and now I finally know who I am. Will you accept me as your granddaughter?" she asked Willie.

"With open arms," he replied, fighting back tears.

They went inside his home, and she met one of Amanda's cousins and an uncle who had come to see her. She spent the rest of the day sitting in Willie's den, talking to him about their lives and learning about all he had endured in Mississippi and fighting with the Black Stuntmen's Association. What made Amanda especially happy is the physical resemblance she bears to Willie. Chin. Cheeks. Lips. Nose. Forehead. They're all the same.

"It's just been the biggest blessing for my life. My soul has peace, and that is something that you can't buy. This is something that has just kind of tormented me my whole life, and I never even had a picture of anybody, and I don't look like anyone on my mom's side of the family at all. Just knowing him, even if he was not my grandpa, I would still want to know him. I would want to be his friend. He has done a lot for me just with words. And I wish there was some way I could repay him, but I love him and I'm just so excited that even though I couldn't have a relationship with him for almost 30 years, I am glad that I am able to come into his life when he is in this season. That I am able to even know him at all."

# 21

## THE GRAND MARSHAL

Growing up in Mississippi shaped Willie. What he saw and experienced crafted his worldview and perception of humanity. He loved the family and friends who had raised him and supported him, but when he got old enough to make his own decisions, he decided that he had to get out. And get out he did, just like half of all Southern Blacks who by 1970 had moved north and west in a quest for economic opportunity and a less oppressive culture. They didn't always find it, but it was worth looking for.

Willie returned home every few years to visit with family and friends, and he kept in close contact with them over the phone. His heart was still in Holmes County—he just couldn't live there. In the fall of 2017 he was invited to be the grand marshal of the Lexington Christmas parade. The invitation came from the mayor of Lexington, a white woman named Robin McCrory.

Willie had to think about it. Lexington and Holmes County were home to him, but they evoked so many awful memories of the monotony of picking cotton, struggling to get a decent meal and keep warm in the winter, Sheriff Dick Byrd, and the way whites completely controlled the lives of Blacks when he was growing up.

"I almost didn't take this because I didn't know what I was walking into," he said.

After considering the pros and cons, he accepted, and Mayor McCrory was excited.

"How important it is for us to turn back the hands of time and bring people back home again and allow us to be able to welcome them and embrace them," McCrory said.

Lexington has been struggling economically for a very long time, and its population has been decreasing steadily since 1950, when it was 3,000, and it was down to 1,500 in 2020. Jobs have left and new ones have not taken their place. While it once took scores of people to farm the massive plantations, the highly efficient cultivating and harvesting machines have made it so just a few people can do the same work. The mobile home factory in town that was a major employer went out of business. There are various factories that manufacture tools and appliances, as well as large catfish and poultry farms, but they are all located 30 or more miles away. It is just easier for people to move away to be closer to their jobs. Tchula, the town closest to Clifton Plantation, was dubbed the poorest town in the poorest state in America in 2015. Holmes is one of the poorest counties in Mississippi, with a third of the residents living below the poverty line.

Despite the challenges, McCrory and the other city leaders worked hard to promote Lexington and encourage its residents to take pride in their hometown through events like the Christmas parade and a fall festival. The city also secured state funding to revitalize Court Square—the political, economic, and social hub of Lexington—by installing brick sidewalks, vintage lampposts, and wrought iron benches.

"Our Court Square is a place that we can all be proud of to drive upon, and it be the front door to our community for all those traveling north and south and east and west. You have to go around that square to get to where you're going. And of course, our courthouse, our historic courthouse, sits in the center and it's just a Norman Rockwell picture to see it," McCrory said.

The Holmes County Courthouse is impressive to behold. Built in 1894, it is listed in the National Register of Historic Places and is a rich red brick building with ornate spires in each of its four corners. It is capped by a soaring cupola that displays clocks on all four sides. The route of the Christmas parade goes all the way around the courthouse, and it is the same courthouse where a 12-year-old B.B. King, who lived in Lexington at the time, was terrified as he witnessed a young Black man get lynched on the courthouse steps in 1938. His alleged crime: touching a white woman. B.B. heard some of the white people who had gathered to watch the lynching say he got what he deserved. In Mississippi, the past is always entwined with the present.

The Christmas parade was held on a rainy Tuesday the first week of December, and Willie's role as grand marshal was announced in a front-page story the week before in the local newspaper. The parade was scheduled to kick off at 6 p.m. and before it started there was a meet and greet event for Willie in the arts council building, located just off the square. There were cookies and the aroma of warm cider wafted through the air. People came out for Willie. They wanted to meet their native son who had left to go to Hollywood and fight to integrate the film industry. The descendants of Peyton Abbott Jones sought him out to chat. The children of the former owners of Brock Plantation, located right next to Clifton, came to say hello, and talk about the old days. Willie mentioned that he would be back the following summer to attend a reunion for folks who grew up on the plantations in Howard. The kin of the plantation owners said they would like to attend as well.

Some of Willie's old friends also came, including Willie B. Davis, whom he hadn't seen since they walked off the basketball court in February of 1960. His friends, most of whom had lived their entire lives in or around Holmes County, asked him why he took it. Why did he agree to be grand marshal?

"I told them me and my mom and my brother used to go to Lexington. It was so evil, walking the streets, and if you see a white woman what you had to do to get out the way and bow your head, and all of that stuff, and I just wanted to say to my mom, 'look how things have changed.' But it could be better, it could be a lot better, but we've come a long way from there," Willie said.

Willie's friend Curtiss Ross was also at the meet and greet. Ross grew up in the cabin next door to Willie's on Clifton, picked cotton in the same fields, and he has lived close to the plantation his entire life. Ross acknowledges that the omnipresent threat of racial terror that permeated their youth is gone, but most whites and Blacks in their part of rural Mississippi, while having more cordial relations, have not yet come together in a meaningful way.

"You've got a few folks that will speak to you now and recognize you to a certain point, but when it comes to getting together you become separated, you understand what I'm sayin'?" Ross said.

Interactions between whites and Blacks in the area tend to be superficial, and Ross believes the veneer of courtesy often masks something sinister.

"I always tell people it's just the icing on the cake. When you cut into the icing you get to the cake, so if anything that is ugly existed, it's still down in the cake. That's the way I put it."

When it came time for the parade to start Willie climbed into a horse-drawn carriage with Mayor McCrory. They were preceded by a police car, a Holmes County Sheriff's Office car, and flag-bearing high school students from the town's ROTC program. Behind them came the school bands, antique cars, decorated cars and fire trucks, and representatives of various church and civic groups.

"We're a small community, and it's nothing fancy, but it's all from the heart," McCrory said.

There were a few hundred cheering people lining the route, and Willie smiled and waved as the procession wound around the courthouse, past the storefronts where his dad used to take him to buy his school clothes, and past the sidewalks where his mom would hold his hand and tell him how to act when they did their errands. Then it headed south down Yazoo Street and returned to the arts council building.

Willie was very thankful for the experience. It was unexpected, and surprisingly pleasant. Mayor McCrory asked Willie if, thinking back on all the turmoil of the old days did he ever think he would come home and be treated this way. The answer was obvious.

Before Willie left town, he went to have lunch with his friends at Gladys' restaurant. There was no other choice. Gladys' is the only place in Lexington where you can get a lip-smackin' down-home Southern meal. Gladys serves up a tremendous variety of comfort food including New Orleans-style seafood gumbo, fried okra, country-fried steak, catfish, trout, and homemade desserts, including her famous three-layer caramel cake. It is open for breakfast, lunch, and dinner and sits on a fork in the road at the edge of downtown. One prong of the fork takes you west toward the plantations and the Delta. The other goes north to Evie Harris' hometown of Carrollton and then on to Memphis. As the only restaurant of its kind in a wide radius, it has become perhaps the only place in Lexington where Blacks and whites regularly frequent and sometimes socialize. It's just the place where everyone goes.

After Willie ate he was as full as a tick, and he said goodbye and walked out. He tread carefully across the parking lot, the gravel crunching under the weight of his shoes and cane, but then he noticed one of his front tires was stuck in a ditch. It had been rainy when he got there and apparently he wasn't paying attention when he parked. He walked around the car to try to figure out what to do. Goddammit, he thought. He was a AAA member, but he doubted that was available in rural Mississippi. Then a white man walked out of Gladys'. He could see Willie was having some kind of issue, so he walked over.

"What is the trouble?" he asked.

"Oh," Willie said," I did a bad job parking and I got myself stuck in this ditch."

The man took a quick look and said "I'll tell you what. I've got a rope in my truck. I'll pull you out."

"That would be great," Willie said.

The man walked over to a Hummer, pulled a rope out of the back, and proceeded to tie one end to the front axle of Willie's car and the other to the back of the Hummer. Then he fired it up and pulled Willie's car right out. Like butter.

The man walked over, and Willie was about to thank him when he said "Mr. Harris, you were the grand marshal of the Christmas parade. I'm sorry, but I forgot your first name."

"It's Willie," he replied.

"It's nice to meet you," the man said. "I live over in Howard, not far from Clifton Plantation."

"No shit?" Willie said. "What is your name?"

"Name is Byrd. Richard Byrd."

Willie's eyes got bigger.

"Byrd? Are you any relation to Dick Byrd?" Willie asked.

"He was my grandpa."

They stared at each other, and they both knew what the other was thinking. Then Willie just burst out laughing.

"Oh, man," he said, "Your grandpa was a son of a bitch."

"I know, I know. I've heard all the stories," Byrd said, smiling.

"Well, thank you very much. I really appreciate it," Willie said.

"Anytime."

Then Willie stuck out his hand and they shook hard.

"You take care now," Willie said. Then he got in his car, and he took off.

<h1 style="text-align:center">EPILOGUE</h1>

Willie contracted the Covid-19 virus at the beginning of January 2021. He was infected just days before he was scheduled to get the Covid-19 vaccine, and about a week into his illness he was hospitalized because he was having difficulty breathing. Cheryl was not allowed to visit him due to the hospital's health and safety protocols and as his disease worsened, she thought she might never see him alive again.

"I thought I was going to lose him. He didn't know who I was, he didn't know the date. He didn't know anything… He came around on our anniversary, January the twentieth I got a call, and when I answered the phone, he said 'Hey, sweetie, how you doin?'"

Willie was never put on a ventilator while in the hospital, but he lay in a bed for about three weeks, and then was sent to a rehabilitation facility for a month so he could relearn how to walk and get more breathing treatments. January and February of 2021 were some of the cruelest months in the Covid-19 pandemic in the United States, with an average of almost 3,000 Americans succumbing to the disease every day. It was a scary time for Willie, as death was all around him.

"I heard them saying 'We just lost one next door,' and you're scared to go to sleep because if you go to sleep you might not wake up, and it was like the old sayin' says: you was right at the pearly gates, but you didn't know which one you was gonna open," Willie said.

Willie returned home in early March and had a lot of side effects from the Covid-19 infection. His strength and energy were depleted, and he was a Covid long hauler. On top of that, he was diagnosed with non-Hodgkin's lymphoma and his doctors prescribed a course of chemotherapy. He wasn't especially concerned about having cancer. The doctors told him it was treatable, and he had survived so many different hardships in his life, this was just another brick on the load.

He received his first chemotherapy treatment in late October, and he was scheduled to get them for eight weeks. However, on November 15 he came home from a doctor's appointment, and when he went into his bedroom, he fell. Cheryl heard a loud noise and Willie calling for help. She found him and his walker on the floor and he was rushed to the hospital. He was alert and speaking, but he was in terrible shape.

"They said that he had broken his neck, his shoulder, he had a fracture of the spine, and he had broken his hip," Cheryl said.

A few days after he went into the hospital things started going further downhill. The recent chemotherapy treatments, an infection, and other factors made it impossible for his body to heal and a breathing tube was inserted. His body was too compromised for the doctors to address all his broken bones, and after he had been in the hospital for about a week the doctors told Cheryl that he was paralyzed. This man's body had endured so much, suffered so much pain, and finally this was all just more than it could take. He died on November 28, 2021.

Cheryl made plans to have him buried at the Riverside National Cemetery, a veterans cemetery that is a 90-minute drive east of Los Angeles. A memorial service and interment took place on December 30. A hard rain fell that day, and Willie's family and friends gathered at the Acheson & Graham Garden of Prayer Mortuary in Riverside to honor him.

Many people spoke about Willie and what he meant to their lives, how he inspired them, how he motivated them, and how they will never forget him. One theme that kept coming up was how big a heart he had.

"Willie was a very, very large man in stature, but his heart was bigger than his body. And I am going to truly, truly miss him and his inspiration, and his leadership, and everything that he has done," Alex Brown said.

Willie's granddaughter Amanda White spoke about how special he was to her, and how meaningful it was when he opened his heart to her.

"He's been just one of the best things that's ever happened in my life, and I'm surprised at just how empty my days are. We talked on the phone all the time about anything, everything. We had so much in common. We were very similar. He loved to call me his Vanilla Willie, because he felt like I looked a lot like him. We just had a lot of things that we shared together, and this is a complex loss for me, losing him. I just didn't get enough time, but I know that he loved me, and I loved him so much," Amanda said.

In addition to Alex Brown, three other members of the BSA were able to attend the service and all of them shared their memories: Henry Kingi, Joe Tilque, and Bill Upton.

"He would get things done. That's what I loved about him. Film industry, politicians, they would listen to him, and he'd get it done. I'm going to miss him. He did a lot for civil rights. He did a lot for the film industry. He did a lot for everybody… but most of all he didn't quit. He didn't quit on anything. If he said he was going to get it done, he would go and get it done, and I'm going to miss him so, so much… Thank you all for coming out to send my best buddy in the whole world out. There will never be another one like him," Upton said.

# ACKNOWLEDGMENTS

I could not be more grateful that I found Willie Harris' phone number and called him for the first time in spring 2016. Having the opportunity to hear Willie's story and ask him hundreds of questions—as well as those of the dozens of people from his past that he connected me to—has been one of the greatest gifts of my life. He lived an extraordinary life, and I am privileged that he was willing to tell me all about it. He told me about the moments in his life that brought him the greatest joy, as well as those that brought the most excruciating heartache. Everything he felt, he felt deeply. His generous spirit and welcoming personality made every one of our conversations something I looked forward to, and I am very thankful that I was able to spend time with him in person on three occasions. I miss him very much.

I am very thankful to everyone from Mississippi who generously shared their stories with me: Wade Murry, Stanford Murry, Joseph Smothers, Dennis Smothers, Dorothy Greer, Al Talbert, Naylond Hayes, Willie Davis, Ollie Johnson, Jean Smith, Rudolphis Hayes, Betty Pearson, Jerry Fisher, Bryant Clark, Phil Cohen, Robin McCrory, and Willie Hoskins.

I am especially grateful to Curtiss Ross, Winford Ross, Harold Quinn, and Joe Lauderdale for the tremendous hospitality they showed me when I visited Lexington, Mississippi, and Clifton Plantation.

I would also like to thank Clifton Taulbert, Elliott Gould, James Meredith, Bernadine Anderson, Dr. Dwandalyn Reece, Howard

Walker, Jay Remaldo, Beryl Warren, and Bill Grady for speaking with me and providing me with so much useful information.

Everyone associated with the Black Stuntmen's Association helped me immeasurably, including Calvin Brown, Bill Upton, Doug Lawrence, Henry Graddy, Henry Kingi, Greg Elam, Jadie David, and Evelyn Cuffee. I would like to especially thank Alex Brown and Marge Ryan Kreeger for their help and support throughout this process.

I am very thankful to the members of Willie's family who spoke to me, especially his brother Robert Harris, his granddaughter Amanda White and his wife Cheryl Harris. Cheryl's constant support of Willie and the book project helped make this possible.

I wish to thank my friends and colleagues who encouraged and advised me on the project, including Miss Kimberly Barrow, Sheril Holbrook, the great Kyshant Moore, Joe Laurito, Kristina Dini, Maryellen Lyons, Peter Hodge, Vince Zandri, Mary Coleman, Karen Stickler, Margaret Otzel, Robert Tinajero, and Carlos Segarra.

Anthony Dini and Gabriel Johnson were especially helpful, and I am extremely grateful to them.

I would like to thank Dan Corbett, Mike Esposito, Ray Seward, Pierre Cast, Janet Barrett, Tucker McCormack, Billy Thurston, Mary-Beth Thurston, Chris Mahoney, Tim Ferguson, Brian Handal, Ed Bresnahan, and Mike Hughes for a lifetime of friendship and encouragement.

Many of my family members provided extremely valuable feedback, including Anna Levine, Ben Greenvall, Kaylee Shea, Carol Esposito, and Tricia Shea.

There are two people who are no longer with us who always inspired me and helped me believe I could do something worthwhile: Peter Sims and my dad, Dave Shea.

I want to thank our four incredible children Tim, Buddy, Megan, and Carly for their recommendations and encouragement, and for making every day so much more meaningful simply by being on this earth.

Most importantly, I want to thank my amazing wife Sue for her constant support, patience, wisdom, and love.

Tim Shea

# BIBLIOGRAPHY

Anderson, Devery S. *Emmett Till: The Murder That Shocked the World and Propelled the Civil Rights Movement.* University Press of Mississippi, 2015.

Anderson, Elijah. *Black in White Space: The Enduring Impact of Color in Everyday Life.* The University of Chicago Press, 2023.

Ayers, Edward L. *The Promise of the New South.* Oxford University Press, 2007.

Blaustein, Albert P., and Robert L. Zangrando. *Civil Rights and African Americans: A Documentary History.* Northwestern University Press. 1992.

Bois, William Edward Burghardt Du. *The Souls of Black Folk.* Courier Corporation, 1994.

Cash, Wilbur Joseph. *The Mind of the South.* Knopf, 1941.

Dessens, Nathalie. *Myths of the Plantation Society.* 2003.

Gerzina, Gretchen Holbrook. *Mr. and Mrs. Prince.* Harper Collins, 2009.

Gossett Jr., Louis, and Phyllis Karas. *An Actor and a Gentleman.* Wiley,

2010.

Hall, B. C., and C. T. Wood. *The South*. Scribner, 1995.

King, B. B., and David Ritz. *Blues All Around Me*. It Books, 2011.

Meyer, Jacob Gibble, and Oliver Stuart Hamer. *The New World and Its Growth*. 1948.

Silver, James W. *Mississippi: The Closed Society*. University Press of Mississippi, 2012.

Sitkoff, Harvard. *The Struggle for Black Equality*. Hill and Wang, 2008.

Thernstrom, Stephan, and Abigail Thernstrom. *America in Black and White: One Nation, Indivisible*. Simon & Schuster, 1999.

Thomason, Sally Palmer. *Delta Rainbow: The Irrepressible Betty Bobo Pearson*. University Press of Mississippi, 2016.

Walton, Anthony. *Mississippi: An American Journey*. Vintage, 1997.

Wilkerson, Isabel. *The Warmth of Other Suns: The Epic Story of America's Great Migration*. Vintage, 2010.

Woodward, Comer Vann. *The Strange Career of Jim Crow*. Oxford University Press, USA, 1955.

# Book Club Discussion Questions

1. What was your favorite part of the book?

2. What was your least favorite?

3. What was your sense of Willie as a person?

4. If you could ask Willie one question, what would it be?

5. What surprised you more: the way Willie and everyone close to him were treated in Mississippi, or the way they were treated in Hollywood?

6. Which person in the book did you identify with the most?

7. Which scene has stuck with you the most?

8. Did you know anything about sharecropping before you read the book?

9. How much did you know about the lynching of Emmett Till before you read this book?

10. How does the book's title work in relation to the book's contents? If you could give the book a new title, what would it be?

11. What did you think of the writing? Are there any standout sentences?

12. Did reading the book impact your mood? If yes, how so?

13. Who do you most want to read this book?

14. Are there lingering questions about Willie's life you're still thinking about?

15. How did your opinion of the book change as you read it?

16. Did Willie's story remind you of any other books or movies?

17. Do you think you will remember Willie's story in a few years?

# About the Authors

Willie Harris was born on August 8, 1941 on a cotton plantation near Lexington, Mississippi. He served in the United States Air Force from 1962 to 1967, and then joined the Black Stuntmen's Association (BSA), a group dedicated to fighting the racist practices that prevented Black men and women from being hired as stunt performers in Hollywood productions. Willie was named president of the BSA in 2004 and was instrumental in the group receiving honors and awards from the United States Congress, the NAACP, and having its story and memorabilia included in the National Museum of African American History and Culture. He died on November 28, 2021.

Tim Shea graduated from Providence College in 1987 with a degree in English. He worked for four years as a newspaper reporter, and since 1993 he has held a variety of posts at a well-known university in New Haven, CT.